# GREAT INVITATIONS

# Great Invitations

David Whitcomb

**AMBASSADOR INTERNATIONAL**
GREENVILLE, SOUTH CAROLINA & BELFAST, NORTHERN IRELAND

# Great Invitations

All Scripture quotations are taken from the English Standard Version copyright 2001 by Crossway Bibles, a division of Good News Publishers, and are used by permission.

Cover design and page layout by David Siglin of A&E Media

ISBN 978-1-932307-93-1

*Published by the Ambassador Group*

Ambassador International
427 Wade Hampton Blvd.
Greenville, SC 29609
USA
www.emeraldhouse.com

and

Ambassador Publications Ltd.
Providence House
Ardenlee Street
Belfast BT6 8QJ
Northern Ireland
www.ambassador-productions.com

*The colophon is a trademark of Ambassador*

DEDICATED TO THOSE FAITHFUL TEACHERS WHO ENTRUSTED
TO ME THE THINGS I MUST TEACH TO OTHERS ALSO
(2 TIMOTHY 2:2).

# TABLE OF CONTENTS

# INTRODUCTION

S ome weeks ago I read an article that revealed that a popular method
for achieving results in modern evangelistic crusades is for hundreds of professing Christians from local churches to sit scattered
throughout the audience. When the invitation is given, these volunteers
get out of their seats and walk to the front in order to encourage sinners
who need to repent to do the same. No doubt the organizers of such cam-
paigns justify this practice as a means of encouraging sinners to go forward
to receive Christ. On the other hand, one might view this practice as a
kind of deception. Furthermore, I have always struggled with the idea that
a person needs to walk an aisle before God is able to do a work in his or
her heart.

That kind of musing brings up a lot of other questions. For example,
some soul winners talk about the need to "draw in the net." That statement
struck me as the kind of thing a car salesman or an insurance salesman
would do. But is that really what the bearer of the good news must do
when he tells a poor sinner that Jesus died to save him from his sins?

Wilson Thompson was a Baptist preacher who had moved from Ken-
tucky to the frontier of Missouri. He was preaching at an open-air meeting
in December 1812 where people gathered from villages twenty to thirty
miles around when an amazing thing happened. He gave this account of
the event:

> I took for a text the saying of Paul: "For the wages of sin is death,
> but the gift of God is eternal life through Jesus Christ". . . . At
> the close of the discourse the large congregation seemed deeply
> affected. I cast my eyes over them, and the general appearance

was a solemn stillness, as though some unseen power was hovering over them. Every eye was set on me, and I felt mute with astonishment, and stood silent for some minutes. I believe there was not a motion nor a sound during the time, until, simultaneously, some twenty or more persons arose from their seats and came forward.

Ian Murray commented about this event by saying, "The Missouri settlers were responding to an alter call which he had not given" (Ian Murray. Revival and Revivalism. Carlisle, Pa.: Banner of Truth Trust, 2002 reprint, 226.). The thing that was most unusual about that true revival was not that God moved among the people, but that they came forward. The concept of the invitation at the end of a service, wherein penitent sinners come to an altar or wailing bench, was not common in the early nineteenth century. What many Christians consider to be normal, an altar call at the end of a preaching service, actually became popular in the 1820's.

The public invitation that is common in conservative Bible preaching circles was popularized by Charles Gradison Finney. It was part of the "new measures" that he and other evangelists and preachers instituted in an effort to create revivals. Finney moved to Jefferson County, N.Y. near the shores of Lake Ontario around 1918. He was an ardent student, an intelligent young man, but virtually self-educated. He never held a degree from any college or university, but he studied law on his own and was admitted to the New York State bar around 1820.

Finney began attending a Presbyterian Church pastored by George Gale. He came to know Christ in a signal experience on October 10, 1821. Almost immediately after his conversion, Finney lost interest in law and decided to preach. His manner was very persuasive, very blunt, and quick witted. Often he preached as if he was an attorney trying to convince the jury. He was the most notable of evangelists to implement the "new measures." These methods were popularized around 1822 and caused much controversy and conflict among ministers in western New York. The concept eventually spread all over the country and even to Scotland and England, primarily due to Finney's teaching.

According to a letter written in May 1825 by Charles Sears, professor at Hamilton College, the controversial issues of the new measures hinged on the use of emotion in revivals. It was not that pastors were opposed to feelings, excitement, or emotion, but they were opposed to Finney's methods for promoting emotions in order to force people to make "decisions" when God was not necessarily moving on hearts. At the "anxious seat" Finney pressured, preached, and argued people into "deciding for salvation." For example, he ended one sermon by pleading:

> Now I must know your minds; and I want that you who have made up your minds to become Christians, and will give your pledge to make your peace with God immediately, should rise up; but that, on the contrary, those of you who are resolved that you will not become Christians, and wish me so to understand, and wish Christ so to understand, should sit still (Murray, 242).

While it is true that such an invitation sounds quite normal to many Christians, one can easily see how the challenge could tempt sinners, who did not experience the conviction of God, to make a decision for Christ for fear of looking bad to the rest of the audience.

At the root of the "new measures" was a terrible theological error on Finney's part. He believed that the Holy Spirit persuades men to be saved when the preacher stirs motivations by emotional appeal. In other words, he concluded that if the preacher could stir the emotions enough, the Holy Spirit could regenerate a soul. That is clearly opposed to the Scripture which states, "He saved us, not because of works done by us in righteousness, but according to His own mercy, by the washing of regeneration and renewal of the Holy Spirit" (Titus 3:5).

Finney also erred in that he did not believe that sinners were controlled by a fallen nature. He believed that every person has the ability and power within himself to commit himself to Christ if he so chooses. Therefore, Finney by necessity rejected the idea that true conversion is an act of God's sovereign omnipotence. Rather, it was his opinion that regeneration occurs as soon as a person begins to obey Christ. He believed that God placed the Holy Spirit at the person's disposal to command, or direct, so that revival must happen if we do the right things. He argued that the total depravity of man was a voluntary condition which the individual can decide to change. (See Charles G. Finney. Lectures on Revivals and Lectures on Systematic Theology.) Denial of man's fallen nature was not original with Charles Finney. That heresy goes all the way back to the Pelagian controversy that church fathers dealt with in the late 4th century.

This brief review of modern revival history helps explain that what we consider to be the normal invitation is actually a method that sincere, zealous, but errant preachers developed in order to get results. Conversely, God requires His people to faithfully proclaim His Word, faithfully tell the good news of salvation to sinners, faithfully plead with them to consider the truth, but then let God the Holy Spirit work through His Word. If the preacher coerces or pressures a sinner to "decide for Christ" when God is not convicting that person through His Word, he will create a person who wrongly believes he is saved and will be quite shocked when Christ sends him to hell. God's messengers must be honest, fair, and careful when inviting sinners to receive Christ.

On the other hand, God's people must invite sinners to receive Christ! That seems like an unnecessary statement. However, the fact is that many of Christ's followers never invite sinners to have faith in Christ's finished work. It is popular for many Christians to spend much time encouraging each other, teaching each other, and splitting hairs over minor doctrines, while spending no time giving out invitations to the Great Marriage Supper. Surely it is profitable to think through several passages of Scripture in both the Old and New Testaments in order to flesh out the teaching and applications of many invitations God has given. God freely invites people to find salvation and security in Him. God expects His people to faithfully offer the same kind of invitations to needy sinners. The Bible records many great invitations. To be impressed with their greatness should drive the reader to pass them on.

# PART I

# GREAT INVITATIONS
# IN THE OLD TESTAMENT

1

# EAT OF EVERY TREE OF THE GARDEN

GENESIS 2:8-17

The value of an invitation is often determined by attendant circumstances. For example, an invitation to a five course meal at a fine restaurant may be warmly welcomed by the average American. But to a political prisoner in a foreign nation who is starving, such an invitation would be astonishing. Not only would it mean that he could finally enjoy a great meal, but it implies that he would also be set free. Invitations to attend a ball game are so common that most people turn down due to lack of time to attend. However, a little boy in a poor family in the Appalachian hills would jump at the chance to attend an actual major league ball game. That might be a once in a lifetime invitation to him. So too, an invitation from a world famous surgeon to perform surgery would not seem very inviting at all, unless of course you knew that you had a deadly disease and that this surgeon would be able to cure you.

Not surprisingly, God's invitation to receive eternal life is not wildly popular. It never has been. Why not? A person will not appreciate the invitation for eternal life unless he is fully convinced that the alternative is eternal death, or worse, eternal judgment! Most people hear the Lord's invitation to receive eternal life within the context of a busy, active, rather satisfying life. If life happens to turn sour and it looks like everything that offered security is disappearing, or is already gone, then folks might think about God's invitation. But under normal circumstances an invitation to enjoy life in the presence of God forever just doesn't have that "must have" appeal.

An invitation to go backstage at a famous rocker's concert has a great appeal to a lot of people. Or maybe an invitation to get into the pits and rub elbows with NASCAR's brightest stars might be the desire of many red blooded American guys. But an invitation to receive eternal life as God's free gift just doesn't have the same attraction. Maybe it is because proud sinners are quite sure that they will be able to achieve everlasting life through their own works. The Bible indicates that many—that is MANY, a lot, more than the average multitude—people will be shocked to discover too late that their good works failed them. They will be astonished to learn that Jesus the eternal Judge will not allow them into heaven.

How does the invitation for eternal life sound in light of the attendant circumstances. The only other choice is eternal death, which is not the same as annihilation. Eternal death is separation from God forever. Eternal death is separation from God's love, protection, peace, and rest. Eternal death is accompanied by eternal punishment, a punishment worse than the human mind can imagine. It is the only other choice apart from the invitation for eternal life. That puts things in a different perspective doesn't it? If eternal life or eternal death are the only choices, anyone in his right mind would choose eternal life. Right? One would think so. But if that were true, Adam was not in his right mind. He lived in paradise. He understood the two choices. God clearly offered him the invitation for eternal life. Adam chose to live life his way and the rest is history.

We are foolish to simplify life too much. But the essence of life still comes down to two simple alternatives—eternal life or eternal death. After all these thousands of years, God's invitation is still that clear. How the individual responds to the invitation has eternal consequences.

## GOD CREATED PARADISE FOR ADAM (vv.8-14)

God planted a beautiful garden, a special garden specifically for the man He created (v.8). Yahweh Eloheim identifies the Master Garden planner and creator as the Creator God. He who established the unique garden is the LORD God who made the earth and the heavens (2:4). He is the LORD God who created Adam from dust (2:7). He is the LORD God who created Eve from Adam's rib (2:22). It is this same God who spoke the perfect world into existence and who, having scrutinized His own work, was satisfied with what He had done (1:1-31). The Bible record shows that when the creation was complete that, "God saw everything that he had made, and behold, it was very good. And there was evening and there was morning, the sixth day" (Genesis 1:31) .

Chapter two begins with the story of God setting aside the seventh day as a special day of rest in order to honor His work of creation. Apparently at some point after the seventh day God created this special garden just for Adam and Eve. He had already created Adam and maybe had not created Eve for him yet. Nevertheless, though the timing of all the details are unclear, it is clear that God made the garden after He made the man. The word for garden speaks of an enclosed place. It typically describes a garden as one would think of it with a fence that sets it apart for the use of the one who planted it. When the Jewish scholars translated the Old Testament into Greek they used the Greek word paradeisos here. This word is obviously the English word paradise. God made paradise for Adam.

The text states that God established this unique garden in "Eden, in the east." That might mean that Eden was east of the place where Moses wrote this history, or that it was east of where Adam was at the beginning of creation, or that Eden was a place or region and God put the garden in the eastern part of it. No one knows for sure which is the correct interpretation. Once God had established the beautiful garden, God directed Adam to go there. The text says that "there God put the man whom He had formed." That is not to say that God miraculously swept Adam up and plunked him down in the new garden, though He could have. Probably God simply directed Adam's heart to go to the new place east of where he was.

Surely when Adam first viewed this magnificent gift from God he was aware or reminded again that God loved him. Verse nine helps explain how God made the garden especially beautiful. The verse says that it was the Creator God who caused things to spring up. The garden did not grow on its own. The process of natural productivity, like the rest of the world, was according to God's design. This beautiful garden was the result of God's special plan. It was His special garden in a special creation to accomplish His special purpose. The very name God gave to the garden, Eden, means delight. The place was a delight because every tree that was beautiful to behold and every tree that was good for food grew there. No doubt Adam's senses were overwhelmed with the beauty, the smell, the aesthetic appeal when he entered that garden.

Moses, under divine inspiration, pointed out that two special trees were in the garden. The rest of the story centers on these two trees. Indeed, the story of humanity revolves around these two trees. The first tree was the tree of life, and the second tree was the tree of the knowledge of good and evil. The story explains the importance of these trees later.

God located the garden in the choicest spot on the earth (vv.10-14). It was a place that declared the Creator's glory through much natural beauty and value (vv.11-12). The story describes the near proximity of the garden as being near the land of Havilah. This part of the world was famous for an abundance of good gold (v.11). Maybe that was still true in Moses day as he wrote this history. It was also in a region known for precious gems (v.12).

Archeologists would love to be able to pinpoint Eden's location so that they could descend on the place with picks and shovels to excavate the glories of the past. That is impossible, in spite of the fact that the named rivers in verses ten through fourteen should easily give away the location. According to verse ten, God put this garden at the headwaters of four rivers. First, was the river Pishon. Flowed through the land of Havilah. No one really knows for sure where Havilah was, nor therefore, where the Pishon was. It is true that the land had much gold, but it is quite certain that the garden was not somewhere near San Francisco.

The second named river is the Gihon. The Gihon River flowed through the land of Cush. That bit of evidence might be helpful because in light of other statements in the Bible this spot might be located. The Bible reveals that Cush was Ham's son and his posterity settled in Ethiopia. Was this the great river of Egypt, the Nile? Maybe. Maybe not.

The third river was the Tigris. Surely the location of the Tigris River is known. The text says in verse fourteen that it flowed east of Assyria. Assyria is easily located as much of present day Iran. In fact, there is still a river flowing through that land called the Tigris. That seems like some very accurate evidence.

The fourth river was the Euphrates. This is another easily identified land mark. The Euphrates River still flows through present day Iraq. Many of God's people today have relatives and friends who have driven over this river more than a couple of times on their way in and out of Baghdad. This is one of the most frequently mentioned rivers in the Bible. Twenty-one times the name shows up in Scripture.

Having viewed all the evidence, is it not likely that we can pinpoint the location of ancient Eden? Not necessarily. The rivers mentioned here existed before the flood. It is possible that when Moses wrote this book hundreds, probably thousands of years after the facts, that he supplied the names of rivers that were extant in his day. But that might not be the case. The Great Flood changed the face of the earth, changed every detail about the landscape of the entire world. The best conclusion is that Eden was located roughly in a region covering the entire Middle East, which is like finding a needle in a haystack. No one really knows exactly where these rivers were nor where this garden was. None the less it was a magnificent garden.

## GOD OFFERED ADAM AN INCREDIBLE INVITATION (vv. 15-17)

God's invitation was very positive, but God set it in the context of serious warning. The negative attendant circumstances lends great importance to the invitation. What were those circumstances (v.17)? God simply forbid Adam to eat of the tree of the knowledge of good and evil. That was a special tree that God planted on purpose. It was also an attractive tree. The next chapter recorded Eve's fall into sin. Satan tempted her to give serious consideration to the tree that God put off limits. "So when the woman saw that the tree was good for food, and that it was a delight to the eyes, and that the tree was to be desired to make one wise, she took of its fruit and ate, and she also gave some to her husband who was with her, and he ate" (Genesis 3:6).

Notice that this forbidden tree appealed to the desire of the flesh. Eve saw that it was "good for food." It appealed to the desire of the eye. "It was a delight to the eyes." It appealed to the pride of life in that it was "to be desired to make one wise." John reminded his readers thousands of years later that those three characteristics are not God-like. Those are the characteristics of the fallen, sinful world-like way of thinking (1 John 2:16). God used this attractive tree in order to present a test for the only part of creation that God made in His own image. Only man has a moral makeup like God's—a will and the ability to reason. This tree did not have some kind of magical fruit so that something in the fruit caused the problem of sin. Rather, eating or not eating of the fruit proved the truth about the inward motivation or character of the person.

The tree of the knowledge of good and evil represented the first principle of humanities relationship with the Creator: obey Him. Adam's relationship with God was built on truth. That principle has continued since the time of Adam. Every meaningful and successful relationship rises and falls on truth. The principle is the same whether it is a person's relationship with God or his relationship with another person. God's standard, command, rule, law, or whatever one wishes to call it, is truth. God's command to Adam was clear, simple and obvious: "Do not eat the fruit of that one particular tree!" The moment God gave the command, the test of Adam's will or heart was set in motion. From the chronology of the story it appears that God gave the instruction to Adam and then created Eve. It was Adam's responsibility to pass on God's standard. Apparently he did that. Now with the law firmly in their minds, would God's created beings obey God's law because they loved Him, or would they disobey God's law because they loved themselves?

This one particular tree represented one of the critical points in Adam's relationship with God, and therefore, it was the tree of the experience of good and evil. The choice to eat caused the eater to step over the boundary of obedience to God. Disobedience opened the understanding to evil. God preferred that His man and woman would be innocent concerning evil, unfamiliar with it, inexperienced in it. Familiarity with evil also makes the contrast between evil and good very obvious. As the record shows, Adam and Eve failed the test. They disobeyed God and that which was normal and typical, the "good," suddenly became a second option.

When God gave Adam the rule, He also promised severe consequences if Adam disobeyed. God said, "Dying you will die." It was a promise of immediate death and of slow lingering death. Death is separation of the soul from the body, or of life from the carcase. Death is also separation from the source of life, the Creator, God. Therefore, disobedience meant that Adam's fellowship with the source of life, God, would be severed immediately. Worse, Adam, for whom God had provided a means for continual life, would forfeit that means of life and die physically. That happened 930 years later. Still worse is the fact that all of Adam's posterity would inherit the death sentence and be subject to physical death. Infinitely worse is that all of Adam's posterity would be separated from God, the life giver, because of the sin principle. Because of Adam's failure, all of his posterity and will be punished forever unless God Himself pays the price to cover the offense of that sin principle.

It was against these attendant circumstances that God gave the marvelous invitation (vv.15-16). God provided paradise and invited Adam to live there because He loved the man (v.15a,16). He loves every person who was born in Adam's line. That includes every person! The Bible makes abundantly clear that God loves the beings He brings into existence. "For God so loved the world, that he gave his only Son, that whoever believes in him should not perish but have eternal life" (John 3:16). God took Adam and put him in the garden because He loved the created being. It was a special beautiful garden. It was paradise. But it was also a proving ground. God gave Adam every tree (apart from the forbidden tree) to enjoy because He loved the man. He desired for the man to be characterized by "eating you shall eat . . ." (v.16). God loved Adam so much that He gave him a tree, the fruit of which, provides eternal life.

Was God wrong to expect Adam to respond to His love with reciprocal love (vv.15b)? God provided everything the man could possibly need because God loved him. God was right to expect reciprocal love. Reciprocal love is built on trust. Surely the man could trust God to love him—the evidence was abundant! Adam could reveal his love for God and trust of God by doing what the Creator told him to do. God put him in the garden to work it and keep it. To work it meant that he should maintain the beauty of the garden which would have been a joy before God cursed the ground because of sin. To keep it meant that he should guard and protect it. From what danger or problem? Maybe a more accurate understanding of the word would be to say that Adam was supposed to be responsible for the garden. In Exodus and Leviticus this same word "keep" almost always refers to worship or keeping God's feasts, laws, ordinances, commands, and such. In other words, God's plan was for Adam to focus on Him and obey Him because He loved Him. Solomon stated this same truth when he concluded, "The end of the matter; all has been heard. Fear God and keep his commandments, for this is the whole duty of man" (Ecclesiastes 12:13).

But Adam and Eve failed. They did not fear God, love God, or obey God—in spite of God's invitation to enjoy everlasting life through His provision. The principle of Adam's sin is passed on to everyone. We all fail to obey God by nature and by choice. Paul warned that, "all have sinned and fall short of the glory of God" (Romans 3:23). That failure is no small matter. Each person who fails (that is everyone) must pay the consequences. "[T]he wages of sin is death," (Romans 6:23a) That is the same serious consequence God warned Adam about. And yet this is the backdrop, the attendant circumstances for the Great Invitation: "but the free gift of God is eternal life in Christ Jesus our Lord" (Romans 6:23b).

Eternal life is available by grace through faith in Christ's finished work. How valuable is God's invitation?

It had hung on the wall of her modest living room for fifteen years. It pictured the temptation of Eve by the Devil. Mrs. Rosemary Cattrell, an Edinburgh art teacher, found out the real value of the painting when she decided to sell it to raise a deposit for a car. Then she discovered that her painting was by a 16th-century German artist, Hans Baldung. The painting, once valued at $50, was auctioned for $537,600.

Indeed, Eve's failure to love God in spite of His gracious invitation for eternal life is the most valuable lesson one can learn. Each person is destined to fail like this. The great news is that the same God who is offended by sin, offers eternal life through His grace. Did Adam receive it? Did you? How important is the invitation? If God offered a five course dinner to a starving man would His invitation be important to the hungry man? The person who has come to grips with the reality of sin and offense against God considers His invitation to be of the greatest importance. We must accept it, embrace it, and tell it to others.

# 2

# COME INTO THE ARK

## Genesis 6:5-7:5

Which came first, the chicken or the egg? The answer to that age-old question is not nearly as difficult as the debaters make it. The answer has been right here in the story of creation for thousands of years. The Bible says, "So God created the great sea creatures and every living creature that moves, with which the waters swarm, according to their kinds, and every winged bird according to its kind. And God saw that it was good" (Genesis 1:21). Surely chickens are winged birds even though they don't fly very well. God did not create the egg, but the chicken—and it produced after its own kind through eggs.

Which came first, faith or good works? Again this is an age-old question. And again, the debaters make the question more difficult than it should be. James declared that a claim of faith that is not demonstrated by good works is no faith at all (James 2:17). However, the writer to the Hebrews states us that without faith it is impossible to please God (Hebrews 11:6). Therefore, the faith must come first, and then good works must follow.

Is that not the picture drawn clearly in this story about God's ark? Most Christians grew up understanding that this passage tells the story of Noah's ark. However, it was actually God's ark. He planned it. It was His idea. He communicated the plans to Noah, and Noah built what God planned. If you hire a contractor to build a new house for you, when he is finished it is not the contractor's house, is it? It is your house. So, too, God conscripted Noah to build the vessel that would provide safety for his family and provide a means for the human race and animal kingdom to survive the great deluge.

How many sermons have preacher's preached on this text over the centuries? "More than the sands on the seashore" comes to mind. Most Christians have heard multiplied sermons on this text. Most of the time the invitation that God gave for Noah and his family to enter the ark is pictured as God's invitation to sinners to find salvation in Christ. There are so many neat pictures here. The ark provided safety from destruction just like salvation offers safety from the punishment of hell. The one door is like Jesus Christ, the only door to salvation. The one window is like prayer, the only way to communicate with God. The three decks are like the Trinity. Really? The analogies go on and on.

The problem with inspiring sermons that draw many kinds of pictures from the ark story is that they often ignore the clear lesson God recorded. God's invitation for Noah to enter the ark is not the same as God's invitation for sinners to enter salvation. The difference is in the fact that before Noah cut the first timber to build the ark, he had already found grace in the eyes of the Lord. That is salvation! If the pictures alone become the basis for interpretation, the result is God inviting Noah to salvation because he did good works. Instead, the story clearly teaches that Noah was a righteous man, blameless in his generation, walked with God, and did all that God commanded, because he had received God's grace.

Therefore, when God invited Noah to enter the ark, it is the same kind of invitation Jesus pictured in the story of the Master who gave his servants talents. When the servant proved faithful with what the Master had already given, "His master said to him, 'Well done, good and faithful servant. You have been faithful over a little; I will set you over much. Enter into the joy of your master'" (Matthew 25:21). The joy of your Master is the reward of heaven. So, too, God drew Noah to Himself. Noah responded with obedience. God invited him to enjoy safety.

That is a perfect picture of the blessed hope that motivates every true believer. Because the believer has already found favor with God, he serves Him faithfully, looking forward to the invitation for eternal safety.

## God Offered An Amazing Invitation

When God offers an invitation to anyone, there is always a need or circumstances that require it. The need for the invitation in this case is spelled out in certain terms (vv.5-7; 11-13). The invitation for safety was necessary because, as God observed, the wickedness of His creation was unprecedented (vv.5-6; 11-12). Imagine how God the creator felt as He observed the wickedness of that which He created for His glory (v.6). He spoke the world into existence because He wanted to. He created man in His image because He wanted to. After that, God carefully looked at all that He had made and said that it was good. Good reflects His glory. As the creator, He had the right to expect His creation to reflect His glory.

But that is not the way it looked at this point in mankind's history. God the creator observed that the wickedness was great in His world (vv.5,11,12). The terminology means that He looked carefully at what was taking place in His creation (v.5). He was investigating in order to come to an understanding. That is God's nature. In His perfect wisdom and omniscience, He knew that the obvious evidence proved that wickedness ruled the day. People were consumed with wicked thinking. Because they thought wicked thoughts they did wicked deeds. That is an unavoidable cause and effect. Jesus said, "The good person out of the good treasure of his heart produces good, and the evil person out of his evil treasure produces evil, for out of the abundance of the heart his mouth speaks" (Luke 6:45).

As a result of wicked thinking and wicked actions among God's created beings, the whole earth was corrupted (vv.11,12). The word means that the creation was spoiled, ruined. Like a beautiful wedding cake left out in the sun for many days, God's creation became putrefied. How long did this take after the fall? If there are no gaps in the genealogy given in chapter five, it might have been only 1000-2000 years. According to verse eleven, this corruption led to violence. Because corruption always leads to violence, the American culture continually requires more and more jails. God said that all flesh was responsible for this corrupting process. Flesh is people. The forefathers of the human race ruined God's creation because they were sinners. Not surprisingly, as time goes on, the same characteristics will be more and more obvious on the earth. How corrupt is society? How much violence is there? How long will God wait until the next judgment? Jesus warned, "Just as it was in the days of Noah, so will it be in the days of the Son of Man" (Luke 17:26).

Because the creation was putrefied, God determined to destroy the living creatures (vv.6-7,13). The proliferation of sin grieved His heart (v.6). When God's heart was grieved, He determined to wipe the earth clean. That does not mean that God suddenly changed His mind and came up with a different plan. Rather the idea here is that God changed His actions toward creation because creation changed its actions toward Him. In His omniscience, God knew in eternity that this would happen.

God planned to wipe away all human and animal life (vv.7,13). The story is a grim reminder that a person's corruption effects more than himself. A sinner's sin is not just his own business. The individual's sin causes grief to God. It also causes grief to friends and family and people the sinner doesn't even know. Recently, a leading senator reported that the cost for society to care for unwed mothers and their babies is $150 billion annually. Among one segment of the culture, illegitimate births account for 75% of all births. Their corruption effects each person in the culture.

God unfolded His plan regarding the invitation in verses fourteen through twenty-one and also in the first verse of chapter seven. God had a plan (vv.14-21). He would continue creation through a selected group of animals, and Noah's family. He planned for Noah to build something that no one had seen before. God did not tell Noah to build just an ordinary boat. Rather He explained the kind of boat, the size, and what it must be capable of enduring. Does it not seem a bit astonishing that the God of creation would pick out this one man from among the millions of people on earth and communicate His plan to him? That is precisely what God did for Noah (6:13-18; 7:1).

God told Noah what to do (vv.13-17). Earlier in the story it is clear that God had already decided what He would do before He talked to Noah (v.7). But why did He tell Noah? Was it because Noah had done something special? No, God picked out Noah to receive His favor. Therefore, God established His covenant with Noah (v.18). The covenant was an agreement between two parties. God drew up the covenant and invited Noah to participate. It was not a matter of equal bargaining. God told Noah to build the ark and that he would be privileged to come into the ark with his family and be saved. That was the agreement. Noah could accept it or reject it. No negotiations, no agents, no clauses.

The end of this part of the story shows that after Noah followed God's instruction, God kept His word and invited Noah into the ark (7:1). In fact, God commanded Noah to "come" into the ark. The word translated "go" in the E.S.V. and "come" in the N.K.J.V. is very common in the Old Testament. It occurs 2307 times. Often it is translated "bring" or "brought" as in verses seventeen and nineteen of this chapter. Most of the time it is translated "come" as it is in verses four, eighteen, and twenty.

That is a good translation for this invitation. For God to say, "Come into the ark" implies that He is already in there.

What a wonderful illustration of God's kindness and grace is demonstrated in this invitation. The whole creation was corrupted. Humans had completely ruined God's perfect creation. God's justice required that He wipe the earth clean of the corrupting beings. Yet, at the same time, God invited a man and his family to come and enjoy fellowship and safety with Him. They would have to come out of the corrupted world in order to enjoy the results of the invitation.

## GOD OFFERED THE INVITATION TO NOAH

Why did Noah, of all the people on earth, receive this privilege (v.8)? The text says that it is because Noah found grace in the eyes of the LORD. That is not to say that God found Noah to be favorable. God was not looking for someone who was qualified to build the ark. God did not look all over the earth for someone who was good enough to be saved. God did not consider several other men first and interviewed Noah after He rejected all the other candidates. There was no interview and hiring process.

The text says that Noah secured favor in the LORD'S presence. It means that God chose to show His favor to this particular man. This man lived in a corrupted world just like all the other people. He, like all the other people, was a son of Adam and shared Adam's fallen nature. Therefore, Noah was prone to sin just like the rest of his world. By nature, he contributed to the corruption of the world. But God's grace and favor made him an anomaly in his world. There is no greater privilege than God's grace that anyone can receive in all eternity.

God poured out His grace and favor on Noah. The result of Noah's privilege establishes a very important lesson (6:9-13, 22; 7:5). Verse nine lists three characteristics by which Noah demonstrated godliness in a wicked culture (v.9). These traits are the result of receiving God's grace. They are found in everyone who receives it.

First, Noah was righteous (v.9). Surely this does not mean that he was naturally more righteous than the rest of the people in his world. Was Noah born with a special unction of righteousness? Of course not. He was born with a nature like the rest of us which Paul describes "as it is written: 'None is righteous, no, not one'" (Romans 3:10). Noah was not naturally a good guy, but was found to be righteous, or just, because God declared Him just. That is still a work of God's grace. We know that God declares us righteous only through the work of Jesus Christ. Paul's desire was to be "found in him, not having a righteousness of my own that comes from the law, but that which comes through faith in Christ, the righteousness from God that depends on faith" (Philippians 3:9). The person who receives God's grace desires to be like Paul and Noah.

Second, Noah was blameless in a very wicked culture (v.9). The word means to be without blemish. It means to be complete or whole. When applied to a person like Noah, the word describes a  man of integrity. A man of integrity will really stand out when he lives ". . . among the people of his time." Noah's peers were extremely wicked, and he was without blame. Did anyone notice? Donald Barnhouse concluded, "Noah and his great-grandfather Enoch proved that a lily can grow in a manure pile" That kind of person will preach righteousness by the very life he lives. No wonder Peter called Noah a "herald of righteousness" (2 Peter 2:5).

Third, the verse says that Noah enjoyed fellowship with God (v.9). Every day his life was characterized by fellowship with God. He loved God with all his heart, soul, and mind. It is not surprising to read that Noah obeyed God (6:13,22; 7:5). He received God's grace which made him righteous, caused him to live without blame, and motivated him to live in fellowship with God. Of course a person like that will obey God, won't he? Obedience to God presumes that the person knows what God requires. Noah heard God's word (v.13). Everyone has the privilege to hear God to some extent. God speaks to everyone through creation (Romans 1:19-20), the conscience (Romans 2:15), and the written word (Romans 3:19). Theologians call these ways through which God communicates common grace.

But when God speaks to the recipients of saving grace, they listen to Him. Paul taught, "So faith comes from hearing, and hearing through the word of Christ" (Romans 10:17). As a result, "The natural person does not accept the things of the Spirit of God, for they are folly to him, and he is not able to understand them because they are spiritually discerned" (1 Corinthians 2:14). The person who hears God's Word and understands God's Word ought to obey God's Word just as did Noah. Verse twenty-two points out that he obeyed God's Word. The writer to the Hebrew Christians said the same thing. "By faith Noah, being warned by God concerning events as yet unseen, in reverent fear constructed an ark for the saving of his household. By this he condemned the world and became an heir of the righteousness that comes by faith" (Hebrews 11:7).

Because Noah esteemed the God of grace he accomplished everything God commanded (7:5). It must of been very difficult for Noah to even decide to obey God in this matter of ark building. Why would a reasonably intelligent man build an ark if there is no rain or no chance of a flood? There had never been rain since creation. Just the construction of the monstrous barge was an astonishing feat that required about 100 years of labor. This boat was 438 feet long by 73 feet wide by 44 feet high. It came complete with three separate decks. The volume was 1,400,000 cubic feet which was equal to the capacity of 522 modern livestock railroad cars. It had a displacement of 18,000 tons. The construction made the boat virtually impossible to capsize. Would we even think about obeying that kind of plan?

God's grace in Noah's life caused him to live obediently to God. As a result, Noah received the invitation to safety and preservation. The story is a picture of the invitation God offers to His faithful servants for eternity. "His master said to him, 'Well done, good and faithful servant. You have been faithful over a little; I will set you over much. Enter into the joy of your master'" (Matthew 25:21). This invitation will only be offered to people who have experienced the new birth. Jesus told Nicodemus, "Truly, truly, I say to you, unless one is born of water and the Spirit, he cannot enter the kingdom of God" (John 3:5). The invitation is an invitation to enter the kingdom of God. It is the believer's blessed hope. People who have received God's grace long to fulfill the promise in Revelation, "Blessed are those who wash their robes, so that they may have the right to the tree of life and that they may enter the city by the gates" (Revelation 22:14).

The people who have received God's grace have been born of the Spirit of God. Only they are able to obey God. Only they receive the invitation to eternal life. That leads one to think through a couple of important questions. First, "Have you received God's grace?" If not, cry out to God for Him to be merciful and gracious to you and forgive your sins. The second question is, "If you have received God's grace, are you living like the kind of person He will invite into His kingdom?" Noah found grace in the eyes of the Lord. Therefore, he was a righteous man, blameless in his generation, and he walked with God.

# 3

# GET OUT OF THIS PLACE!

Many years ago a man told me a sad story. He told me that his parents had been faithful Christian folks who took him to church every Sunday. As a young boy he understood the gospel and realized his personal need for a Savior. He accepted Jesus Christ as his Savior from sin and, later when he was a teenager, he was quite sure that God wanted him to prepare for full-time ministry as a pastor. He thought long and hard about that and just couldn't bring himself to make the commitment. He decided instead that life offered too much fun and he didn't want to miss out. So he put off going to school to study for the ministry. But he was sure that one day he would follow the will of God.

Well, months turned into years, and before long the man had grown teenagers of his own. He had quit attending church long before the kids were born, so they never had the experience that he had grown up with of Mom and Dad hauling them off to church services. In fact, the children grew up hearing very little about God's plan of salvation. It was not that the parents considered the truth of God's Word to be unimportant but that everything else in life was more important. Long ago the man had turned away from God's will to follow his own pleasures, and now he was so deeply sunk in the quicksand of pleasure that there was just no time for God.

As one might expect, by the time the kids grew into teens, one of the sons began to get into a lot of trouble. The older man said that he tried unsuccessfully several times to talk to this rebellious young man about his need to clean up his life. With tears in his eyes, the man confessed that his son always rejected the gospel saying that if it wasn't good enough for Dad, it wasn't good enough for him. He lamented, "What could I say? I had been such a bad testimony all his life that it was better for me to keep my mouth shut about the gospel."

Just a few years after that conversation, the man passed away. He was tired and worn out; a broken man who looked many years older than he really was. The years of struggling with a rebellious son had taken their toll on him. Sadder yet was the day, only about two years later, when the rebellious son died of a drug overdose.

It is hard to imagine the pain and hopelessness that man felt every day. Lot must have understood the feeling. He too made some really bad choices in his life. He too came to a point of crisis in his life. He too attempted to draw his future sons-in-law out of the path of destruction. But when he gave them the invitation to escape destruction, they thought he was kidding. His life was so opposed to the nature of the invitation that the people who knew him well could not take him seriously. Thus, Lot watched as people he loved were destroyed by God's fire and—worse—were consigned to the same kind of eternal punishment forever. In a matter of hours, Lot witnessed the devastation of his home, his livelihood, and his entire family. He alone was saved. His invitation was valid. His invitation was tremendous. His invitation was sincere. But his invitation was so jaded by his chosen lifestyle that people who were closest to him laughed it off as a joke.

This sad story is repeated often. God offers the sinners of the world an invitation to escape certain and eternal destruction. He offers this tremendous invitation through His people. But often, His people have chosen to live like they are not His people. As a result, when they attempt to tell the good news, people who know them cannot possibly take them seriously. Griffith Thomas concluded, "When the testimony of the life does not agree with the testimony of the lips, the latter always goes unheeded. It is the life that is the true light" (W.H. Griffith Thomas. Genesis, A Devotional Commentary. Grand Rapids: Eerdmans Publishing Company, 1946, 172.). That principle is true for us who wish to be God's mouthpieces who invite sinners to escape that wrath that is to come.

## GOD SENT HIS MESSAGE OF IMPENDING DOOM (VV.12-13)

God observed the wickedness that abounded in Sodom and Gomorrah and decided to destroy the cities. He sent word of His decisions to Lot by way of a couple of divine messengers, one of which seems to be a pre-incarnate Christ (v.13). Lot's culture was exceedingly sinful, even worse than ours. Even way back in Genesis 13:13, which tells the story of Lot first going to Sodom, God concluded that the men were wicked. The word means that they were bad, harmful, or malignant. Furthermore, that verse reveals that they were great sinners against God. That is not to say that they were great people, but that they were people who sinned greatly—and that against Yahweh! Another part of the story about the sinful people in these cities seems to indicate that God, in His kindness, chastened them in an effort to get them to repent and humble themselves. At one point, while Lot was living there, four kings made an alliance and captured the people of the cities (Genesis 14:10). In spite of the fact that the kings Sodom, Gomorrah, and company ended up in a tar pit, it seems that no one was interested in repenting. Their sin was very grave (Genesis 18:20). It was so "heavy" or "weighty" that it caused a great cry to rise up to God demanding that He deal justly against it. (Genesis 18:20).

God told His friend Abraham, Lot's uncle, that He was going to destroy the wicked cities because of their great sin. Abraham interceded for the sinners and asked God to forego judgment if fifty righteous people could be found (Genesis 18:24-32). The word righteous can refer to people who are lawful according to man or according to God. Neither was the case for the people in Sodom and Gomorrah. God could not find even ten righteous people (18:32). It came down to Lot, his wife, two daughters, and two fiancees—a total of six people. But all of them were not righteous. The two fiancees of Lot's daughters rejected God's invitation to escape. Lot's wife disobeyed God and was killed in a most unique way. The two daughters committed gross sin with their father and thus proved to be unrighteous. That leaves Lot who was not exactly a shining example of righteousness.

Sin abounded in Sodom, and yet life looked pretty normal. Jesus taught that normal life in Lot's day in Sodom looked a lot like the way normal life will look in the world just before God pours out judgment in the last days. He taught, "Likewise, just as it was in the days of Lot—they were eating and drinking, buying and selling, planting and building" (Luke 17:28). But normal life in a wicked world causes stress to righteous people. Peter used Lot to illustrate God's astonishing grace. He argued that, "if He rescued righteous Lot, greatly distressed [worn out] by the sensual conduct [outrageous, shameless, licentiousness, unbridled lust] of the wicked [one who breaks through the law's boundaries in order to gratify his lusts]" (2 Peter 2:7). What a terrible place that must have been!

The story that tells how the citizens of Sodom treated Lot's guests illustrates the horrible extent of sin in that city. The men of the city acted like animals (vv.4-5). The text says, "All the people to the last man, surrounded the house." They demanded that Lot turn over his guests to them that they might be able to sexually abuse them. Incredible! How could a culture become so perverted? The men proved that God's warning about the cycle of sin is true. Romans 1:19-25 explains how individuals, and even entire cultures, become so incomprehensibly sinful. God states that (regarding sinners) that "What can be known about God is plain to them, because God has shown it to them" (v.19). "For his invisible attributes, namely, his eternal power and divine nature, have been clearly perceived, ever since the creation of the world, in the things that have been made" (v.20). Therefore, according to the last part of verse twenty, "They are without excuse" (v.20b). However, "Although they knew God, they did not honor him as God or give thanks to him, but they became futile in their thinking, and their foolish hearts were darkened" (v.21). "Claiming to be wise, they became fools" (v.22). Their folly is revealed by the fact that they "exchanged the glory of the immortal God for images resembling mortal man and birds and animals and reptiles" (v.23). "Therefore God gave them up in the lusts of their hearts to impurity, to the dishonoring of their bodies among themselves, because they exchanged the truth about God for a lie and worshiped and served the creature rather than the Creator, who is blessed forever! Amen" (vv.24-25). That is how a person, a family, an organization, a culture becomes so perverted that nothing is sacred and no one is safe.

When I was a young man, pornography was pretty much limited to a few magazine publishers and some underground movie makers. Now it is a multi-billion dollar, world-wide, in-your-face industry. It is available through every media imaginable. Sex outside the bounds of marriage was frowned upon forty years ago. Now it is so expected that the President is mocked and ridiculed for suggesting that the best means for preventing HIV and AIDS is abstinence and sex only within the bounds of marriage. A generation ago, homosexuality was kept in the closet because it was considered a perversion. Now it is a protected and flaunted right of the citizens. What happened? People who scoffed God's warning about the cycle into perversion demanded that society accept them as normal. This led more and more people to step over God's boundaries. The degeneration of the American culture is proof positive that sinners and perverts are not satisfied to be sinners and perverts themselves but must recruit others to join their march to destruction. Sin loves company.

The wickedness in Sodom was great. God would destroy the cities because of it. But at the same time, God kindly warned some of the people to escape (v.12). God warned Lot and his family because He is kind. Because He is kind, God forewarned Abraham because He had made an agreement with the man (Genesis 18:17). He forewarned Lot because He is extremely long suffering. Nevertheless, God destroyed because He is just. He will not tolerate sin forever. Sinners are not ignorant of that fact. God has revealed what can be known about Himself. One of the things that can be known about Him is that sin offends Him. He has warned that He will judge sin.

On numerous occasions God has illustrated His judgment against sin. Often He has demonstrated His judgment against sin through individuals. For example, God killed Onan because what he did was wicked (Genesis 38:10). Sometimes God has illustrated His judgment against sin by judging entire cities. The classic illustration of that principle is this story of how God wiped out Sodom and Gomorrah. One might also consider cities like Pompeii and Herculium. Some people also think that examples of God's judgment against whole cities or nations should include events like the recent Indonesian Tsunami or the plight of New Orleans after Hurricane Katrina. One day we will know the full extent of how God destroys whole cities because of their sin. At this time, some conclusions to that end might be speculative.

Sometimes God has obliterated entire cultures because they became exceedingly sinful. He made this point clear when He sent Israel into the Promised Land. God instructed through Moses, "But you shall devote them to complete destruction, the Hittites and the Amorites, the Canaanites and the Perizzites, the Hivites and the Jebusites, as the LORD your God has commanded" (Deuteronomy 20:17). Is it not true that God judged the whole world in the flood? "The LORD saw that the wickedness of man was great in the earth, and that every intention of the thoughts of his heart was only evil continually. And the LORD was sorry that he had made man on the earth, and it grieved him to his heart. So the LORD said, 'I will blot out man whom I have created from the face of the land, man and animals and creeping things and birds of the heavens, for I am sorry that I have made them'" (Genesis 6:5-7).

Those illustrations should serve to remind all people that God will judge the whole world again in the end. Jesus warned that "the day of the Lord will come like a thief, and then the heavens will pass away with a roar, and the heavenly bodies will be burned up and dissolved, and the earth and the works that are done on it will be exposed" (2 Peter 3:10). God has spoken. Who is listening?

## GOD'S WEAK SERVANT TRIED TO INVITE OTHERS TO SAFETY (v.14)

Lot heard the message from the angelic messengers. He believed what they said and immediately went out to explain the impending doom to people he knew and probably loved. In fact, Lot did not just offer the invitation. He adamantly invited sinners to escape the coming wrath. Lot sternly warned his sons-in-law to escape the coming destruction. An invitation that commands people to be saved is an invitation that understands the seriousness of the impending doom. If we really believe that the Holy God will reign retribution on the earth because of sin and will punish on repentant sinners forever, we would not hesitate to command people to be saved.

Is it possible or even right to command sinners with an invitation? Yes. Consider for example some of the imperative verbs Scripture uses to invite sinners to salvation. These are commands! God called out to wandering Judah through the prophet Isaiah, "Turn to me and be saved, all the ends of the earth! For I am God, and there is no other" (Isaiah 45:22). Jesus offered, "Come to me, all who labor and are heavy laden, and I will give you rest" (Matthew 11:28). Peter preached his heart out on Pentecost, "And with many other words he bore witness and continued to exhort them, saying, 'Save yourselves from this crooked generation'" (Acts 2:40). When the Philippian jailer asked Paul and Silas how he could be saved, they did not offer optional advice. They commanded, "Believe in the Lord Jesus, and you will be saved, you and your household" (Acts 16:31). A command conveys the idea that this must be done.

Maybe Lot was driven to offer the invitation so adamantly because He had a relationship with the sinners. These two men were betrothed to Lot's daughters. This relationship must have given them opportunity to observe Lot for a long time. Surely this time had allowed them to establish a special relationship with Lot which caused him to be concerned for them. They would be no different than our loved ones, neighbors, and co-workers. Maybe Lot even had sons in the city. The angels' command might imply that. They told Lot, "Have you anyone else here? Sons–in-law, sons, daughters, or anyone you have in the city, bring them out of the place" (Genesis 19:12). The daughters and sons-in-law are obvious in the story, but what about the sons?

One cannot tell from the story how many different family members Lot had in the city. It is clear that Lot demanded that the sons-in-law accept the invitation to safety because he really believed God.

The saddest part of the whole story must be the fact that the sinners rejected Lot's invitation. They thought the man was joking. Apparently, this was not the Lot they knew. They had come to know Lot as the man who was a leader among the people. But for the first time, it seems that someone in town was surprised that Lot wasn't like them. This should not be the case at all for God's people. Peter expressed the expected response from sinners when he said, "They are surprised when you do not join them in the same flood of debauchery, and they malign you" (1 Peter 4:4). Suddenly, Lot looked like one of these kinds of people Peter was describing, and it didn't fit.

How did this happen in Lot's life? How did it all come about? The Bible gives enough information to reveal Lot's decline into the wicked culture. In the beginning, he chose Sodom and Gomorrah as the place to live because he saw the external advantages. "And Lot lifted up his eyes and saw that the Jordan Valley was well watered everywhere like the garden of the LORD, like the land of Egypt, in the direction of Zoar. (This was before the LORD destroyed Sodom and Gomorrah.)" (Genesis 13:10). So Lot pitched his tent near Sodom (13:12). Then Lot lived in the city and was captured by the allies (14:12). Soon one finds Lot sitting in the gate (19:1). Finally, we are shocked to hear Lot offer his two virgin daughters to the perverted mob that they might sexually abuse them (19:8). He had become very much like his wicked culture.

Now in a time of crisis Lot appeared to be righteous, and his culture was surprised. The mob must have been surprised to hear Lot talk about how the men came under the protection of his roof (v.8b). Since when did Lot act so different? He witnessed to the truth of God's coming judgment, and his closest associates mocked him. The world does not respect a compromising Christian. "When the testimony of the life does not agree with the testimony of the lips, the latter always goes unheeded. It is the life that is the true light" (W.H. Griffith Thomas. Genesis, A Devotional Commentary. Grand Rapids: Eerdmans Publishing Company, 1946, 172.).

They were destroyed. What a sad conclusion. In an earlier judgment, God saw that sinful humanity had corrupted (destroyed) His creation and, therefore, He destroyed it(Genesis 6:11-13). Here the culture of Sodom had destroyed God's standard of purity, and now He would destroy them. We live in this scenario on a wholesale basis now. Our world is the city destined for destruction. Our world is deserving destruction. The world, which is not a ball of dirt but is the system opposed to God, is the reason for promised destruction. The world, all of the people who are opposed to God, will endure eternal destruction. So? What will you do? We must go to them and cry out, "Get out of this way that is against God! God will destroy!"

Do we really believe that God will destroy sin and sinners? Are we concerned that real people should escape certain judgment? Based on the way we live, will people listen to the invitation when we offer it?

# 4

# COME UP TO THE LORD

## Exodus 24

The Bible does not teach the doctrine of the second blessing. That is the erroneous idea that some Christians get a second, and greater, dose of the Holy Spirit at some point after salvation. The Holy Spirit is a person. When a sinner confesses sin and receives Christ as Savior by faith, he or she is immediately indwelt by the person of the Holy Spirit—all of Him. However, there are Christians who experience a closer walk with God, an almost mystical fellowship with God, that the masses of Christendom never experience.

A. W. Tozer was one of those people. He was a unique servant of the Lord. He enjoyed an intimate companionship with God that most Christians will never know—a walk that causes many of us to stand in awe, wondering what it would be like. Many would say that Tozer was a mystic. Maybe he was, but he walked with God as did Enoch.

In his biography about A.W. Tozer, James Snyder wrote:

Tozer discovered that the companionship of Christ had to be cultivated. That is why he withdrew so often and spent so much time alone. "You can be straight as a gun barrel theologically," Tozer often remarked, "and as empty as one spiritually." Perhaps that was why his emphasis was not on systematic theology but on a personal relationship with God. For him it was a relationship so real, so overpowering as to utterly captivate his attention. He longed for what he fondly referred to as a God-conscious soul—a heart aflame for God. (James L. Snyder. In Pursuit of God: the Life of A.W. Tozer. Camp Hill, Pa.: Christian Publications, 1991, 159.)

One might expect such a man with a heart aflame for God to say, "There are occasions when for hours I lay prostrate before God without saying a word of prayer or a word of praise—I just gaze on Him and worship"

(Tozer, In Pursuit of God, 2). That is a testimony from a mere human, like us, and yet a servant who bore a unique testimony of walking on a higher plane with the Lord than most of God's people will ever know.

Moses was a servant of God like that. God called the lineage of Abraham out of Egypt to be His special nation, His unique people. When God delivered His people from Egyptian bondage, He fulfilled His promise to Abraham. Having delivered them, and having destroyed Pharaoh's pursuing army, and having provided bread and water for the multitude, God gathered them at Mount Sinai. At that place, God organized the mob into a nation that could serve and worship Him according to His standards. God never expects people to guess about what it takes to please Him. Pagan gods, the gods of man's imagination, are like that. Imaginary gods love to keep their followers in the dark. But the true God delights to reveal His "eternal power and divine nature" to His people so that they will know how to please Him.

In this story, when God unfolded the details about what it takes to walk in fellowship with Him, He offered three different invitations. God invited the people to gather around the base of the mountain and observe some of His might and power. He invited the elders of the people, and those who would be priests, to come part way up the mountain and observe more of His splendor. Finally, God invited Moses to enter into His very presence and be enveloped in His shekinah—the outward expression of His glory.

Paul told the Corinthian Christians, "We all, with unveiled face, beholding the glory of the Lord, are being transformed into the same image from one degree of glory to another. For this comes from the Lord who is the Spirit" (2 Corinthians 3:18). On which level of glory are you? Have you not received the invitation from the Lord who is the Spirit, to come up to the higher level?

## GOD'S INVITATION TO THE PEOPLE (vv. 3-8)

God invited the people in general to come to the base of the mountain (19:10-13). There they would be able to observe His magnificent glory (v.13). God told the people, through Moses, that He would come down and His presence would be manifested on the mountaintop. This was a very broad invitation given to all of the people. All of God's people, without exception, had the privilege of seeing His glory.

The invitation was broad and generous, yet God couched it with warnings. He warned the people to maintain awesome respect for His glory when they responded to His invitation (vv.10-12; 24:3-8). First, the people would need to be set apart (consecrated) unto God before they participated in the event (v.10). If, for whatever reason, someone chose not to respect God's ordained boundaries, God expected the rest of the people to execute him (v.12-13). God does not take disrespect from mere humans lightly. God took the initiative to offer the invitation to behold His glory. The people needed to take the initiative to discipline themselves and show respect.

The day came when God did exactly what He promised. His presence came down on the top of Mount Sinai. The people were gathered around the base of the mountain; and when God descended, they were astonished at His glory. They revered God and displayed the awesome respect that God required from them. They had been careful to take care of the consecration thing earlier. Moses had consecrated the people and set them apart unto God (24:4b-8). He had rehearsed God's covenant and rules with them (vv.3-4). He had taken charge of offering sacrifices so that the people would be cleansed and set apart by the blood (vv.5-8). And when God descended, the people feared Him mightily (Exodus 20:18-21). They trembled with fear (v.18). They begged Moses to intercede (v.19). They stood far off (v.20).

So far the picture of the people's character looks pretty good. These trembling souls are the same folks who had earlier agreed to do everything God required of them. In fact, they agreed to do what God told them even before they knew what God was going to say (19:7-8). When they responded to Moses' initial instruction with the words, "All that the Lord has spoken we will do" (19:8), they might have been thinking about Moses' introductory words in this grand event. He had relayed to them God's message, "You yourselves have seen what I did to the Egyptians, and how I bore you on eagles' wings and brought you to myself. Now therefore, if you will indeed obey my voice and keep my covenant, you shall be my treasured possession among all peoples, for all the earth is mine; and you shall be to me a kingdom of priests and a holy nation" (Exodus 19:4-6). Therefore, the masses might have meant, "We will do that! We will keep God's covenant, whatever that is."

The people's response might also have revealed their desired attitude for everything that would be coming from God. For example, He had yet to give Moses all of the laws and requirements of the covenant. Surely the people were sincere when they said, "We will do whatever God says." In fact, even after they heard Moses read the words of the covenant, they still felt the same way (24:3, 7-8). The sad truth is that this resolve lasted only a matter of days until they yielded to the desires of their flesh. They proved to be stubborn and stiff-necked people. None of those people gathered at the base of the mountain who declared, "We will obey God," entered the Promised Land. God killed all of them for stubbornness and disobedience except for Caleb and Joshua who was with Moses at the time. Their view of God's glory did not have much lasting effect.

## GOD'S INVITATION TO THE LEADERS (vv. 1-2, 9-11)

The leaders in this story were the elders of the people and the future priests (vv.1-2). Because they were leaders, they needed close fellowship with God (v.1,14). Aaron and his sons, Nadab and Abihu, would be priests who interceded between the people and God. At this point in the history of God's people, they did not have a job. However, as soon as the events at Mount Sinai were over, they had a very important responsibility before God and the people. They would be responsible to maintain all of the outward symbols of worship. They were responsible to offer the sacrifices of God's people. The High Priest would take the atonement for the nation's sins into the very presence of God. God had very high standards and special requirements for this group of people.

The elders were also held to a higher standard than the general populace because they represented the people and led them. Each of the seventy elders represented families into which they were born. In that sense, their position of authority and service was predetermined. On the other hand, each elder was chosen to be a representative because he was skillful and trustworthy.

The story reminds us that the leaders of God's people should be the first to obey God's invitation. God still says, "Come up to Yahweh . . ." (v.1). He still invites us to know Him, the everlasting God, better. He still invites us to find Him in His Word. He still invites us to fellowship with Him. How do twenty-first century leaders of God's people respond to God's invitation to "come up?" Often leaders erroneously see themselves as just normal, run-of-the- mill folks. Many forget that they are leaders in their home, leaders on the job, leaders in their church, or leaders in their community. Leadership is a serious responsibility and, therefore, God holds the leaders to a higher standard. James warned, "Not many of you should become teachers, my brothers, for you know that we who teach will be judged with greater strictness" (James 3:1). God invites leaders to come up and experience His glory.

The leaders of Israel observed an astonishing display of God's glory (vv.9-11). They saw God's glory manifested even though God kept certain limitations on what they would face (vv.9-11). They went to a level above the masses of the congregation. Therefore, they saw things the congregation didn't see. They saw a manifestation of the God of Israel (v.10). They did not see God Himself because, as God warns, no one can see the exact being of God and live. Shortly after this event, Moses begged God to show him His full glory. "But, [God] said, you cannot see my face, for man shall not see me and live" (Exodus 33:20). Therefore, it is clear that God did not reveal His full glory to the leaders. This is such an important point because the text records the fact that God did not punish them (v.11). He did not kill them. They saw precisely the amount of glory God wanted them to see. They rejoiced in the experience. They feasted in celebration (v.11).

What did the leaders see? According to the description here, it seems like they saw the glory of God seated as King. They saw a beautiful blue pavement of some sort that was probably clear like a precious gem. The whole scene reminds us of the vision John described in the Revelation.

And he who sat there had the appearance of jasper and carnelian, and around the throne was a rainbow that had the appearance of an emerald" (Revelation 4:3). From the throne came flashes of lightning, and rumblings and peals of thunder, and before the throne were burning seven torches of fire, which are the seven spirits of God, and before the throne there was as it were a sea of glass, like crystal (Revelation 4:5-6a).

But even they did not experience what Moses would experience on the highest level.

Based on what the leaders saw, they should have stood firm in God's standards when the time of testing came (32:1-6). No doubt the test came much sooner than the leaders expected. According to Exodus 32, the people quickly turned to rebellion (v.1). They grew impatient waiting for Moses and resorted to the religion of their pagan neighbors. Their disrespect of God led them into gross sin. The saddest part of the story is that Aaron, who would become the High Priest, let the people become an abomination to God (vv.2-6). It appears that he did nothing to dissuade them. Why didn't he steadfastly refuse? Where were the elders? Where was Hur (v.14)? Where were Aaron's sons? Well, subsequent evidence proves that Aaron's sons, the nation's first priests, were probably in favor of the fiasco. Some time later it was necessary for God to destroy the two older boys because they engaged in a similar action of offering unacceptable worship to God (Numbers 3:4). Their vision of God's holiness did not make them more holy. They were like many professing Christians. They were like the people the writer to the Hebrews warned about. "For it is impossible to restore again to repentance those who have once been enlightened, who have tasted the heavenly gift, and have shared in the Holy Spirit, and have tasted the goodness of the word of God and the powers of the age to come, if they then fall away, since they are crucifying once again the Son of God to their own harm and holding him up to contempt" (Hebrews 6:4-6). It is a sad situation when people who have observed God's glory come to see no reason to protect His glory.

## God's invitation to Moses (vv.12-18)

Moses went up into the mountain when God invited him  (vv.12-16a). He and his faithful assistant, Joshua, heeded God's call (vv.12-14). They did not barge up the mountain seeking to be the first ones to get to the highest level. That response is expected from junior high boys, not of God's chosen servants. God invited first (v.12). God invited Moses to come to the highest level of glory so that He could give His servant the tablets of stone. These tables map out God's character and the people's responsibility to Him. Nothing in all of God's revelation in creation more clearly describes God than His law and covenant. His law reveals His unattainable standard of holiness, and His covenant reveals His mercy.

Moses and Joshua moved ahead in spite of the terrible glory of God. They left the other leaders on level two. They willingly moved into an unknown situation. They demonstrated the truth that God does not ask us to approve of the circumstances before we move up another level with Him. He invites and we either move or reject His invitation. Moses accepted the invitation and went further than anyone else. And there he waited (vv.15-16a). He had left Joshua behind. He went into the cloud of God's glory and waited six days. Often the move to greater fellowship with God is through the clouds of patience. God invites us to follow Him to greater glory, and suddenly we are in circumstances through which we cannot see, issues that we do not know, and events that we do not understand. What is the servant of God to do? What did Moses do? God invited him into the unknown, and Moses simply trusted God.

Because he responded to God's invitation, Moses was enveloped by God's glory (vv.16b-18). Moses enjoyed intimate communion with God for a long time there. Forty days and forty nights is a long time. Some scholars think that the term is not to be taken literally, but that it means a long time. Actually, remaining forty days and nights in a frightening cloud is a long time. What did Moses do all that time? He was receiving the law of God. He was enveloped in a "devouring fire." What did the people think? Often the deepest fellowship with God is found in the most fearful circumstances. God's glory is a fearful thing and most humans hesitate to accept His invitation to go there.

God invited Moses to the highest level of glory so that he would be prepared to represent God to the people. Because of the invitation, Moses would have God's law and commandments. Those truths were a great rock to which he could cling when He took difficult stands. They put him in good standing as he interceded for the people. As a result, Moses became an enduring example of faith for God's people in every age to follow. He, like Paul, counted all earthly accomplishments as loss that he might gain Christ. Gain Christ? Moses did not even know about Christ, did he? He must have known something about the promised Redeemer because God said, "He considered the reproach of Christ greater wealth than the treasures of Egypt, for he was looking to the reward" (Hebrews 11:26). What an example Moses is for believers. It is interesting to discover that the believers who come out of the Tribulation will sing the song Moses wrote. "And they sing the song of Moses, the servant of God, and the song of the Lamb, saying, 'Great and amazing are your deeds, O Lord God the Almighty! Just and true are your ways, O King of the nations!'" (Revelation 15:3). The man who responded to God's invitation to come up higher learned well that God's ways are great and amazing. He learned that God's ways are just and true. Those truths are discovered most clearly in deep, intimate fellowship with God.

Have you begun that fellowship by accepting God's invitation to eternal life in Christ? Have you accepted God's invitation to deep intimate fellowship with Christ? On which level of glory are you willing to dwell?

# 5

# THE INVITATION TO
# HONEST COMMITMENT

## JOSHUA 24:14-24

G od's people had been in the Promised Land for about seven years when Joshua gathered the people at Shechem to renew the stipulations of God's Covenant. Shechem was in the center of the new nation. It was a place of great significance to the Israelites. Here Abraham stopped on his way out of Haran (Genesis 12:4-9). The LORD met him at this place and promised to give that very land to his posterity. This was God's first promise regarding the Promised Land. Abraham built an altar signifying his respect for the God who promised. Later, Abraham's grandson, Jacob, stopped at the same location, bought a piece of land, and built an altar to remember the God of Israel (Genesis 33:18-20).

Now, at least all of the leaders of the nation gathered at the same spot, and probably many of the people joined them. Joshua rehearsed to the multitude how God had summoned their forefather Abraham out from among the pagan idol worshipers in Haran beyond the Euphrates River (vv.1-3). He reminded them that God had delivered their forefathers from the bondage and idolatry of Egypt (vv.4-5). He rehearsed how God had defeated their enemies along the way, putting to shame the army of Pharaoh (vv.6-7), defeating the Amorites (v.8), protecting them from Balaam's curse (vv.9-10), and driving out the pagan idol worshipers who once occupied the very land where they now lived (vv.11-13).

Having set the backdrop of God's faithful deliverance from cultures and natures that were sunk in idolatry, Joshua offered the great invitation to God's people. He invited them to choose for themselves whom they would serve. They could serve this God who delivered them, or they could serve the idols of the people whom God defeated. What kind of a choice is that? No one in their right mind would pick the wrong side of that invitation. Who would want to serve idols if God had been kind enough to deliver them from the sin of idolatry? The invitation appears to be pointless.

Idols are not only the bars of gold Achin stole or the family idols Rachel stole from Laban. John Calvin was right when he concluded, "The human heart is an idol factory, tear down one idol and it will build another." Because this is true, the human heart has the ability to make almost anything an idol. So in the history of God's people, Jacob was Rebekah's idol, Jacob's favorite wife, Rachel, was his idol, and Bathsheba was David's idol, and Solomon's many wives were his idol. Idols can be almost anything or anyone, and they always separate God's child from God. In the end, they always cost God's child much pain and sorrow.

This sad reality led F. B. Myer to conclude, "Our only hope is to be strong in our choice of God. The negative destruction of self is unsatisfactory. We must deliberately set ourselves toward God. Our will must crown him. Our soul must make him first. Our life must be subdued to the least syllable of his command" (F.B. Myer. Joshua the Land of Promise. Fort Washington, Pa.: Christian Literature Crusade. 1977. 204). Modern day people of God, must respond to Joshua's invitation to make a wise choice. We will not serve God accidently. We will not forsake idols as a matter of chance. We must do what Joshua invited God's people to do. We must choose to serve God!

## JOSHUA INVITED THE PEOPLE TO EMULATE HIS RESOLVE (vv.14-15)

At this important meeting in this important place, Joshua invited the leaders and the people of God to choose to serve God (vv.14-15a). The circumstances of the event set the tone for not only the invitation, but for the entire meeting (v.14). Joshua had just rehearsed God's history with His people (vv.1-13). His words, "Now therefore" appeal to the context of a legal setting of the covenant. This was no small matter. This was not an insignificant gathering. The root issue, the foundation upon which every statement stood, was, "Fear the Lord."

There is no question that "fear the Lord" is a frequently stated and, therefore, important Old Testament requirement. Before he died, Moses reminded the people that they were well aware of God's plan. He reminded them "how on the day that you stood before the LORD your God at Horeb, the LORD said to me, 'Gather the people to me, that I may let them hear my words, so that they may learn to fear me all the days that they live on the earth, and that they may teach their children so'" (Deuteronomy 4:10). Moses also reminded the Israelites, "The LORD commanded us to do all these statutes, to fear the LORD our God, for our good always, that he might preserve us alive, as we are this day" (Deuteronomy 6:24). Because the command is so plain, there should never have been any doubt in the minds of God's people about what God expected from them. God's people should maintain an awesome respect of Him. They should always remember that God is fearsome, but He is kind.

But when we come to the New Testament, it appears (according to some scholars) that there is a kinder, gentler God who does not require such deep respect. However, "fear the Lord" is also a requirement discovered in the New Testament. For example, Peter wrote, "Honor everyone. Love the brotherhood. Fear God. Honor the emperor" (1 Peter 2:17). The plan is simple.

There is a reason why God requires His people to respect Him. Awesome respect of God keeps His people from playing with idols. Idolatry indicates that we are comfortable with that which is opposed to God. Sometimes it is the simple practices of life betray our lack of respect to God. In light of God's plan for His people to fear Him, Woudstra concluded, "Whatever resembled an alliance other than that with the Lord, be it in manner of dress, sacrificial practices, common mores, and the like, was forbidden. Some things prohibited by law were not necessarily immoral when viewed by themselves, but their connection with the cultus of foreign gods rendered them unusable for Israel" (M.H. Woudstra. The New International Commentary on the Old Testament. "The Book of Joshua." Grand Rapids: W.B. Eerdman's Publishing Co., 1981, 351.). Is the principle out of date? Should we not think along the same lines today?

Proper respect for God is the foundation necessary to "serve Him in sincerity and faithfulness . . ." as Joshua challenged his peers. This is a call for uprightness and integrity, as opposed to pretense and outward symbolism. Do not worship lesser gods in private, while pretending to worship the true God outwardly in order to please men.

The invitation requires God's people to put away idols. Joshua challenged the Israelites to abandon the gods their forefathers served beyond the river and in Egypt. The river he referred to without name must be the Euphrates. Abraham came from a family that worshiped the moon god in Ur on the east side of the Euphrates River. Idolatry was a learned trait for Abraham, but he forsook it to trust God. Likewise, Egypt was a spawning ground for idolatry. Israelites participated in it while they lived there for 400 years in slavery. The golden calf incident at Mt. Sinai, after God had delivered them from Egypt, shows how deeply ingrained in God's people idolatry was.

Joshua also challenged the people to abandon the idolatry of the Amorites (v.15b). The fertility gods of the Amorites, which emphasized licentious behavior, appealed to their flesh. The sexual perversion was an appeal to the lust of the flesh. The promise of a great harvest, if their worship pleased their god, appealed to human wisdom. Human wisdom is impressed by the fact that a good harvest is guaranteed if we do the right kind of things in human strength. It makes us look pretty good. Because the Israelites were farmers, this idol was a serious temptation. They depended on good crops.

Earlier Joshua had confronted the people about fooling around with the idolatry of Moab. He rebuked them saying, "Have we not had enough of the sin at Peor from which even yet we have not cleansed ourselves, and for which there came a plague upon the congregation of the LORD" (Joshua 22:17).

Hundreds of years later, Stephen's sermon revealed that idolatry had a strong hold on God's nation. Stephen reminded the Israelite leaders that, "God turned away and gave them over to worship the host of heaven, as it is written in the book of the prophets: 'Did you bring to me slain beasts and sacrifices, during the forty years in the wilderness, O house of Israel? You took up the tent of Moloch and the star of your god Rephan, the images that you made to worship; and I will send you into exile beyond Babylon'" (Acts 7:42-43).

This proven propensity to fall prey to idolatry is why the people needed to make a choice (v.15). Notice how Joshua posed the invitation. "Does it seem evil. . .?" Did it seem unreasonable, inconvenient to serve God? Why wouldn't they choose to serve God? In fact, it seems strange that such people would even need the invitation to choose since God had already chosen them to be His people. What choice did they have to make? In reality, as far as justice goes, they had no choice. They must fear God and serve Him. Therefore, they, like us, could choose to do the right thing or choose to do wrong. It is a choice we make every day. We can easily become like rebellious Israelites on Mt. Carmel. "Elijah came near to all the people and said, 'How long will you go limping between two different opinions? If the LORD is God, follow him; but if Baal, then follow him.' And the people did not answer him a word" (1 Kings 18:21). Indeed, when God's people are challenged to serve the God who has already chosen them, what can we say?

The man who presented the invitation to God's people had already made the choice himself. He did not ask them to do something he was not willing to do himself. He chose to lead his family in serving God (v.15b). Joshua made the choice for his house. Was that fair? It was good for him to choose to abandon idolatry for himself. It was good that he chose to put away the false gods. It was very noble, yea righteous, for Joshua to recognize the problem and choose to fear God. But was it fair for him to make his choice the choice for his entire family?

Because Joshua was the head of his home, it was his responsibility to lead the family in the correct lifestyle. It did not guarantee that every member would become a true Israelite. That is not the responsibility of the head of the house. Each member of the family is responsible for his or her relationship with God. However, fathers, or the heads of home, must make the choice first to serve God. That choice does not guarantee that his children will grow up to be born again and serve God. However, it gives them every opportunity to know God so that they are without excuse. Conversely, when fathers make the wrong choice, they entrench their families in exceeding sinfulness.

Joshua made the choice to commit to serving God, and then he invited others to follow his example. "Choose whom you will serve," he offered. Who would make an honest, actual choice to serve false gods instead of the true God? That question might be answered by another question: "What kind of example have you set?"

### The People Were Resolved To Serve God (vv.16-18)

They remembered what God had done for them (vv.17-18a). They admitted that God delivered them from bondage (v.17). They made some very meaningful confessions in response to Joshua's invitation. They confessed, "He is the LORD our God." They acknowledged, "He brought up our fathers and us from slavery. He did many wonderful signs in our sight. He preserved us." These were deeply personal confessions. Everyone admitted that they had personally witnessed God's kindness. This is the proper testimony for every saved person.

The people also admitted that God had defeated their enemies along the way (v.18). God drove out the pagan idolaters who were in the land. In particular, He drove out the Amorites who worshiped the fertility god (v.15). It sounds like they were glad to be rid of that temptation. Every Christian must acknowledge that God provides victory over sin. Our claim is Paul's challenge to, "Let not sin therefore reign in your mortal bodies, to make you obey their passions. Do not present your members to sin as instruments for unrighteousness, but present yourselves to God as those who have been brought from death to life, and your members to God as instruments for righteousness. For sin will have no dominion over you, since you are not under law but under grace" (Romans 6:12-14).

Because the people remembered how kind and gracious God had been to them and their forefathers, they were determined to serve Him (vv.16, 18b). They emphatically vowed a commitment (v.16). "Far be it from us to serve idols . . . ," they said. They were emphatic. Their's was a response from the mind, will, and emotions. They confessed to love the Lord with all their heart, soul, mind, and strength. The people were as sincere as people can be (v.18b). They vowed to serve based on what God did. Would they continue to serve if things got confusing and it looked like God was not protecting them in the way they thought He should?

## JOSHUA WARNED THE PEOPLE THAT SERVING GOD IS COSTLY (vv.19-24)

He pointed out two important traits about God (v.19-20). The leader reminded the people that God is holy and jealous. Because He is holy, He is unapproachable apart from a covering for sin because He is sinless and does not tolerate sin. Because He is jealous, He is zealous to protect His holiness from the infection of sin. He will maintain His holy honor at all costs.

Serving such a God demands much from a human perspective. Because God zealously protects His holy honor, Joshua told the people, "You are not able to serve" according to human wisdom or strength. Your human abilities will fail you in your attempts to serve God. Be assured of this. This forces an honest appraisal of our commitment. If we really think that we can abandon our idols and serve the true God in our own strength, we are sadly mistaken. We need to hear Joshua's assurance that we are destined to fail.

The reminder that God is so holy that we cannot serve Him in human strength is a bit shocking. But Joshua's next statement is more stunning. He told the people that God "will not forgive your transgressions or your sins." What? How could he say that? This is an extreme statement meant to teach that no one should presume that God will forgive sin. Does God forgive? Yes, but not because He has no other choice. God forgives because of His merciful grace. You cannot force God to forgive you. God does forgive, but He who knows the heart does not deal superficially with sin like we are prone to do. Therefore, never presume on God's grace. Make your commitment to God in fear and trembling, trusting Him to provide the grace to do what you promise.

The word transgressions speaks of those times when people who ought to serve God miss the mark of God's righteousness. It happens when God's people leave things undone, or when our best wasn't good enough. The word sins speaks of stepping over the boundary. These are acts of commission when, in rebellion, we choose to do what God forbids or choose to ignore what God prescribes. These statements remind us that our deepest soul must be pervaded by an awful reverence of God's holiness. Because we are so special to God, because we are the objects of His favor, we must be especially careful about our attitudes toward idolatry. Thus, Amos the prophet said of these people, "You only have I known of all the families of the earth; therefore I will punish you for all your iniquities" (Amos 3:2). We, too, are that privileged.

The standard was strict. Joshua's reminder was pointed. Nevertheless, the people affirmed their choice to serve God (vv.21-24). This is a second and more emphatic affirmation of service (v.21). Joshua called them to be witnesses against themselves if they failed to keep their commitment (vv.22-24). They witnessed that they accepted the invitation to serve God (v.22). All right then! If so, they needed to get rid of the current idols immediately (v.23). They really wanted to obey God (v.24). The people's determination and emphatic vows remind us that outward expression validates inward commitment. They vowed to serve God, and they did so as long as Joshua was alive (v.31). But after Joshua and this generation died, the posterity seemed to forget what their forefathers did. According to Jeremiah people who grew up with the same advantages and privileges forgot how wonderful God had been and that they should commit to serve Him out of fear and love. He thundered to their posterity:

Hear the word of the LORD, O house of Jacob, and all the clans of the house of Israel. Thus says the LORD: "What wrong did your fathers find in me that they went far from me, and went after worthlessness, and became worthless? They did not say, 'Where is the LORD who brought us up from the land of Egypt, who led us in the wilderness, in a land of deserts and pits, in a land of drought and deep darkness, in a land that none passes through, where no man dwells?' And I brought you into a plentiful land to enjoy its fruits and its good things. But when you came in, you defiled my land and made my heritage an abomination. The priests did not say, 'Where is the LORD?' Those who handle the law did not know me; the shepherds transgressed against me; the prophets prophesied by Baal and went after things that do not profit" (Jeremiah 2:4-8).

May such never be the case for us. God is gracious to invite us to follow Him. God is gracious to invite sinners to abandon their idols and pursue Him alone. How foolish it is for people to hear the invitation from a gracious and loving God and then choose instead to walk a path of sin that will certainly result in judgment. The wise man or woman hears God's invitation and quickly and thoroughly leaves that hobby, habit, friend, our dream that stands between them and God. God will not share attention with anything or anyone. Choose today which you will follow: the God of grace and mercy or the gods of your own making that will fail you in the time of need. Embrace this wonderful invitation.

# 6

# SHALL A FAULTFINDER CONTEND WITH THE ALMIGHTY?

### Job 38:1-3; 40:1-14; 42:1-6

The life of a typical American goes something like this: We are born in a comfortable hospital with all the latest technology to assure a healthy beginning. We grow up in comfortable homes, attend well equipped schools, participate in many different fun activities, and prepare for a particular program in college or vocation in life. We attend college or learn a trade with the purpose of preparing to make a comfortable living. We graduate, marry a helpful spouse, get a good job, and live in a nice house, with the latest conveniences, in a nice neighborhood. Along the way we insure ourselves against any possible problem and prepare for a comfortable retirement. Finally, we reach retirement age when we sit back and enjoy the fruit of our labors until we die.

All in all that is a pleasant scenario, and it is not altogether unbiblical. However, it is obvious that the people in that scenario have the desire and the opportunity to insulate themselves from difficulty. Who wouldn't do that given the opportunity? No sensible person intentionally sets himself up for problems. In fact, the day may soon come when typical American citizens will face a multitude of trouble their forefathers never had to face.

Facing problems in life is not as bad as it sounds. James wrote: "Count it all joy, my brothers, when you meet trials of various kinds, for you know that the testing of your faith produces steadfastness. And let steadfastness have its full effect, that you may be perfect and complete, lacking in nothing" (James 1:2-4). Trials often take away a person's self-confidence or self-sufficiency. Trials have a way of making folks feel vulnerable. For some people, the trials of life drive them to a closer walk with God. Is it possible that this is the reason why some people seem to have one trial after another in life? Do they tend to wander away from God unless God keeps the pressure on them?

The silver lining in the cloud of trouble is that people who are sensitive to God's will, people who respect God's Word, tend to turn to Him in prayer and ask if He has a purpose in the trial. It is astonishing that the Creator God of the universe would even want mere people to converse with Him. But He does! This is the God who said to the stumbling, sinning Israelites, "Come now, let us reason together, says the LORD: though your sins are like scarlet, they shall be as white as snow; though they are red like crimson, they shall become like wool" (Isaiah 1:18). That is an amazing invitation! God invites mere people to come and reason with Him. The stated result of that reasoning is that the sinner's sins will be covered over, and he or she has the privilege to come into right fellowship with God.

That is not to say that sin is atoned for through a process of arguing with God. Rather, it means that when a person truly comes face-to-face with God, he will see God as He is and see himself as he is and humble himself before God. That is the story of Job. Job endured troubles that most of people cannot imagine. He did not understand why he had to face these trials. He wanted to argue his case with God, but complained that he could not find Him. After allowing Job to complain for some time, God spoke to him. God invited Job to "dress for action." God said, "I will question you and you make it known to me."

In the face of difficulty, God's people are prone to question God like Job did. We wonder why He allows us to have problems. We wonder why He doesn't have better control of things. We wonder where He is when things go haywire. Some folks even wonder if He exists. God invites troubled people who are facing troubling times to come and defend their case to Him. When a person really comes face-to-face with the truth about God, he quickly discovers, like Job, that he has no case. Would to God that we would all be humbled before God as was Job. God invited Job to go through two interrogation scenarios in order to help Job see that he was nothing and God is everything. In the end, Job achieved the anticipated result: humility of self and complete faith in God. The result proved how great the two-fold invitation really was.

## THE FIRST INVITATION (38:1-40:5)

God invited Job to answer His questions (38:1-39:30). It is important to realize that God offered this invitation to a righteous man. Job was no mere sinner. He was not even a mere person. He was an unusual man. The Bible says that Job was the most righteous man in the earth. That is how God chose to introduce Job from the very outset of this book about the unusual man (Job 1:1). That is the same terminology God used when He described Job to Satan (Job 1:8). Imagine a person who God could introduce to Satan as the most righteous man in the world.

Because Job was righteous, there were at least four obvious traits in his life (Job 1:1,8). He was blameless, he lived an upright life, he had deep respect for God, and he avoided evil. He revealed his character by his practice. The introductory words of the book reveal that Job regularly consecrated his children and, after they had partied together, he offered sacrifices to God in their behalf in case they had sinned (1:5). Obviously, Job tried everything possible in human strength to do right. It is almost certain that Job was a more godly person than anyone we know.

But Job needed to grow in grace. He was still human and, therefore, plagued with the sinful human nature. Evidence of his need to grow is seen in the way he responded to accusation. This man tried hard to live righteously and did not appreciate being accused of failing in righteousness. The story is full of his arguments and the arguments from his friends. His friends were quite convinced that Job must have really sinned at some point, or he would not be enduring such terrible trials in life. The truth is that Job's facts were right. He was not suffering because of personal sin. That made his trial even more difficult. Who among us would respond to false accusing friends any more lovingly?

Worse than arguing with friends was the fact that Job displayed a fiery attitude toward God also. Listen to some of his arguments: "For he is not a man, as I am, that I might answer him, that we should come to trial together. There is no arbiter between us, who might lay his hand on us both. Let him take his rod away from me, and let not dread of him terrify me. Then I would speak without fear of him, for I am not so in myself" (Job 9:32-35). "Only grant me two things, then I will not hide myself from your face: withdraw your hand far from me, and let not dread of you terrify me. Then call, and I will answer; or let me speak, and you reply to me. How many are my iniquities and my sins? Make me know my transgression and my sin. Why do you hide your face and count me as your enemy?" (Job 13:20-24). "Oh, that I had one to hear me! (Here is my signature! Let the Almighty answer me!) Oh, that I had the indictment written by my adversary!" (Job 31:35).

Actually, responses like this might cause one to wonder about Job's righteousness. Have we never questioned God? Have we not argued about His apparent will for us? Who has not at some point complained about the row God has given him to hoe?

Job needed to grow in grace. He would do that through a process of the revelation of God's eternal nature and divine power. Job desired a bill, a statement listing what he had done wrong. God did not comply with Job's desires. God didn't do anything that Job expected Him to do. God's response to Job's complaints reminded Job that God is not subject to anyone—not even a righteous man. Just before God interrupted the foolish men and invited Job to answer His questions, Elihu said that if God showed up it would be in golden splendor or awesome majesty (37:23). God didn't obey Elihu either. Instead, God spoke out of a terrible storm. Some people foolishly wait for God to send a choir of angels to announce His will for them. That is probably not going to happen. More often than not, God chooses to speak quietly out of the storms of life.

Furthermore, God never told Job about Satan and the whole plan. Surely one might expect this story to end like the novels men and women write, with God unfolding the whole situation so that Job can live happily ever after. As far as it is possible to tell, Job never knew about God's conversation with Satan.

Not only did God fail to respond in a way Job expected, but He also did not answer Job's questions. Throughout the story, Job either directly or indirectly addressed multiple questions to God. But God never answered even one of them. He is not interested in arguing with humans on their level of understanding. Rather, God desires for His people to learn more about Him and more about themselves. His desire is for people to learn the helpful things along the way like Job did. Thus, God taught Job about His majesty and Job's insignificance through a series of rhetorical questions. That is not to say that God's questions could not be answered, but it is clear that Job did not answer them. It is as if God took Job "outside" and showed him around His world. God did not intend for His questions to crush Job with His obvious superiority or to humiliate Job because of his ignorance. Job should have rejoiced that God even desired to converse with him.

It is important to remember that Job had no Bible. He did not have God's Law nor was he aware of the sacrificial system that God would introduce many years later. Through such means God revealed His nature, power, and personality to His people. But Job did not have those advantages. So God took Job to His handiwork in nature and said, "Look at what I do. Trust me!" That really should be sufficient evidence for anyone. That is Paul's argument to the Roman Christians. He said, "What can be known about God is plain to them, because God has shown it to them. For his invisible attributes, namely, his eternal power and divine nature, have been clearly perceived, ever since the creation of the world, in the things that have been made. So they are without excuse" (Romans 1:19-20). It is good for God's people to take time to learn about God's handiwork as it displays His glory.

With rapid fire questions, God drew Job's attention to the fact that He is the Creator of this magnificent universe (38:4-15), that He rules over inanimate nature (38:16-38), and that He rules over animate nature (38:39-39:30). Therefore, Job is without excuse. What can Job say? Where does the man who complained that God was not being fair stand now? "And the LORD said to Job: 'Shall a faultfinder contend with the Almighty? He who argues with God, let him answer it'" (Job 40:1-2). Job was in deep trouble if he wanted to argue with God at this point.

Job's response to the first line of questioning is recorded in 40:3-5. It appears that God's questions reduced the man to silence. There is obviously no more rage, no more anger, no more accusations against God. Most folks would be satisfied with this. God was not. God understood that Job's response here indicated more accurately that he was determined to hold his ground. The fact that Job talked about being silent did not convince God. Silence is not the same as change, acknowledging error, or repentance. But didn't Job say, "I have no answer"? Did he not show deep respect for God when he replied, "I lay my hand over my mouth"?

Observe and listen to all that Job said in this reply. Consider especially verse five where Job said, "I have spoken once, I will not answer." Another way of expressing his sentiment is to say, "I have said what I have said. I will not change." It seems likely that Job concluded, "I am settled." He offered no confession of sin. He offered no retraction of the accusations he made against God. He demonstrated no submission to God's will at this point. Job's condition at this juncture was too much like that of Christians who have concluded that they cannot wage war successfully against God, so they just grit their teeth and try to endure life. That is not acceptable.

## THE SECOND INVITATION (40:6-14)

God proceeded to offer another challenge and another series of questions to Job (40:6-41:34). God invited Job to prove Him wrong (40:8). God's invitation to Job reveals that He has the authority to question His created beings whenever and however He chooses. Would we try to prove God wrong in an effort to appear to be right (40:8)? That sounds so utterly foolish, and yet God accused Job of that very attitude.

Therefore, God invited Job to match His majesty (40:9-14). What will the puny human do when God invites him to clothe himself with the splendor of God (v.10)? No person can even begin to do that. That is the point. Having offered the challenge for Job to put on the majesty of God, He then challenged Job to humble those who are proud (vv.12-13). Surely that question hit Job like a brick. This is the key issue in the argument. The honest person must admit that he has a hard enough time humbling himself. How can he truly humble someone else? If I attempt to make someone humble, they will probably respond by getting angry or maybe by setting their jaw and remaining silent in Job-like fashion.

That is precisely God's argument against humanity. If we were actually able to be like God, we could save ourselves (v.14). But we are not like God so we cannot save ourselves from destruction. In order to help Job and us understand how unlike God we are, how un-majestic we really are, God threw out two very simple illustrations of His power. He asked Job if he was able to take control of the Behemoth (40:15-24). Then God asked Job if He could take control of Leviathan (41:1-34). No one is exactly sure what these beasts were, but they were obviously mammoth and powerful. Obviously no ancient person could control them. But God does! Are we enough like God to save ourselves? Not even close!

This last line of questioning brought Job to the conclusion he desperately needed. Job repented (42:1-6). His repentance was not an emotional response to a sad story. His repentance was based on his newly refreshed knowledge of God. He confessed, "I know that you can do all things, and that no purpose of yours can be thwarted" (Job 42:2). We, like Job, must come to the settled conclusion that God is all powerful and able to do whatever He wants to do. We must also conclude that God is all wise and always does the right and good thing.

Second, Job's repentance was based on newly discovered knowledge of himself. God had said: "Who is this that hides counsel without knowledge?" Now Job confessed: "Therefore I have uttered what I did not understand, things too wonderful for me, which I did not know." He said, "It was me." God said: "Hear, and I will speak; I will question you, and you make it known to me." Job confessed: "I had heard of you by the hearing of the ear, but now my eye sees you; therefore I despise myself, and repent in dust and ashes" (Job 42:3-6). He repented in dust and ashes. That was the right conclusion.

Job had accused God of unfairness (3:11-23; 10:18; 6:4; 7:14-20; 9:17-23). So do we. Job's opinion of God was infected with human finiteness just like ours. God said, "Let us make man in our image." Man said, "Let us make God in our image." And so we have. That gives us the freedom to say, "That's not fair" a lot. Human wisdom concludes that it is not fair for God to destroy Sodom but not America. We decide that God is not fair to allow the false religion of Islam to spread unchecked. God was not fair to allow the December tsunami to destroy 200,000 lives. Fair according to human wisdom or according to Divine infinite wisdom?

Mere humanity does not understand God, therefore, He must be wrong. Why does He allow sickness, death of the innocent, accidents, failed relationships, rebellion in a Christian family, rejection of the gospel, professing Christians falling into utter ruin, government that robs people of freedom, and such?

The person who demands that God governs things according to his understanding or plans does not trust God. The person who insists that God must save souls according to his many prayers and efforts, or change the hearts of rebels, or heal the sick, or give him a satisfying job, or make him happy, or change his spouse, or bring offenders to justice, or any other number of things, does not trust God.

We need to see ourselves in light of the truth about God in order to arrive at Job's conclusion. James set Job up as an example of coming to the right conclusion after testing. He said, "As an example of suffering and patience, brothers, take the prophets who spoke in the name of the Lord. Behold, we consider those blessed who remained steadfast. You have heard of the steadfastness of Job, and you have seen the purpose of the Lord, how the Lord is compassionate and merciful" (James 5:10-11).

Maybe the most amazing part of the story is that "Job is brought to contentment without ever knowing all the facts of his case" (D.J. Wiseman, ed., Tyndale Old Testament Commentaries "Job." Francis Anderson. London: Inter Varsity Press, 1976, 270). Job is satisfied only that God spoke to him. That was sufficient to reveal that all things were okay between him and God. If all things are okay between God and His child, what happens doesn't matter. Satan accused God of protecting Job. Job needed to learn to trust God alone apart from any human wisdom, effort, or good works. He just needed to know God, love God, and trust God for who He is. Therefore, he did not need to know all the facts. Job could never say, "Oh, now I understand. I see all the facts." Rather he would always have to be content to say, "I have no idea why these things happened. But I know that God is faithful and I trust Him."

In the end, Job accomplished what Eliphaz challenged him to do, but could not show him how to do. Eliphaz told Job, "Agree with God, and be at peace; thereby good will come to you. Receive instruction from his mouth, and lay up his words in your heart" (Job 22:21-22). But Eliphaz, like most people of the world, did not have a clue about how to accomplish this task. God did. He took Job through the trial and then invited Job to learn how to trust Him. Compared to Job, do we really trust God?

# 7

# COME, FEAR THE LORD

## PSALM 34

The title of this Psalm reveals the circumstances surrounding its writing. David wrote the Psalm when he had escaped from Abimelech (Achish). The story is recorded in more detail in 1 Samuel 21:10-15. There it is revealed that Saul had threatened to kill David because he feared David's popularity. Saul was insanely jealous of David and was plagued with an evil spirit that caused him to react violently toward him. Finally, the wicked king could not endure David any longer and vowed to kill him. Jonathan, Saul's son and heir to the throne, was David's dearest friend. He warned David to flee for his life, which David did. But where would he go to escape Saul's furry? David, the man who had experienced God's protection when he killed a lion, killed a bear, killed Goliath, and slain his tens of thousands, ran like a frightened rabbit. He decided it would be safer to live with Achish, the king of the Philistines, instead of trying to live with Saul. Notice that the name Achish is interchangeable with the name Abimelech. It appears that Abimelech was a title similar to king or pharaoh and was used to identify at least five different Philistine kings.

This was a bad choice. Why didn't David simply trust God who had already proven in several situations that He would care for David? In a moment of human weakness, David chose to ally himself with God's enemy. When he and his little band of supporters showed up in Gath, one of the chief cities of Philistia, the Welcome Wagon did not joyously embrace them. In fact, the king's cabinet of advisors said to the king, "Is not this David the king of the land? Did they not sing to one another of him in dances, 'Saul has struck down his thousands, and David his ten thousands'?" (1 Samuel 21:11).

David was a pretty bright fellow and right away he realized that Achish would perceive him as a threat to the throne. What was he to do? Human wisdom might recommend that David go to the king and tell him that things were not well in Camelot and old, cranky King Saul made it impossible for him to live there. We would have told David to just ask Achish, in a nice way, if he couldn't stay in Philistia until things cooled down. Things did not work that way in the kingdoms of 1000 B.C. If King Achish saw David as a threat, he would remove the threat by killing David. Political issues were generally simple and straight forward in that day.

Therefore, David resorted to shrewdness or human wisdom. He decided that if he acted like a crazy man the king would simply reject him and run him out of the country. So David wrote graffiti on the door, let spittle run down his beard, and probably talked like a crazy man. Achish bought into the charade and ran David out of town.

In response, David breathed a sigh of relief and praised God for his deliverance. This leads to an interesting question. Did God actually deliver David? Is it not true that the deliverance was the result of David lying or at least pretending to be something he wasn't? Notice that there is not one mention of David's lapse in this Psalm. First, he made a bad choice by going to the enemy for safety. Second, he made another bad choice by misrepresenting his condition. And yet in spite of the bad choices, God really did deliver him from certain destruction.

Modern believers ought to be able to identify with this picture. Who can point back to a spotless, blameless life in which he has never made a bad choice or dumb decision? But God still cares for us. People who have experienced this immeasurable love and mercy of God ought to fear Him. We who know God's deliverance from the penalty and power of our sins, and even from our foolishness, ought to know how to fear God. We ought to teach others that same fear. Here is the great invitation: "Come, O children, listen to me; I will teach you the fear of the Lord."

## Hear The Testimony Of One Who Fears The LORD (vv.1-7)

Thinking back to how God had delivered him from a very dangerous situation in Philistia, David declared, "I will bless the LORD" (vv.1-3). That kind of praise should characterize the LORD's people (v.1). But talk about praising the Lord, blessing the Lord, exalting God is so common that it almost seems meaningless. It especially seems meaningless when the people who make the most noise about praising the LORD demonstrate lives that are no different than the lives of their unsaved neighbors. What is missing in this picture? To bless the LORD is to kneel before Him and praise Him. It is the same idea one finds in worshiping the LORD. Worship reveals the true heart. A heart that exalts God and bows before Him will truly bless the LORD. A heart that is focused on self will actually exalt self instead of blessing God. It is Human nature to exalt self and, at the same time, hold on to God for insurance.

God's people should be characterized by continual praise for Him on their lips. David appears to have had a hymn of praise for God in his heart. Only people who have high respect for God will do this. Only people who fear God can even understand this idea. As a teenager, I listened to a steady diet of rock music. I didn't know a teenager who didn't. When I went to a Christian college, I discovered that the administrators of the school thought that real Christians ought to have a better standard of music. I didn't fight the rules. In spite of my background, I obeyed completely. That is when I discovered how sensible this principle is. Why would a person who truly respects God want to have praise for sins and fleshliness in his mouth?

The believer's praise should encourage others to join him or her (vv.2-3). David was sure that humble people are glad to hear someone boast about the LORD (v.2). Humble people have acknowledged their sins to God, and have said the same thing about their sins that God says. Humble people have confessed God's pure magnificence. Therefore, because God is supreme, and they are His humble servants, they are glad to hear boasting about God. A humble person does not require coercing to magnify God.

A few weeks ago, I attended a teen rally where our son Mark was leading the singing—if it could be called singing. Most of the teens were from Christian schools, and like most Christian school kids, they had no desire at all to exalt God and sing His praise. Mark addressed the matter at the end of the song by telling the kids that if they did not have a genuine relationship with God through faith in Jesus Christ, they did not have a reason to praise God and would do well not to sing at all. The sad truth is that there are not many humble young people in Christians schools these days.

Humble people respond to the invitation to praise the LORD (v.3). They are glad to join others in exalting God's name. In fact, people like David are uncomfortable with anything that detracts from God's glory. Whether it is an arrogant, boasting athlete, or a politician, or so-called Christians who call attention to themselves, people who fear God disdain such self-glorification. People like this cringe when hypocrites exalt their own name while pretending to praise God.

David proclaimed with confidence that he had good reasons for praising the LORD (vv.4-7). First, he had just learned again (for the umpteenth time) that the LORD delivers (v.4,6-7). The person who fears God has learned this cause-and-effect principle that David described in these verses. He said, "I sought" and the result was "God delivered" (v.4). He said, "I cried" and the result was "God heard and saved" (v.6). The petitioner's attitude is very obvious in this scenario. He is seeking because he has great fear (v.4). He is crying because he is aware of his spiritual poverty (v.6). Self-reliant, arrogant, proud people do not fear God and have never experienced this joy.

David was a mighty warrior and a popular guy, but he found himself in a very precarious position. It is not a bad thing for God's people to suddenly discover that circumstances are out of control. That is when the child of God is more likely to cry out to God. Sometimes difficult circumstances point out spiritual poverty. Thank God for the times when His people literally cry out to God because they have no strength or ability to make it on their own. Like David, the humble person who cries out to God discovers how the LORD encamps around him. Because he has learned this truth, he is confident in God. He knows that God will deliver. That is the attitude of the person who has learned how to fear God.

Another reason to praise the LORD is because He never fails (v.5). Verse five states that people who look to the LORD are radiant. Their faces shall never be ashamed. People who trust God exude confidence. When David described these people as the ones who look to the Lord, he used a word that means to regard with expectation, not simply to notice. When we trust God alone it shows. Co-workers, neighbors, family, and fellow church members know if their professing Christian peer actually trusts God or if he is trying to make it on his own.

People who trust God completely have a glowing countenance about them because they never have any problems. Woe! God never taught that or implied it anywhere in the Bible. In fact, David admitted in verse nineteen that people who trust God do experience trouble (v.19). Saints experience troubles the world cannot imagine. We experience the same problems with health, jobs, families, finances, and everything else that our unsaved friends and neighbors must face. Beyond that, people who fear God also struggle with persecution on various levels because they do not fit in the world system. Even more trying sometimes is the fact that real Christians fight real spiritual warfare every day.

God's people face problems just like everyone else, but we have learned how God is faithful to deliver. Does God always deliver? Yes. Sometimes God delivers His people from the trouble by removing the troubling circumstances. Sometimes God removes the saint from the trial by moving him to another location or maybe even by moving the one He loves so much to be in His presence in heaven. Sometimes God delivers His child within the trouble by offering sufficient grace. People who fear the LORD are very privileged people. We continually praise Him because He gives us so many reasons.

## Learn To Fear The LORD (vv.8-14)

Why wouldn't a person want to be like the one described in the first seven verses of this Psalm? Who wouldn't want to have praise for God on their minds and lips continually? Who wouldn't like to enjoy God's deliverance? To people who contemplate such things, this invitation sounds wonderful. David invited everyone to come like teachable children and learn the benefits of fearing the LORD (vv.8-10). The first benefit is that those who fear the LORD are blessed (v.8). In essence, this is an invitation to experience God. "Oh taste and see that the LORD is good" is not an invitation to just be familiar with Him, like most so-called Christians who are actually only religious. It is an invitation to come into an intimate relationship with the LORD. That kind of relationship requires complete trust. It is also built on awesome respect for God. A person who only wants a casual relationship with God, one that does not require ultimate love and respect, needs to look elsewhere. God does not do shallow relationships.

Those who accept the invitation are blessed. In other words, they are happy. Really? Sure, everyone who finds refuge in God is happy. The person who claims to trust God alone, but at the same time is miserable, displays a conflict. The obvious conclusion is that the person really does not trust God alone.

A second good reason for learning to fear God is that those who fear the LORD have no lack of good (vv.9-10). The young lions suffer lack (v.10), but not the people who fear God. The young lions offer a picture of strength and prowess. It is an illustration of people who are confident in their own ability. They are confident that they can provide for themselves all that is necessary for life. To a point that might be true. But such self-sufficient people will suffer lack that they will never see until it is too late. Eternal spiritual lack is infinitely worse than any lack of the materialism and pleasure of this world.

Conversely, people who maintain an awesome respect for God will have no lack. That is not to conclude that God's people will have abundance of all things in life. Sometimes they do. Sometimes they do not. People who fear God will often lack what the flesh claims are needs, but they will never lack anything of eternal value. One day each person who has lived will stand before God. In the radiance of His majesty and glory, in the reality of eternity, nothing that was important on earth will be matter, and most of the things that the world despised and rejected will be of extreme value. Those who truly fear God will never lack what matters.

There are many blessings promised for the person who fears the LORD. Therefore, David offered the invitation for everyone to come in childlike faith and learn the requirements of fearing LORD (vv.11-14). This is more than an invitation from a faltering fellow-human. In essence, the LORD Himself invites people to learn (v.11-12). It is interesting that this invitation implies that a person must learn the fear of the LORD (v.11). Obviously, the fear of the LORD is not a natural thing. Of course not. The natural flesh avoids elementary fear. Thrill seekers might use fear as a stimulant, an adrenalin rush. But normal people run from that which makes them afraid. Nevertheless, it is good for people to learn to be afraid of God. Jesus admonished the disciples, "And do not fear those who kill the body but cannot kill the soul. Rather fear him who can destroy both soul and body in hell" (Matthew 10:28).

It is necessary for people to learn how to fear the LORD because the natural person does not respect God. At best, human nature creates its own model of God so that it can still be in control. That means that folks who live in a culture of disrespect must learn to have unnatural respect for God.

In order to really fear the LORD, one must also learn what constitutes good (v.12). The world offers something that they call good. They conclude that it is good to be well liked, it is good to have nice things, it is good to have pleasure. But the world's concept of good is not the same as the divine concept of good. God warned through Isaiah, "Woe to those who call evil good and good evil, who put darkness for light and light for darkness, who put bitter for sweet and sweet for bitter!" (Isaiah 5:20). That is an apt description for the world in any age, but especially in the modern age. The important lesson here is that people who would enjoy pure goodness, eternal days, must first learn to fear God.

Another important principle in the lesson about fearing the LORD is that to fear the LORD is to shun evil (vv.13-14). First, shunning evil applies to spoken words. People who fear God have sanctified tongues (v.13). They don't talk like unregenerate people. Second, they are characterized by turning away from evil (v.14). This means that the person is capable of identifying evil. It is astonishing how many professing Christians are incapable of this practice. Having identified evil, the person who fears the LORD chooses to avoid it.

## LEARN THE REASON FOR FEARING THE LORD (vv.15-22)

One good and positive reason to fear the LORD is because He blesses those who fear Him (vv.15,17-20, 22). David was confident that the LORD hears the righteous (v.15). He watches over them all the time and listens for their cry. When they cry out for help, the LORD delivers the righteous (vv.17-20). Notice that David was sure that the Lord hears and delivers His people from all troubles (v.17). God delivers from all of our troubles? Is that true? Indeed it is. God delivers His people through His promises and through His grace. Many people who claim that God does not keep this promise have never learned to respect Him. With the awesome respect comes complete trust. With complete trust comes the ability to recognize and apply His grace. With His grace comes perfect peace.

It is good that God delivers, but even better is the fact that He also is near to the brokenhearted (v.18). The broken heart is a sweet sacrifice to God. This same Psalmist who wrote this Psalm concluded, "The sacrifices of God are a broken spirit; a broken and contrite heart, O God, you will not despise" (Psalm 51:17). The brokenhearted person knows a special closeness of God.

Third, God delivers from the many afflictions (v.19). Sometimes He delivers His people from their problems in this life. If not, His people can be certain that God will deliver those who fear Him from trouble for all eternity.

Fourth, the LORD protects completely (v.20). This promise of no broken bones appears to be a little extreme. It must be taken figuratively. God-fearing saints do have accidents and have received broken bones when they were martyred. What does this mean? It is a picture of the Passover lamb which was not to have a broken bone when the offerer sacrificed it. It is a picture of the Perfect Lamb, Jesus, who though crucified had no broken bones. So, too, God never loses one who fears Him. Those who fear Him are as important and precious as any sacrificial lamb. He protects His own for eternity. This is extreme care.

On the other hand, there is a good negative reason to fear God. The LORD is against the wicked (vv.16, 21). He is opposed to people who do evil (v.16). More exactly, God is turned away from the wicked person. He who rejects God is on his own. At best, the person who rejects God receives common grace such as rain, sunlight, or air. At worst, God becomes his adversary to remove his name from the earth.

The wicked person's own sin will destroy him (v.21). God has already condemned sin and therefore sinners. His wrath is already poured out against sin. Paul pointed out that "the wrath of God is revealed from heaven against all ungodliness and unrighteousness of men, who by their unrighteousness suppress the truth" (Romans 1:18). So because of God's abiding wrath, the evil person's sin kills him physically and spiritually. There is no hope. Either a person fears God or he doesn't. There is no middle ground. Either you hold Him in highest esteem and give Him respect, or you hold yourself in esteem and respect your own desires. God invites you to learn the difference. God invites you to learn how to fear Him. A wise person will accept His invitation.

# 8

# COME AND SEE WHAT GOD HAS DONE

## Psalm 66

Many years ago my wife and I were in the market to buy our first house. Like many young couples, our first house would need to be somewhat meager. College kids generally don't have a lot of money to sink into a nice house in an upperclass neighborhood. We looked at several options with a relator friend and were consistently disappointed. The problem was that the amount of money we budgeted for a mortgage payment fell painfully short of our impeccable taste. Well actually, a lot of those houses were pretty bad. In spite of the fact that we had reasonable expectations, we couldn't find a descent house in a descent neighborhood that we could afford.

One day while looking through the classified ads, I spied an advertisement for a house in the upper end of our price range. It seemed to be in a fairly good neighborhood. But the thing that attracted my attention was the closing statement. It was a simple statement consisting of two words: "Must see." Sometimes "must see" leaves the inquisitor quite disappointed. "Must see" gives the idea that whatever the object might be, it is better than words can describe. More often than not, one might conclude that the advertiser has a very limited vocabulary if he can't describe the mediocre item he is trying to sell. But that was not the case with this little house. It was just what we were looking for, and it satisfied our needs for seven years before we outgrew it.

The epitome of "must see" is God's work. That is essentially the invitation of the entire Bible. God gave the world His Word to point out all of the many reasons why people must see what He has done. God, like an artist, puts His works on display so that everyone can see them and glorify Him for His power, majesty, grace, and mercy. When one beholds the works of God, he must conclude there is no person and no other god that is like Him. The more we see of God, the more astonished we should be. The more that He reveals of Himself, the more His created beings realize that God is virtually incomprehensible. His works should drive everyone to worship Him.

This Psalm was a song that God's people sang as praise to Him. It is possible that it was sung during the Passover celebration. It appears that the people might have sung it responsively. The leader challenged the people to praise God (vv.1-3), and the people sang back their response such as, "All the earth worships You . . ." (v.4). He challenged them to "come and see what God has done . . ." (v.5), and they responded by recalling God's mighty deeds (vv.6-12).

In this psalm, God invites everyone to come and see what He does for the benefit of all people. God invites the whole world to observe. Obviously, the whole world is not interested. The world— the product of God's creative acts—is so infected with sin that it rejects God's invitation and prefers to look at itself in the mirror of narcissism. Sinners are transfixed with their own reflection.

God also gives His invitation to people who ought to be impressed with His work. The ancient Israelites were eyewitnesses of God's many miracles. They tasted of His power. They received His grace. But for the most part, they walked away from God and chose to serve the gods their pagan neighbors served. They illustrated the same failure found among religious people today. Many religious people have attended church services for years where they heard the truth about God. Sadly, that truth doesn't mean much to them, and they prefer to walk in close fellowship with their sinful world.

Finally, God offers His invitation to the people who are truly His. People who enjoy a right relationship with God, people who fear Him, people who observe His many works of grace. Surely Christians are also aware of God's mighty displays of power. But it is His work of grace that melts the redeemed sinner's heart. People whose hearts have been melted by God's grace respond to His invitation by offering sacrifices of thanksgiving.

God offers the invitation for everyone to come and see His mighty works. Everyone should sing praises to God because of what He has done. However, only those few who fear Him will respond to the invitation in an honorable way.

## AN INVITATION FOR THE ENTIRE WORLD (Vv.1-4)

The Psalmist declared that everyone should give God praise (vv.1-2.4). Most of God's people would agree with Him. It is a good thing to praise God. Therefore, God offers the invitation in this psalm for the whole earth to praise Him (vv.1,4). The phrase "all the earth" must include all of creation (v.1). The first part of creation one thinks about is probably the human part. Surely thinking, reasonable humans should praise their Creator. But even the heavens shout for joy because of God's work. Yea, the heavens are more consistent in praising God than the human part of creation is. David rejoiced that "the heavens declare the glory of God, and the sky above proclaims his handiwork" (Psalm 19:1).

According to the fourth verse in this psalm, "All the earth worships" God. That isn't true, is it? It is true that all of the earth will one day praise God. This statement has to be taken in a future sense because the whole world does not praise God at this point in the ages of humanity. In fact, most people in every age have refused, and continue to refuse, to acknowledge God. Most people disallow His creative acts and prefer to embrace theories of man that might in some hard-to-believe way explain how the world began. The world is impressed with itself, not with God. It doesn't praise Him. But in the Millennial kingdom the whole world will shout God's praises. At that time all of the earth will worship God, sing praises to Him, and sing praises to His name. But that is not now.

This song invites the whole earth to praise God in worship (vv.1-4). It is interesting to recognize how the Psalmist piles up command on top of command to describe how the world should declare God's worth. First, the earth should shout for joy (v.1). This is a command to shout for joy continually. The shout is like the shout an athlete makes because of victory or the shout of an army going into battle. No little noise! Nor is this an angry or fearful shout. It is a shout of joy offered up to God.

Second, the earth should sing (v.2). The whole earth should make music unto God, music that praises God, music that points out the glory and majesty of God.

Third, the whole earth should praise (v.2). This word speaks of a hymn of adoration or thanksgiving. The wording indicates that everyone on earth should determine to do this. It is a matter of putting praise in the right place. It is planned praise, not spontaneous emotion.

Fourth, the earth should "say." (v.3) The word refers to common talk. It might mean to talk about or it can also mean to speak in one's heart silently. These commands cover the gamut of declaring God's worth. Sometimes it is an outward shout of joy. Sometimes it is the silent words of praise kept in one's heart. Always it is focused on God's greatness.

Consider the essence of worship the earth should offer but refuses to offer until the Millennium. The shout for joy is not generated by the winning of the lottery or by some other mundane, passing benefit. It is supposed to be a shout for joy to God. We are supposed to sing the glory of His name. The whole earth should give Him praise. In other words, worship must focus on the glory of God. Is your praise an expression about your feelings and opinions, or is it an expression of who God is and what He does? Does your praise declare God's worth or does it demonstrate desires and abilities of your flesh? Praise that declares God's worth must be different than praise that declares man's sinfulness.

How can a person possibly use the same vessel to transport thoughts of sex, drugs, and hedonism, as well as thoughts of God's holiness, purity, and righteousness? The two different objects of praise require two different kinds of vessels. The Old Testament priest dared not use a vessel dedicated to the temple worship to transport the ordinary or mundane and certainly not to transport manure or waste. One of the greatest act of desecration occurred when Belshazzar used the temple vessels to honor the pagan gods of gold, silver, bronze, iron, wood, and stone (Daniel 5:2-5). God invites the whole earth to engage in praising Him.

Everyone should praise God because He displays great power (v.3). The Psalmist said that the citizens of earth should tell God that His deeds are awesome. The word awesome has fallen into a sad state. These days it simply means cool, hot, heavy, or some other meaningless thing. It is more accurate to go back to the original meaning and let it stand for that which causes fear or dread. It is good to recount how mighty and terrible God can be.

But stories like the one that tells how God opened the ground and swallowed up Korah, his fellow rebels, and all of their families are not well received by the world. The story that recounts God saving Noah and family while He destroyed the rest of humanity because of their sins is so ridiculous to the world that sinners reject it out of hand.

That is why the Psalmist also said that the earth should say to God or tell God that His deeds make sinners cringe. This is the whole point. God's works are mighty. God's works cause terror. And sinners cringe at the thought of God's mighty works. It is hard to imagine, but this is a form of praise. To acknowledge that God's works strike terror in the hearts of those who hate Him is to talk about God's glory and value. Therefore, God's people must continue to invite the world to praise God, knowing full well that the whole world will not praise Him until He reigns supreme.

## AN INVITATION FOR THE VISIBLE BODY OF GOD'S PEOPLE (Vv.5-12)

The entire corporate or visible body of God's people should praise Him for what He has done (vv.5,8). This invitation is directed to people who belong to God—at least it appears outwardly that they belong to God (v.8). The context of the invitation deals specifically with works that God did for Israel. Israel was God's chosen people. Who in all the world should have praised God continually for His works but the very people He chose to be his own? They had to know more about God's works than anyone. They should have a better understanding of what God did, and why He did it, than any other people. But many of the chosen people chose to forget God's mighty deeds. This is a grim reminder of Paul's warning that not all of the people who claim to be God's people are truly God's people. The principle remains the same today. There are millions of Jews, who consider themselves to be God's special people. But in reality, they rejected God a long time ago and are not really His people at all.

Likewise, many "professing Christians" choose to forget God's works. There is a vast difference between a professing Christian and a genuine Christian. Professing Christians have tasted and seen some of the mighty works of God. But in spite of what they have experienced, they are not truly born again. The writer to the Hebrews warned these people about the danger of their condition:

For it is impossible to restore again to repentance those who have once been enlightened, who have tasted the heavenly gift, and have shared in the Holy Spirit, and have tasted the goodness of the word of God and the powers of the age to come, if they then fall away, since they are crucifying once again the Son of God to their own harm and holding him up to contempt (Hebrews 6:4-6).

God invites people like this who are supposed to belong to Him to observe His awesome deeds toward humanity (v.5).

They should praise God because He displays power and grace (vv.6-7, 9-12). Some of God's works display His might (vv.6-7). Verse six made a quick reference to two of the stupefying works that God did. First, He caused the people to cross the Red Sea on dry ground (v.6). Second, He allowed the people to cross the Jordan River on dry ground in order to take the Promised Land (v.6). The people rejoiced at the time. But soon the same people, or at least their posterity, became rebellious and exalted themselves in spite of having seen God's power (v.7). Likewise, multitudes of people who have been in church most of their lives continue to respond the same way.

Some of God's works display His grace (vv.9-12). He puts His people to the test (vv.10-12). That is a good thing because in the midst of the test God's people discover that He always sustains His own (v.9). How sad that many people have watched God test and sustain His people, and yet they reject God in spite of being familiar with His grace.

## AN INVITATION FOR THOSE WHO ARE RIGHT WITH GOD (vv.13-20)

Finally, the Psalmist offered an invitation for those people who truly fear God. People who fear God should praise Him (vv.13-16). These people saw God's mighty works and spoke about how terrible He can be (cf. v.3, 5). They understand that the God who can create worlds with a word and can condemn a world of sinners to eternal hell with a word. They understand that He is perfectly holy, and that sin is a great offense to Him. They admit that they have sinned and are personally responsible for offending God. They fear that God will destroy them forever!

That is not a terrible, self-damaging conclusion as human wisdom would have us believe. It is good for a sinner to come to this understanding. In this process, a needy person learns to highly respect God. These people have discovered that God's grace offers the acceptable sacrifice to cover their sins. By faith they have accepted the sacrifice of God the Son to reconcile them to God. Being reconciled, having God's love poured out in their hearts, they love God supremely. Therefore, people like this hate sin and avoid it in order not to offend God whom they love and respect. That is what it means to fear God in a mature sense. It would be sad indeed for God's people to spend all of eternity quaking in fear that

God might push a button and send us to hell. That is elementary, immature fear. To fear God is to love Him.

People who fear God worship Him (vv.13-15). The Psalmist pictured how the Old Testament saint came into God's house with offerings and sacrifices. He was familiar with that kind of response to fearing God. He understood this way. They offered a sacrifice that pleased God. They paid their vows. Worship was all about honoring God. In a very similar way, the New Testament saint comes before God with offerings and sacrifices. We offer ourselves wholly to Him for His service and glory. That is what Paul meant when he told the Romans, "I appeal to you therefore, brothers, by the mercies of God, to present your bodies as a living sacrifice, holy and acceptable to God, which is your spiritual worship. Do not be conformed to this world, but be transformed by the renewal of your mind, that by testing you may discern what is the will of God, what is good and acceptable and perfect" (Romans 12:1-2).

New Testament saints show their worship to God through the kind of lives they lead. We are supposed to live like dedicated, sanctified priests and offer our works as spiritual sacrifices. Peter said, "You yourselves like living stones are being built up as a spiritual house, to be a holy priesthood, to offer spiritual sacrifices acceptable to God through Jesus Christ" (1 Peter 2:5). Modern Christians certainly should appear to love God like their Old Testament counterparts did.

God's people should praise Him because of His grace (vv.17-20). We cry out with praise to the God we respect (v.17-18). His praise is on our tongue—not cheap, mindless chatter about cheap, mindless things. His people avoid sin knowing that it prevents genuine praise. As a result, we discover that God affirms the certainty of His grace to us continually (vv.19-20). God listens and attends to our prayers (v.19). Praise God because of His steadfast love (v.20). Only people who are in a right relationship with God can buy up the invitation to see what God has done and praise Him for it. The people who have expressed genuine faith in Christ and live in a way that shows respect for God love to praise God for what He has done.

How have you responded to God's invitation? Do you really see what God has done in the earth? Do you really praise God or do you express the desires of the flesh? Do you fear God? People who are in right fellowship with God know what God has done. They love Him and highly respect Him because of His work. They praise Him through worship that honors Him.

# 9

# COME PRAISE THE LORD
# WITH ME!

PSALM 95

Many Christians have been involved with some kind of church visitation effort. Maybe this amounted to working in a bonafide visitation program in which you went door-to-door throughout a neighborhood inviting folks to Christ. More often than not, especially in the Greenville, South Carolina area, you invited folks to visit our church because most of the people you met assured you that they are indeed born again. Did they show up at church? Probably not. Some of you have invited your friends to come to church. Sometimes they actually attend. Others regularly invite family members, co-workers, club members, or whoever it might be, to join them in a church service. Seldom do people accept our invitations. Why?

According to the experts in church growth, the problem is the vast distinction between a church's style of worship and the kind of entertainment friends, neighbors and co-workers are accustomed to. Hence, the solution to the problem is to make the church worship look a lot like the friend's, neighbor's and co-worker's venues of entertainment. That is an illustration of human wisdom at its best.

Why do modern church growers think that people who live in God-offending sin every moment of every day want to come and meet with the God they continually offend? That should not make sense to even human wisdom! It would be nice for sinners to meet with God's people and get a true, honest glimpse at the holiness of the Almighty, unchanging, unsearchable God. But most sinners are not interested in that. Most sinners know that being in the presence of the thrice holy God would make them uncomfortable.

That explains why sinners generally refuse a sincere invitation to attend church services. But what about Christians? Why would a Christian, who has the privilege and the invitation to attend worship services at least twice a week, choose to go shopping or stay home and watch television instead? It is very confusing to learn that Christians make this kind of choice on a regular basis. Maybe they do not understand who God is. Or maybe they do not understand who they are. David concluded, "When I look at your heavens, the work of your fingers, the moon and the stars, which you have set in place, what is man that you are mindful of him, and the son of man that you care for him? Yet you have made him a little lower than the heavenly beings and crowned him with glory and honor. You have given him dominion over the works of your hands; you have put all things under his feet" (Psalm 8:3-6).

Have you looked at the heavens lately and thought about what you are in comparison? You are one of about 300 people in this place. This place is located in a city which is small compared to many cities in the world that have populations in the millions. This city is located in the state of South Carolina, which is a comparatively small state among the fifty that make up the nation of the United States of America. While the people in this building are part of a significant nation in the world, still we are almost an unknown entity in a sea of people numbering over three billion on this planet. The earth seems quite significant when compared to half the planets in our solar system. But when compared to the other half of the planets, the earth suddenly seems small and insignificant. Our insignificance is multiplied when compared to the center of our solar system, the sun. The sun makes the earth look like a pinhead. But when compared to other stars like Sirius, Pollux, and Arcturus, the sun looks like a pinhead, and our mighty earth disappears from sight. God also spoke into existence the star Antares. That star makes the earth's sun look like a pinhead and suddenly the earth is not even a figment of the imagination. And Antares is only the fifteenth brightest star in the universe — as far as scientists know at this point!

In light of such sheer size and magnificence, human logic must dictate that there is not even a word capable of describing the insignificance of us earth dwellers. We are less than nothing compared to the universe. We are circles with the rings rubbed out! And God invites us to come into His presence and shout for joy because He loves us. That is astonishing. Yea, that is humbling. The God of creation, who holds the entire universe together by His word, invites insignificant earth dwellers to come and sing His praise together. The invitation should make the recipient feel so honored that he naturally invites others to join the praise—right? Only if the person has come to understand and accept this invitation.

Charles Spurgeon concluded about this Psalm, "It is a Psalm of invitation to worship. It has about it a ring like that of the church bells, and like the bells it sounds both merrily and solemnly, at first ringing out a lively peal, and then dropping into a funeral knell as if tolling at the funeral of the generation which perished in the wilderness" (C.H. Spurgeon. The Treasury of David.). This Psalm is one of the great invitations of the Bible.

## Come Let Us Adore Him (vv.1-7a)

The invitation of this Psalm rings out with the clarity of church bells on Christmas morning: Come and worship (vv.1-2,6). The God-inspired Psalmist invites us to come and make a joyful noise to the LORD (vv.1-2). Obviously God's people are the ones who receive the invitation. "Let us sing" isn't the kind of invitation that is offered freely to the sinners of the world who have no love for God or even a concern that He exists. To sing is to make a ringing cry in joy; it is exaltation and praise. It is the kind of response that exploded from the lips of God's people when He displayed His pleasure with an approved sacrifice. When Aaron offered to God the first sacrifice under the Law, "fire came out from before the LORD and consumed the burnt offering and the pieces of fat on the altar, and when all the people saw it, they shouted and fell on their faces" (Leviticus 9:24). They thought that it was really important for God's people to be pleasing to Him.

Isaiah uses this Hebrew term for sing fourteen times in his writings. Every time it appears, the word emphasizes holy joy which is celebrated by Israel. In contrast, the cessation of such emotion is portrayed as one of the grimmest aspects of Moab's fall. Isaiah described the sad state of affairs by writing, "And joy and gladness are taken away from the fruitful field, and in the vineyards no songs are sung, no cheers are raised; no treader treads out wine in the presses; I have put an end to the shouting" (Isaiah 16:10). When God's people are in fellowship with Him, we want to sing aloud to praise Him.

Second, the Psalmist invites us to "shout." Most English translations use the phrase "make a joyful noise," but shout is a very accurate rendition.

Some people claim they can't carry a tune in a bucket, and, therefore, they are exempt from singing. However, almost everyone can shout God's praise. The word means to raise a noise like shouting. That makes sense. However, a more exact definition points to the use of an instrument as the primary means for making the joyful noise to God. This was God's prescribed sign for His people to gather for worship according to His Law. Moses taught them, "When the assembly is to be gathered together, you shall blow a long blast, but you shall not sound an alarm" (Numbers 10:7).

God's people are often reticent to do this. Why? Scripture shows other parts of God's creation engaged in what Christians should be doing. When the Ark of the Covenant was delivered to the tabernacle in Jerusalem, David composed a song in which he declared, "Then shall the trees of the forest sing for joy before the LORD, for he comes to judge the earth" (1 Chronicles 16:33). Job exclaimed, "When the morning stars sang together and all the sons of God shouted for joy?" (Job 38:7). In spite of sin's encroachment on God's creation, it shouts His praise. Likewise, in spite of our insignificance, God invites us to come and shout joyful praises to His name for His glory.

God invites His people to come and praise Him. Then God's people declare the invitation for each other to participate. David said, "Let us sing." The invitation implies personal experience. Praising God through song is the privilege of God's people in every age. David invited God's people in his day. But this was not a privilege saved for ancient Israelites alone. The author to the Hebrew Christians applied the same principle in the Church age by quoting part of this Psalm. He told first century Christians, "Today, if you hear his voice, do not harden your hearts" (Hebrews 4:7). Obviously then the wonderful invitation to sing praise to God goes out to Jews and Gentiles alike in every age.

Praise must be God-ward, not directed toward fellow God-fearers. God's people do well to sing to the Lord, not to each other. So much of modern church music is for the benefit of the listener and to the glory of the performer. Christians have chosen to emulate a pop culture that is all about self. We wander far from the standard of "singing unto the Lord" if we do not intentionally set up safeguards.

Furthermore, when God's people gather to praise His name in song, they do well to remember that they have "come into His presence with thanksgiving." Meetings for corporate worship bring God's people right before His face. Christians gathered in church meetings should be aware of the very presence of God at such times. Isn't it true that God is omnipresent—He is everywhere all the time? Yes, but some settings heighten the sense of God's presence. For example, when God's people in Old Testament Israel brought sacrifices to the tabernacle or temple, they were more keenly aware that they had come before God's face. God revealed this truth to Isaiah who wrote God's wonderful promise: "These I will bring to my holy mountain, and make them joyful in my house of prayer; their burnt offerings and their sacrifices will be accepted on my altar; for my house shall be called a house of prayer for all peoples" (Isaiah 56:7).

The same principle stands for modern gatherings of God's people. Jesus promised the disciples, "Where two or three are gathered in my name, there am I among them" (Matthew 18:20). Is this still true? Do God's people really believe it? Do God's people have a sense at all that they gather before His face to worship?

David said that God's people gather in His presence in thanksgiving. In other words, genuine praise flows from a heart of thanksgiving (v.2). Thanksgiving calls to mind God's faithful works of the past. Therefore, hope for the future is built on what Jehovah has already done in the past. Apart from the finished work of Christ, there is no reason to hope. Because of Christ's work, there is great hope in eternity. People who have no experience of God's redeeming work in the past have no reason to hope and, therefore, have no reason to thank God. People who have no reason to thank God really cannot praise Him. That might explain why much so-called worship, whether dead traditional or contemporary, focuses on the performer and the audience instead of the Mighty God.

Another important part of this invitation is found in verse six. God invites His people to come together to sing and make a joyful noise in praising Him. Another description of that is to worship the LORD (v.6). God invites us insignificant, faltering people to enter, to come into His presence, and worship Him. Notice how the Psalmist laid down three verbs in rapid succession to convey the idea of what God's people should do. We must worship, bow, and kneel. All three verbs point to the same response. All three illustrate the proper attitude of praising God. Humility before God is the key attitude. Praising God is not about how the praising person feels. It is about God's glory. If the worshiper detracts from God's glory, if he steals some of God's glory for himself, he is not praising God nor is he really worshiping. God invites His people to engage in true worship.

Why should God's people should respond (vv.3-5, 7a)? Let's be honest. That is the kind of question many people think about, whether they articulate it, when they receive the invitation to join in worshiping God. One good reason for people to worship God is because He is almighty (vv.3-5). He is the Great God (v.3). He is the Great King above all gods (v.3). Another good reason for singing praise to God is because He controls the mighty, often unknown, powers in nature (vv.4-5). David declared that Yahweh holds the depths of the earth in His hand. One trite song puts it like this: "He's Got the Whole World in His Hand." That song doesn't begin to articulate God's magnitude of greatness. It is not just that God controls the obvious things. He knows the secrets about this earth well. He knows things that brilliant minds throughout the ages have not yet discovered or truths they have misinterpreted.

Super deep wells drilled in Russia and Germany reveal super deep secrets of the earth. The scientists' findings reveal that with all of the modern technological advancements, scientists are still ignorant about much of the earth. One super deep well on Kola Peninsula in Russia reaches a depth of over 12,000 meters. A hole drilled in the Black Forest of Germany revealed that at 9,100 meters, the temperature in the earth was 265°C. That is 509°F. That is almost incomprehensible. But that is one small bit of knowledge that had been unknown for centuries. Furthermore, the heights of the mountains are God's. Men sacrifice their lives to climb the highest, most imposing mountains. But God put the mountains in place and sits far above them, knowing things about those hills that the most experienced climbing guide never imagined.

David rejoiced that the sea and dry land belong to God. Scientists learn new facts about the sea every day. Many of the brightest minds are intrigued with what might lie in the ocean's depths. Scientists working on the ship JOIDES Resolution drilled a deep hole about 800 Kilometers from Costa Rica and made an astonishing discovery. Their research identified a 15-million-year-old region of the Pacific Ocean that formed when the East Pacific Rise was spreading at a rate of more than 200 millimeters per year, much faster than any mid-ocean ridge on Earth today. What amazing facts! Maybe most amazing is the age of that region! The things of life that amaze us are nothing to God. All things are in His hand. Praise Him!

A greater reason to praise God is because God is ours (v.7a). This is the greatest reason to praise Him. He is our maker (v.6). People did not just happen. Humanity is not the process of evolution. Individuals are each unique products of God's creative processes, brought into life for His glory. Therefore, it is only fitting for to conclude that He is our God and we are His people (v.7a). He is our Shepherd and we are His sheep (v.7a). He cares for us, guides us, feeds us, heals our wounds,  and protects us like a shepherd does for his sheep.

He is our Rock of salvation (v.2). The rock is a picture of fortitude, safety, and security. The rock concept speaks of salvation in this present life, but more important, salvation for all eternity. The same man who invites us to praise God because He is our rock of salvation declared, "The LORD is my rock and my fortress and my deliverer, my God, my rock, in whom I take refuge, my shield, and the horn of my salvation, my stronghold" (Psalms 18:2). Our Rock gives us every reason to praise His name, to make a joyful noise because of who He is and what He does.

## Do Not Harden Your Heart (vv.7b-11)

The last part of verse seven and the first part of verse eight offer an interesting challenge. David warned the reader, "If you hear His voice do not harden your heart." The simple statement reveals that not everyone hears God's voice. Everyone is aware of the evidence of God in nature and in conscience. But not everyone hears God's voice. Many people choose to suppress the truth about God. They don't want to hear God's voice. God complies with their resistence against Him until finally God's voice is deadened. God's voice does not bother such people any longer. They see evidence of His grace abounding, but they do not understand what they see. That explains why God gave such strange advice to Isaiah when the prophet volunteered to be God's spokesman. "And [God] said, 'Go, and say to this people: "Keep on hearing, but do not understand; keep on seeing, but do not perceive." Make the heart of this people dull, and their ears heavy, and blind their eyes; lest they see with their eyes, and hear with their ears, and understand with their hearts, and turn and be healed'" (Isaiah 6:9-10).

People who do hear God's voice must be careful not to harden their hearts. A serious reminder here is that each individual is  responsible for hearing God's voice, and each individual is responsible for responding in obedience to it. A right response will keep God's people from following the many examples of failure that have gone before. In particular David calls on all people to avoid the examples of failure that the Israelites left (vv.8-11). These were God's chosen people. They knew the better way, but put God to the test anyway (vv.8-10). They had seen God's power and heard God's Law. And yet they chose to live according to the dictates of their flesh.

The ancient Israelites responded the way all flesh desires to respond. God's people must learn to discipline the flesh because it will always tempt the person to stop listening to God's voice and praise self instead of God. That is why Paul warned the Roman Christians to "clothe yourselves with the Lord Jesus Christ, and do not think about how to gratify the desires of the sinful nature" (Romans 13:14 NIV).

The sad result of hardening of the heart is stated in verse eleven. God judged the people (v.11). He refused to allow the stubborn Israelites to enter the Promised Land. It is a picture repeated many times since that day. How many people have resisted and resisted listening to God' voice and obeying Him until finally God allows the judgment to fall? We do well to heed Solomon's warning, "He who is often reproved, yet stiffens his neck, will suddenly be broken beyond healing" (Proverbs 29:1). We do well to ask ourselves if we really understand this invitation to praise God. Do you praise God or do you prefer your own way to the hardening of your heart?

# 10

# LET THE SIMPLE TURN IN HERE

## PROVERBS 9:1-6

For the past couple of weeks the citizens of the land have observed news clips and a few short articles about the incoming congress. The news sources would have the nation believe that America is now privileged to enjoy the fresh new breeze that is blowing out of Washington. Some folks have not been convinced. Some of us are not convinced that wisdom now resides within the "Beltway."

Recently as some of the new leaders confidently espoused their plans and goals, it sounded a lot like the folly of human wisdom. Human wisdom perceives itself to be broad-minded and far-reaching in its thinking. Human wisdom has deceived itself into thinking that it has a solution for the consequences of sin. Or worse, human wisdom errantly believes that there is no sin, only social problems. It concludes that there is no sin because there is no Creator who identifies sin. Therefore, human wisdom needs no Divine Savior. Human wisdom is its own savior. How sad that horrible destruction awaits any and all who dare walk that pathway of reasoning.

America is writhing in the grip of sin's consequences—and her leaders imagine that the nation is on the brink of utopia! What could be more foolish? It is the manifestation of the conflict God has taught, illustrated, and demonstrated throughout Scripture. Sin is wreaking havoc on the world, while the inhabitants of the world insist on denying the existence of the dreadful monster. The citizens of the world are clutched in the ever-tightening coils of the sin constrictor all the while pretending to comfort each other by talking about the beauty of the snake's skin pattern.

Into that setting steps Wisdom personified with a much needed invitation. God Himself cries out to the fools who travel the road to certain destruction, begging them to turn out of the way and to enter and enjoy the sumptuous banquet He has prepared.

## WISDOM HAS BUILT HER HOUSE (8:1-9:2)

Wisdom, who builds a house, is explained in some detail in chapter eight. These verses indicate that this Wisdom is the essential character of God (8:1-36). Of course such wisdom must be manifested in practical living or no one would see it or be challenged by it (8:1-21). She cries out with truth to the human race (8:1-11). Understanding, which is a synonym for wisdom, raises her voice in places where people will hear (8:1-3). The great desire for Wisdom is that all people will hear her as she cries out (8:4). She pleads with the simple ones and challenges them to leave their foolish ways (8:5). Her message is one of noble, true, and righteous words (8:6-8). While her words sound strange and unacceptable to the fools of the world, they make perfect sense to those who seek understanding and knowledge (8:9). Those who seek truth discover that wisdom is more valuable than precious metal or jewels (8:10-11). They love the message of Wisdom. They long for everyone to embrace this message.

What is there about the message of Wisdom that causes seekers of truth to embrace it? She promises great blessing (8:12-21). And yet that blessing can only be enjoyed by humble people because wisdom is opposed to pride and arrogance (8:12-13). Effective leaders lead by wisdom (8:15-16). Citizens who live under the rule of such leaders rejoice. In fact, years of blessing come to those who seek wisdom (8:17-21).

It is obviously a wonderful message! What a great promise. Only a fool would intentionally reject that which is more precious than gold or jewels. What kind of simpleton would ignore that which guarantees quality life? It seems that a person with common sense would quickly embrace such a message. So where does one find this precious possession? Men and women have searched over the entire earth and often expended all of their time, financial resources, and energy seeking this elusive treasure. They consult teachers who advertise wisdom that they have found in human reason and meditation. But time and again the seekers have been disappointed. They have sought in the great libraries of the world, read the works of those who are purported to be the great authors of the race, but conclude that all is vanity. Solomon illustrates that frustration of humanity in its quest for wisdom. Indeed, Solomon, whose wisdom is demonstrated in this collection of Proverbs, led the way in plumbing the depths of human wisdom to the point of frustration. Solomon, who prayed that God would give him the wisdom necessary to lead God's people, abandoned the source of true wisdom and attempted to climb the peaks of human wisdom. His journey is recorded in Ecclesiastes. (See Richard Mayhue. Practicign Proverbs. Ross-shire, Scotland: Christian Focus Publications, 2003, 18.)

The book that begins with "vanity of vanities" and ends with the same cry of despair, "vanity of vanities," is a record of a man's search for wisdom. He who received God's wisdom through grace counted that wisdom too unimportant for real life. He climbed one mountain of human wisdom after another. He experimented with man's knowledge, with self-indulgence, with building, with work, with money, and with women. When he finally climbed the last peak in his old age and peered over the precipice—there was God. He was right back where he started. How amazing that the simple wisdom that God gave in the first place was sufficient for all things.

Since Wisdom is the essential character of God, it is manifested best for all to see in Christ and His Work (8:22-36). This Wisdom existed before the creation of the world (8:22-26). Wisdom was with God when He made the sky, sea, and land (8:27-29). Wisdom was always with God (8:30-31). By wisdom God created the worlds. Earlier Solomon had said, "The LORD by wisdom founded the earth; by understanding he established the heavens" (Proverbs 3:19).

Those sound like statements other passages of the Bible have made about Jesus Christ. Indeed, Christ is the complete fulfillment of God's wisdom. He was in the beginning with God (John 1:2). He made all things (John 1:3). He is the expression of God's wisdom. Paul taught, "He is the source of your life in Christ Jesus, whom God made our wisdom and our righteousness and sanctification and redemption" (1 Corinthians 1:30). All that Christians know about wisdom, righteousness, and sanctification comes through Christ.

Therefore, the first step in wisdom is a right relationship with God. That is Solomon's point when he concluded, "The fear of the LORD is the beginning of wisdom, and the knowledge of the Holy One is insight" (Proverbs 9:10). But it is not possible for a person to simply decide that he will be right with God and then accomplish enough good works to gain favor with God. Mature fear of the LORD, awesome respect of God, is possible only through Jesus Christ's reconciling work. It is impossible to establish a relationship with God apart from the work of Wisdom personified.

The message of Wisdom as it cries out is more than common sense in living (though it is that). The full message of Wisdom is that humans can have abundant life through a right relationship with their Creator God. It is the message that blessings, both temporal and eternal, come from the hand of the Creator, through the work of the Savior.

Wisdom is prepared to welcome and benefit all who will respond (9:1-2). She has built her beautiful house (v.1). She has decked her house with seven pillars. Surely the number seven speaks of completion or perfection. That conclusion is based on the many other illustrations of completeness in the Bible that employ the number seven. For example, in the beginning there were seven days of creation (Genesis 2:2). Noah took seven pairs of clean animals on the ark (Genesis 7:2). In the law, God honored the seventh day as the Sabbath on which He expected His people to cease from work as He did. Likewise the seventh year is Sabbath year during which the Israelites were supposed to allow their fields to lay fallow (Exodus 25:2; Leviticus 25:4). But the Revelation, the last book of the Bible, the prophecy of completing events, contains the most references to the number seven. There are seven spirits, seven churches, seven lampstands, seven stars, and on and on the list goes. Altogether there are at least eighteen different "sevens" in the final book of the Bible.

So what do the seven pillars of Wisdom's house represent? One must be careful not to supply ideas or interpretations for which the Bible does not allow. Some Bible teachers have concluded that the seven pillars are equivalent to the seven spirits mentioned in Revelation 1:4, 3:1, 4:5, 5:6. That is an interesting conclusion. However, one must wonder what exactly the seven spirits are or what they represent. It has been suggested that the seven spirits have been clearly identified in Isaiah 11:2: "And the [1]Spirit of the LORD shall rest upon him, the [2]Spirit of wisdom and [3]understanding, the [4]Spirit of counsel and [5]might, the [6]Spirit of knowledge and the [7]fear of the LORD" (Isaiah 11:2). Those are all traits of the promised Messiah and Savior.

Such interpretations are interesting and this one might even be plausible. But it is better to exercise caution with questionable texts. Many years ago J. S. Wardlaw warned regarding this passage, "I have no doubt, that those who are fond of the system of spiritualizing, would find the distinct mystic symbol of something spiritual in each one of the pillars, and bring out of the seven a whole body of divinity. This however, would not be exposition, but the mere play of a conjecturing fancy; and how excellent soever the truths exhibited, they would be educed from that which the Holy Spirit never meant to contain them" (J.S. Wardlaw. Lectures on the Book of Proverbs. Vol. 1. Minneapolis: Klock & Klock Christian Publications, Inc., 1981 reprint, 208.).

Not only has Wisdom built a beautiful house, but Wisdom has also prepared a sumptuous feast (v.2). The picture seems to be that of a beautiful home with the messengers welcoming passersby to enter and enjoy the feast of roast lamb or beef along with wine that was mixed with spices or mixed with water to make it palatable (a thought that was a later Greek custom).

The fulfillment of the picture is far more important than the picture. The LORD still invites people to sit at the table He prepares. David acknowledged, "You prepare a table before me in the presence of my enemies; you anoint my head with oil; my cup overflows" (Psalms 23:5). In a later Psalm, he affirmed, "The afflicted shall eat and be satisfied; those who seek him shall praise the LORD! May your hearts live forever!" (Psalms 22:26). God is gracious indeed, and He does picture fellowship with Him at a great meal. But the greatest banquet, the best fulfillment of this picture, will be during the last events of history. Jesus revealed to John that those who receive Wisdom's invitation will sit down with the Savior at the Great Wedding feast. "And the angel said to me, 'Write this: Blessed are those who are invited to the marriage supper of the Lamb.' And he said to me, 'These are the true words of God'" (Revelation 19:9). What a feast that will be! But only the people who have accepted Wisdom's invitation will be present.

## WISDOM INVITES THE SIMPLE TO ENTER HER WAY (vv.3-6)

Wisdom's messengers invite the simple (vv.3-4). She has sent them out with the wonderful news that simpletons do not have to continue on the road to destruction. It is interesting how this simple text reveals that the messengers proclaim the essential message of wisdom (v.3). Wisdom herself cries out. The story in 8:1-3 pictures Wisdom in the busy thoroughfares of life trumpeting the invitation to the simple ones. But more than that, Wisdom sends her messengers with the same invitation (v.3).

Yea, Wisdom speaks through them as if speaking herself (v.4). Notice that the messengers' invitation is, "'Whoever is simple, let him turn in here!' To him who lacks sense she says, 'Come, eat of my bread and drink of the wine I have mixed'" (Proverbs 9:4-5). Those are the very words of Wisdom. If we would be Wisdom's messenger, let us be sure to proclaim Wisdom's message and not one of our own.

The message is directed to the simple (v.4). The simple person is actually referred to by three separate terms in the collection of Proverbs. First, he is called the simple. This person is gullible and easily led astray. He is naive and believes almost anything. But at the same time, he is stubborn and irresponsible. His irresponsibility is highlighted by the fact that he chases after vanities. Solomon taught about the simple person by contrasting him to the wise worker. He concluded, "Whoever works his land will have plenty of bread, but he who follows worthless pursuits lacks sense" (Proverbs 12:11). In the end, it is plain that the simple person followed worthless pursuits.

The same kind of person is also called a fool in this collection of Proverbs. He assumes that wisdom is owed him and, therefore, someone will give it to him rather than admitting his need to search diligently for it. He loves to express his opinion, but eventually his "wise" remarks are seen as foolish. Sadly, this person does not realize how foolish he is or sounds. That is not to conclude that the simple person is mentally foolish. In fact, the fellow might be quite bright intellectually, but he is spiritually foolish. Because he is spiritually challenged, he proves his folly by being enslaved to sin. "Like a dog that returns to his vomit is a fool who repeats his folly" (Proverbs 26:11). Try as he might, the fool proves that human effort cannot un-enslave him. That is why it is possible to "crush a fool in a mortar with a pestle along with crushed grain, yet his folly will not depart from him" (Proverbs 27:22).

The third term describing this needy person in Proverbs is scoffer. He is proud. "'Scoffer' is the name of the arrogant, haughty man who acts with arrogant pride" (Proverbs 21:24). He dislikes correction. "Whoever corrects a scoffer gets himself abuse, and he who reproves a wicked man incurs injury" (Proverbs 9:7). Not surprisingly then, the man is also a source of arguments. Many have learned the truth of the maxim, "Drive out a scoffer, and strife will go out, and quarreling and abuse will cease" (Proverbs 22:10). Such people are in great need, but seldom do they know it or admit it.

Wisdom invites the simple to forsake his way (vv.5-6). This person needs to leave his simple ways (v.6). The invitation from Wisdom is a call for self-reflection and humility. When the proud, arguing, irresponsible sinner admits the truth about himself, God will give him grace to be humbled. But what about good sinners? There are many sinners in life who are not proud, arrogant, enslaved to sin, and all the other unsavory characteristics that the simple person in Proverbs demonstrates. It is true that there are sinners who appear to be above the cut for simpletons and fools. Nevertheless, measured against God's standard, they are still simple and arrogant against God.

Those who have embraced Wisdom's invitation must cry out for the simpletons and fools to leave that path of destruction! We must realize that such people need to enjoy wisdom's bounty (vv.5,6b). God invites the simple one to feast on what He has prepared. He who accepts Wisdom's invitation will live in a new way, a way that demonstrates insight and understanding of God's truth. Is it possible that someone can appear to be righteous, but in reality be a proud fool? It is good for everyone to be sure that he has admitted his foolish sinfulness and accepted Wisdom's (i.e. Christ's) invitation. Then we must call out Wisdom's invitation to the foolish. The one who has found refreshing grace in Christ will surely want other weary sinners to enjoy the same refreshment. The invitation still stands. Who will articulate it to the needy wanderers?

# 11

# COME AND DISPUTE
# WITH GOD

ISAIAH 1:18-20

S ome people enjoy debate. Some of those people even study debate
in highschool or college. Those people who have been involved in
debate know that the debater must abide by clearly stated rules.
If a debater breaks the rules while arguing, it really does not matter how
sound his arguments were, nor does it matter how passionate he was
about his topic. If he breaks the rules, he loses.

Attorneys spend several years in law school learning how to argue
within the proper boundaries of courtroom decorum. A defendant does
not want a defender who has great passion but no understanding of
courtroom procedures. To be represented by a boisterous fool in court is
a certain recipe for failure. Wise judges and jurymen are not impressed
by zeal as much as by sound reasoning. By sound reasoning, a case is
presented and the evidence should be sufficient to acquit or condemn
the plaintiff.

God invited the citizens of Judah into the same kind of setting. This
was His nation—what was left of it. By the time God called Isaiah to proclaim His message, the ten tribes of Northern Israel were in a serious state
of declining. Assyria had already made devastating forays into the nation,
and by 722 B.C. they had overrun the Northern tribes of Israel and scattered the citizens to distant lands. God sent the words of this text to the
people in Judah during the waning days of their northern counterpart.
The handwriting was on the wall. God's promises of judgment because
of sin were not empty threats. It was obvious from His responses to Israel
that God intended for His people to love and obey Him.

God sent Isaiah to people who were very stubborn, very religious, and very sinful. He warned them that there was only one right response to Him. It is the response that results in blessing. He invited them to come before His bench, as it were, and to argue the evidence of their lives. They must argue according to His rules. What would the evidence prove? Were they loving and obedient, and thus deserving of God's blessing? Or were they rebellious, disobedient, and deserving God's judgment?

God continues to offer the same invitation. The world is His. Every person in the world is supposed to belong to God because He is creator of all. But the whole world, and everyone in it, was hijacked by sin. As a result, sin and offense permeates every person to the core. Nevertheless, many people believe that if they are dedicated enough, religious enough, or kind enough to needy people, God will bless them instead of judging them. Many people do many religious deeds in order to gain God's favor. Many people need to hear God's invitation to come and dispute their position with Him. Tell God the evidence of your life, and let God the righteous Judge determine whether you should receive blessing or judgment.

### The Invitation (v.18)

God offered this wonderful invitation through Isaiah to people in need (1:1-17). Yea, they were in great need? According to whom? Probably the people themselves did not think they had many needs at all. That is why it was necessary for God to identify the need (1:1-10). The text of God's message did not address a felt need, nor did it deal with an emotional/psychological lack identified by government specialists or social workers.

The opening words indicate that people who should have belonged to God were experiencing a serious need. Notice that God calls on the rest of His creation (heavens, earth) to bear witness to His words (v.1). With the witnesses in place, God laid down evidence that affirms the offenses of His people (vv.2-10). He pointed out that He created and reared children who should have grown to respect and honor Him. Instead, the very children He brought into existence reject Him (v.2). Even dumb animals are more respectful than the people God made (v.3).

God laid out one incriminating evidence after another in a list that quickly becomes heavy with guilt. His people, who He intended to be holy unto Him, became a sinful nation (v.4a). They are heavy with depravity (v.4b). Each of the citizens were born in evil (v.4c). They are children of those who ruin everything that is good (v.4d). These are not pleasant words. This is not a general, non-committal description. The words are pointed and painful. Why does God use such terrible words to describe people who called themselves by His name? God continued with the bombardment of evidence. He accused them of forsaking the LORD (v.4e). The LORD is the eternal, self-existing God who promised to provide for these people. They have despised the Holy One (v.4f). As a result, their sin has completely cut them off from fellowship with God (v.4g).

This barrage of evidence sounds a lot like Paul's assessment of people in the New Testament. He wrote,

as it is written: 'None is righteous, no, not one; no one understands; no one seeks for God. All have turned aside; together they have become worthless; no one does good, not even one.' 'Their throat is an open grave; they use their tongues to deceive.' 'The venom of asps is under their lips.' 'Their mouth is full of curses and bitterness.' 'Their feet are swift to shed blood; in their paths are ruin and misery, and the way of peace they have not known.', 'There is no fear of God before their eyes' (Romans 3:10-18).

This familiar accusation from Romans is not about Judah or Israel. This is God's assessment of all humanity. What God said about Judah is precisely true about all of us. It is a great need because all people who respond to God like this are worthy for judgment. According to verses five through nine, Judah was already reaping some of the consequences of sin. Indeed, Paul warned that God's wrath is already abiding on sinners who reject His truth (Romans 1:19). The whole human race is in serious trouble just like Judah was in the eight century B.C.

However, as verses eleven through seventeen point out, the needy people are often ignorant. The folks in Judah did not even acknowledge their desperate condition (1:3b). God proved how senseless His people were by saying, "The ox knows its owner, and the donkey its master's crib, but Israel does not know, my people do not understand" (Isaiah 1:3). They were either very ignorant or living in denial. Instead of acknowledging that they were in hot water with God, the people actually thought that they were very devout followers of God. They did far more than their pagan neighbors did to honor God. These people offered multitudes of sacrifices (v.11a). Isn't that what God's law requires? Not really. God's overarching requirement is obedience from a heart of love. That foundational trait must undergird every thought, motive, and action. People in Judah didn't have it. Neither do the majority of the human population today.

The people who should have been God's people were proud to keep or observe all the special days with a passion (vv.13b-14). God acknowledged that they kept the feast days and Sabbaths. Didn't God require His people to observe the feasts in His law? Of course. Were they not, therefore, obeying God? Not necessarily. God requires obedience from a heart of love.

God even acknowledged that the people prayed regularly (v.15). In fact, it appears that they prayed seriously. Doesn't God delight in the prayers of His people? Not always. God desires fellowship out of a heart of love for Him. Vain repetition does not impress God. It might impress the false gods created out of man's imagination. But the only true God is not moved by empty, mindless words flowing from the mouths of religious people who do not love Him.

God expects a far different kind of evidence (vv.16-17). First, He told the people that there were some things they needed to jettison. They needed to get rid of sin and its putrefying effects by purifying themselves and making themselves clean. This would require them to remove evil deeds from their life and stop doing evil. On the other hand, the people (sinners) needed to do some positive things like learn to do good, seek justice, judge the oppressor, defend orphans, and contend for the widow's case. Those are good social causes.

God is the prosecutor and judge. He has just laid out His case. People who are expected to be His people are not His people at all. They prove they do not have a relationship with God because they do what they should not do, and they neglect what they should do. This is the evidence against the whole human race. Extreme religious practice not withstanding, people whom God created to bring glory to Him actually glorify themselves. Self-love causes us to do the wrong things and neglect the right things. God still desires obedience to His will out of a heart of love. He lays down the stipulations. They are clear. But who is able to do these things? Who naturally avoids the wrong thing and embraces the right thing? Not people who love themselves! God invites all people to come to His judgment seat and argue their case.

That brings the reader of the prophecy to the amazing invitation. God, the prosecutor, jury, and judge, invites sinners to acknowledge their need (v.18). The words, "Come now" are really more than an invitation. It is an imperative, that is, a command. It is a command by the Almighty, Holy God to sinful people. It does not leave an option. All must appear. Nor is this an offer for equals to meet and negotiate. It is a command from the Superior to the inferior. Yet, attached to the particle "now" the command is softened to an invitation.

This is God's command for sinners to come and "let us reason together." That makes it an invitation to discuss together the LORD's accusations against His people. God has already stated the charges (vv.1-17). There is no question about the evidence that leaves each person guilty before Him. God's messenger says, "Now let's talk about it!" It is an invitation for the accused to approach the Judge's bench and argue with Him about His accusation. On one hand, Judah (as well as all of us) is indeed a sinner. On the other hand, God is ready and willing to forgive. So God argues, "What is the wisdom of continuing the path of destruction when I am offering forgiveness?"

To reason with God is to be forced to accept His argument. Since He is the infinitely wise God, there is no other option. Job learned this. In the midst of his trial Job blurted out, "Though he slay me, I will hope in him; yet I will argue my ways to his face" (Job 13:15). That sounds honorable enough. Did he not accept God's invitation to come and argue His cause? However, when God finished the questioning, Job was speechless. He humbly confessed, "I had heard of you by the hearing of the ear, but now my eye sees you; therefore I despise myself, and repent in dust and ashes" (Job 42:5-6). No one should ever look at God's invitation to reason with Him as an opportunity to convince God that he or she is okay and deserves blessing. That is not going to happen.

God is the author of sound reason. It is not a concept to which He must submit. He invented it. Therefore, to reason with God is to agree with His conclusions and submit to His commands. All sin is outside the bounds of God's reasoning. The first step in repentance is to acknowledge that one's thoughts, attitudes, or actions are not in keeping with God's reasoning. Therefore, this is a command to be judged in light of God's law, to admit guilt, to ask for and receive forgiveness. John Calvin observed, "For the Lord declares that the Jews will have nothing to reply, and that, even though they obtain an opportunity of clearing themselves, they will still be speechless" (Calvin, p.66).

God promises results for everyone who receives His invitation. The invitation or command in God's "saith the LORD" reminds the reader that this is not the prophet's idea, command, or invitation. God promises, "If your sins are becoming as double-dipped scarlet, they shall be as white as snow. If they are becoming red as crimson, they shall be like wool." Sin is pictured as being red like a garment deeply stained with blood. The person who has cut his finger and bled on his white shirt understands the picture well. The blood stain penetrates deeply. So, too, scarlet was a deep, fixed color. Albert Barnes described it by saying, "Neither dew, nor rain, nor washing, nor long usage, would remove it. Hence it is used to represent the fixedness and permanency of sins in the heart. No human means will wash them out. No effort of man, no external rites, no tears, no sacrifices, no prayers, are of themselves sufficient to take them away. They are deep fixed in the heart as the scarlet colour was in the web of cloth and an almighty power is needful to remove them" (Albert Barnes. Notes on the Old Testament. "Isaiah," vol. 1. Grand Rapids: Baker Book House, 1978 reprint, 72.). Sin and its staining effect is so deeply entrenched in the human being that no person can ever remove it.

But God can cleanse away sins so that the once stained garment is pure and colorless. He promised to make penitent sinners who are deeply stained by sin as white as snow. White speaks of purity—no hint of stain. It is what Daniel saw when He looked at the vision of God's glory. He confessed, "As I looked, thrones were placed, and the Ancient of days took his seat; his clothing was white as snow, and the hair of his head like pure wool; his throne was fiery flames; its wheels were burning fire" (Daniel 7:9). This is the kind of purity the disciples saw when they gazed upon the transfigured Jesus. "And he was transfigured before them, and his face shone like the sun, and his clothes became white as light" (Matthew 17:2). It is the kind of sinlessness that Jesus promised to first century saints when He told John to write, "Yet you have still a few names in Sardis, people who have not soiled their garments, and they will walk with me in white, for they are worthy" (Revelation 3:4). Ultimately, white is the purity one finds around the throne of God in heaven. John saw, "Around the throne were twenty–four thrones, and seated on the thrones were twenty–four elders, clothed in white garments, with golden crowns on their heads" (Revelation 4:4).

God's grace makes sin colorless, non-existent. This is justification: God declaring the sinner free from the stain of sin.

## POTENTIAL RESPONSES TO THE INVITATION (vv.19-20)

There is a positive response to debating with God and learning the truth about oneself (v.19). The debater can be willing and obey. The phrase, "if you are willing," can mean something like, "if your mind be ready and your will be disposed to obey." More exactly it means, "If you are being willing (imperfect tense verb), you are obedient (perfect tense verb)." The condition of the heart determines the actions. Hearts that are ready and willing to take heed to God's Word are obedient. That is not "might be obedient" or "could be obedient." They are obedient.

But who is willing? Did ancient Israel or Judah have the ability to change the way they thought or acted? Does any sinner in any age have the ability, in and of himself, to be willing to listen to God's command? If we review again God's assessment of the nation in the first seventeen verses of this chapter, we must conclude that the people were hopelessly sunk in sin. They were totally consumed with self and sin. How can people like that respond favorably to God's invitation? No healing from within themselves is possible. No reform can come from within. They need help from without. That is the whole argument! God invites sinners to come and argue their position. They will discover that they are impossibly sunk in sin, and God is ready and willing to wipe every stain of the sin away.

The result of God's heart-changing work is beneficial. For Judah it would mean that the nation could continue to enjoy the bounty of God's Promised Land. For all sinners, it is the promise that penitent sinners can enjoy abundant life. Abundant life is life as God intended for His people to live now. It is a perfect life for eternity.

However, the nation chose otherwise. So do most people. A negative response to God's invitation is common (v.20). The debater and be willing and obey, or the debater can refuse and rebel. Again the phrase means, "If you are refusing (imperfect tense verb), you rebel (perfect tense verb)." People with a rebellious heart refuse to listen to God. People who refuse to listen to God never—ever—accept this invitation. Since God has already gone on record as being willing to forgive sins, if Judah (or sinners) choose not to accept His invitation, they are responsible for their own destruction.

The consequences of this choice are deadly. For Judah it meant that instead of eating God's provision, they would be eaten by the sword. For sinners today, rejection of the invitation means eternal death. Paul wrote quite simply, "The wages of sin is death, but the free gift of God is eternal life in Christ Jesus our Lord" (Romans 6:23). Eternal death is worse than the human mind can begin to imagine. Escape it at all costs. The promise is certain. ". . . for the mouth of the LORD has spoken." Have you ever heard God's invitation? If you have heard the invitation, have you responded and pled your case to God? If you pled your case, you lost. Then have you received His forgiveness for the sin that God says you committed? Has God declared you to be stain-free from sin because you have received by faith the finished work of Christ as your payment for sin?

# 12

# TRUST IN THE LORD

## Isaiah 26:1-4

The Revelation that Jesus Christ gave to John, while he was exiled on Patmos, has been the source of arguments and various interpretations since John received it and wrote it. The most controversial, the most debated part of that writing is not the identification of the beast or the false prophet, not the nature of the various judgments, not the identification of the 144,000, or not even the mark of the beast. The most debated issue in the book is the short description of a 1,000 year reign of Christ and His saints. John wrote,

> Then I saw an angel coming down from heaven, holding in his hand the key to the bottomless pit and a great chain. And he seized the dragon, that ancient serpent, who is the devil and Satan, and bound him for a thousand years, and threw him into the pit, and shut it and sealed it over him, so that he might not deceive the nations any longer, until the thousand years were ended. After that he must be released for a little while. Then I saw thrones, and seated on them were those to whom the authority to judge was committed. Also I saw the souls of those who had been beheaded for the testimony of Jesus and for the word of God, and who had not worshiped the beast or its image and had not received its mark on their foreheads or their hands. They came to life and reigned with Christ for a thousand years. The rest of the dead did not come to life until the thousand years were ended. This is the first resurrection. Blessed and holy is the one who shares in the first resurrection! Over such the second death has no power, but they will be priests of God and of Christ, and they will reign with him for a thousand years. (Revelation 20:1-6)

Is this a literal kingdom that endures for 1,000 years on earth? Is this a symbolic kingdom that lasts for a long time? Is it something entirely disconnected with kingdoms?

Premillennialism teaches that Christ will return to the earth at the end of the Great Tribulation and will establish this kingdom. The kingdom will be the fulfillment of the kingdom God promised to Israel, the extension of David's kingdom. In this kingdom, Christ, the seed of David, will reign supreme over the world and Israel will be the chief of nations. This reign will last for a period of 1,000 years during which time millions of people will be born. At the end of the period, Satan will be released from bondage and will put the "newbies" to the test. Many will side with Satan in one last-ditch effort to unseat Christ. Christ will be victorious, condemn Satan and his followers to hell forever, wipe out the current heavens and earth, and establish the eternal heaven where we will live with Him forever. That has been the favorite teaching in dispensational circles for many years.

Postmillennialism teaches that this will be an actual 1,000 year kingdom, but it will not be established directly by Christ. Rather, because of the preaching of the gospel, nations will turn to Christ and the result will be worldwide peace. Christ will rule in the hearts of men and women around the world which will bring utopia for 1,000 years. After that time, Christ will return to earth. Some of the great minds of the past, such as Jonathan Edwards and Benjamin Warfield, held to this view. No doubt Postmillennialists today believe that the Muslims will usher in a worldwide kingdom of peace. Probably not!

Amillennialism teaches that this kingdom is symbolic of a long period of time during which Christ reigns in a spiritual kingdom. This view teaches that Christ bound Satan at the cross and now reigns in the hearts of His followers. At the end of the age, Christ will come again and bring all things to an end for His glory. Martin Luther believed this view as well as more modern thinkers like William Hendriksen and Jay Adams.

With that background, we come to this great invitation in Isaiah chapter twenty-six where Isaiah promised the people of Israel (technically just Judah and Benjamin because the northern tribes had been captured) that "In that day . . ." things were going to be different. This appears to the a promise of the same kingdom that John saw in Revelation 20. It is the same utopia Isaiah described in 2:1-4 ("For out of Zion shall go the law, and the word of the LORD from Jerusalem") and 11:1-16 ("the lion will lie down with the lamb"). It must have been wonderful news for people who were looking at almost certain destruction to hear that one day God would indeed send His Messiah to lead the restored nation of Israel.

While this is a wonderful promise to the nation, it is a greater invitation to all people. To people who were anxious about the future, to people who were unsure if they would even be alive next year, God said through Isaiah, "You keep him in perfect peace whose mind is stayed on You, because he trusts in You. Trust in the LORD forever, for the LORD God is an everlasting rock" (Isaiah 26:3-4).

But when will Christ establish this kingdom? Will Christ actually establish it, or will we the people finally convince the sinful world to live more godly? If God's people

knew the answers to questions like these, it would be far easier to trust God. That is the point. The person who embraces this invitation trusts God. Period! If the penitent sinner can trust God to dismiss his offenses against Him and give him everlasting life, he does not need to know when everlasting life begins. Real faith trusts God to take care of the details. If He has to explain the details of life to us, we really don't trust Him.

When I step on an elevator, I typically see a sign that tells me how much weight the elevator can hold. I never worry about it. I never fear that it might not do what the owner of the elevator says it will do. I never take a survey of the passengers and add up their weight and compare it to the posted information. Now if I can trust a sign on an elevator, I surely ought to be able to trust the God of eternity. Born again people trust God. We should trust Him completely.

## IN THAT DAY . . . (vv. 1-2)

God promised His people through Isaiah that in that day Judah would sing a song. What day? Isaiah described that day so that the reader has some idea of the circumstances of this promise (24:1-25:12). That day will be (would be) a time shortly after God has judged the earth (24:1-23). For several chapters leading up to this statement, God had promised through His messenger that He would level complete destruction against neighboring nations. The list is almost depressing as it goes on and on. He authored an oracle against Assyria (14:24-27), an oracle against Philistia (14:28-32), an oracle against Moab (15:1-16:13), an oracle against Damascus (17:1-14), an oracle against Cush [Nubia] (18:1-7), an oracle against Egypt (19:1-15), a promise of Babylon's fall (21:1-15), an oracle against Jerusalem (22:1-25), and finally, an oracle against Tyre and Sidon (23:1-18).

All of these oracles and promises came to pass at about the same time as Jerusalem's destruction. Therefore, on the one hand, it is safe to conclude that God has already carried out these promises. On the other hand, it is also fair to say that God will issue a similar kind of devastation in the days of the Great Tribulation, only it will be on a much broader scale. In that day, the destruction will be worldwide.

But coming to chapter twenty-four, it appears that God has broadened the picture. The description of God's judgment in chapter twenty-four reveals a day of great devastation. In this case, the whole earth will be effected (vv.1-3). Though it is true that the term "earth" can just as easily refer to "the land," the context of the entire chapter seems to portend something bigger than the description in the previous chapters. In this judgment, everyone on earth will mourn (v.4). God warned that the destruction would be because of earth-wide sin (vv.5-6). The destruction will be accompanied by supernatural cataclysm (vv.18-20). Not only will the earth quake in judgment, but even the sun and moon will be effected (v.23). This sounds very much like the outpouring of God's wrath in the seven seals, seven trumpets, and seven bowls that one reads about leading up to chapter twenty in the Revelation.

The grim promises of chapter twenty-four are followed by the refreshing promises of chapter twenty-five. That "day" will also be a time when God will exalt Jerusalem (25:1-12). Everyone will glorify God (vv.3-4). No doubt much of the rejoicing will be in the fact that the LORD will make a feast in Jerusalem (v.6). In connection with God judging all of the nations, the LORD will also remove the reproach from His people (v.8). The LORD will fulfill the promises for which His people had waited and for which they had longingly looked (v.9). "It will be said on that day, 'Behold, this is our God; we have waited for him, that he might save us. This is the LORD; we have waited for him; let us be glad and rejoice in his salvation.' For the hand of the LORD will rest on this mountain . . ." (Isaiah 25:9-10a).

That day will be a day of great rejoicing (26:1-2). Rejoicing will erupt because it will be a day when God establishes salvation (v.1). This will not be the work of earthly kings or wise men. All of God's people will know that God has done this wonderful work. Everyone will know that it was the LORD who destroyed His enemies and the enemies of His people. Being eyewitnesses to God's hand of judgment against their life-long enemies will certainly motivate people in Judah to rejoice. The surrounding middle eastern people have been the Jew's enemies for centuries.

But in a matter of days, God will change all of that. Isaiah promised that the LORD will set up salvation like walls of a mighty city. Indeed, God will build an actual phenomenal city in that day. When Christ comes to earth again, He will stand on the Mount of Olives. Zechariah promised that the hill will split in two (Zechariah 14:4). A new temple mount will rise up between the two halves upon which the LORD will build a new temple (Ezekiel 40-48). A river of living water flows from the city both east and west (Zechariah 14:8). Then all of the nations will come into the city to worship God (Zechariah 14:16). What a picture this is. No wonder unbelievers dismiss the whole idea out of hand. It is too wonderful to comprehend. It is also no wonder that the people in Judah will sing a song. What a change that will mean for people who have been despised and mistreated for centuries. What a hope for people who had been looking at certain destruction as their only future.

The walls of salvation are erected. The nation is singing praise to God, and the city gates are opened for the righteous nation (v.2). The LORD is responsible to have the gates opened and to invite people to come and worship. The term "righteous nation" must refer to everyone on earth who is righteous. Righteous people are the ones who maintain faith in God. Abraham believed God (faith) and God accounted that faith to him as righteousness (Romans 4:3). Only people like Abraham, only people who fully trust God, would want to worship Him in His city at His temple. Many people in every age want freedom from the problems and the ramifications of sin. But few are willing to humble themselves before God and confess their sin. They do not trust Him. But people who have faith in God willingly bow before Him in worship.

This was an astonishing picture and promise to people who were concerned about a real enemy who threatened to annihilate them. The threat of Assyria, and later Babylon, were very real. Likewise, we live with people who are in bondage to sin all the time. The evil taskmaster threatens to destroy them with the consequences of their sin. Many are in poor health and emotionally distraught because the taskmaster of sin demands its wages. What hope can you give them? Tel them that the LORD will keep His promises. The LORD will bring to pass all that He ever promised. In perfect accord with His eternal plans, and in keeping with His perfect timing, the LORD will establish His earthly kingdom, fulfill all of His promises to the nation of Israel, and then set up the new heaven and new earth where He will live in perfect fellowship with every person who trusted Him for eternity. Can you believe it?

## TRUST IN THE LORD (vv.3-4)

God gives peace to those who trust Him (v.3). In this, one of the great verses of the Bible, God promises perfect peace. Perfect peace is not the absence of trouble. Trouble-free peace is what the world promises and never delivers. Conversely, God gives peace in spite of difficult circumstances. It is a calm assurance that God is in control of the hurricane. It is steadfast confidence that all things work for good for God's glory. It is a certainty that God is in control of all events, so I don't have to be.

People who are looking the enemy in the eye need this kind of confidence that only God can give. In the example of this story, the citizens of Judah needed perfect peace. They were essentially surrounded by powers that threatened to overrun them and end their freedom. They had been for years. They needed the peace of God to face such fearful circumstances. In a similar way, sinners need to escape the taskmaster of sin that always causes doubt and fear. They need to flee to freedom in the arms of God where they find peace. Saints need to quit worrying about what they cannot change and rest in the peace of God.

The LORD promises perfect peace. Perfect peace eclipses human comprehension. It is a peace that human wisdom or logic cannot explain. Therefore, it is not available through human cogitations but only by having complete trust of God. God promises this kind of peace, this Godlike peace, to those who have fixed their minds on Him. The requirement of a mind fixed on God might help explain the nature of this peace. The mind that is settled on God is the mind that trusts Him completely. Complete trust of God leaves no room for trust in self. Self is insufficient. The flesh will fail in the time of need. Too often people who claim to trust God alone actually face trouble through their wisdom and simply use God as a backup if things get out of hand. Proud, self-sufficient folks are sure they can develop a way out of most problems. However, if things get tougher than they expected, they can always turn to God Who is right there behind them.

God's plan does not conform to that foolish plan hatched in human wisdom. A mind fixed on God has put God first in all things. It is a mind that meditates on God's person and God's Word all the time. That kind of mind sees God in every event and seeks God in every circumstance. That mind truly believes that God not only has a vested interest in everything but controls all things for His own glory.

Isaiah concluded that folks who have a mind fixed on God surely ought to trust Him (v.4). The requirement is to put full trust in Him alone. Of course, the rest of the Bible makes it clear that the redeemed saint must trust God alone for salvation. That is not as easy to do as one might think because confession and repentance of sin spells death to self. If self is dead, only God can give life and move the lifeless corpse according to His will. Therefore, humble faith does not attempt to help God in salvation. Humble faith must trust God because it has given up on trusting self. Humble faith knows that human effort does not gain God's favor.

Some people have trusted God alone for salvation, but then act like they don't trust God for life. Real faith depends on God every day. Real faith is impressed by what God does, not what people do. Real faith in the LORD alone lives out the words to the song In Christ Alone written by Keith Getty and Stuart Townsend. The text expresses Isaiah's thoughts well:

In Christ alone my hope is found
He is my light, my strength, my song
This Cornerstone, this solid ground
Firm through the fiercest drought and storm
What heights of love, what depths of peace
When fears are stilled, when strivings cease
My Comforter, my All in All
Here in the love of Christ I stand

Do we trust in the LORD alone, not only for salvation, but for power to live for His glory?

Isaiah understood why everyone should trust in God alone. He is worthy of trust because He is an everlasting rock. The rock is a symbol of strength and safety. It stands strong in a storm. No storm of sin or Satan will ever effect Christ. Stand secure in Him alone. Do we? The person who stands secure on the rock of the LORD enjoys the peace that only He gives. That peace will effect how you respond to Satan's accusations against you. If Christ the Rock offers eternal peace through salvation, does He not also offer peace in the trials of life? Certainly He does.

# 13

# SET FORTH YOUR CASE

## ISAIAH 41:21-24

I saiah proclaimed God's messages to His people and to the enemies of God's people for a period of about fifty years. The book that bears his name identifies the beginning of his ministry as the year that King Uzziah died. The Bible states that Uzziah died in 739 B.C. No one knows for sure when Isaiah's ministry ended, but it must have been somewhere toward the end of King Hezekiah's reign. Probably Isaiah's ministry ended somewhere between 690 B.C. and 680 B.C.

The first thirty-nine chapters of this prophecy contain contemporary messages. That is, God sent messages to people who were living contemporaries of Isaiah, whether they were fellow-Israelites or neighboring Gentiles. For the most part, the messages and warnings of the first part of Isaiah's book do not look beyond his lifetime.

However, the second part of Isaiah (chapters forty through sixty-six) deals almost exclusively with events that would come to pass after the death of Isaiah and his contemporaries. The subject matter in the latter part of the prophecy deals with Judah's captivity in Babylon, God's deliverance of His people from captivity through King Cyrus of Persia, the restored nation, the coming Messiah, and Messiah's earthly kingdom. Sometimes the merging between the promises about the restored kingdom after the Babylonian captivity and the final kingdom of Messiah are so subtle that the two almost blend into one. Often, the ideas of Israel's restoration are blended into both kingdoms, and it requires careful scrutiny to determine which kingdom God is talking about.

An example of this is found in the current text. God promised His people that He would deliver them from Babylonian captivity. No doubt such promises escaped the understanding of Isaiah's contemporaries because the captivity itself was still about one hundred years in the future. However, one can only imagine how encouraging these words would have been to people who, at a later time, languished in captivity to the Gentile Babylonians. They must have wondered where God went and why He wasn't fulfilling His promise to protect His people. The words of this chapter would have been very encouraging to people like that.

In this text, God calls the Gentiles who persecute His people to come to His court and defend their reason for choosing to worship and serve false gods. With these words, God invites His people to remember that He is the true God, that He is the God of blessing and protection, that He raises up kings and puts down rulers according to His desires. With these words, God taught that everyone who chooses to serve lesser gods is an abomination to Him. The words must have been very encouraging to captive Israelites. The words are still encouraging to the people of God who live under the intense pressure of a culture wholly given to idolatry. Where is the true God in the midst of this perverted, abominable culture? When will God's people abandon their chase after the next American idol?

## THE TRUE GOD COMFORTS HIS PEOPLE

God presented clear evidence against the nations that proved they were guilty of serving and worshiping unrealistic gods (vv.1-7, 25-29). Isaiah drew a picture of God issuing a subpoena for the nations to appear in court and defend their choice of gods (vv.1-7). He ordered the coastlands and the peoples to appear with Him in court. The terms refer to the Gentile nations surrounding Judah, and they also include all the cultures in the world other than His chosen people. God expected these people to appear in court with Him and argue their position.

God knows that when the pagans show up with their evidence, it will be clear they chose to serve idols. Now they must listen in silence while the God of Creation, the only true God, lays down the evidence of their offense against Him. They who talk so endlessly and confidently about the attributes of their god must answer to the evidence of God's mighty power (vv.2-4).

God began the courtroom proceedings by asking the offending Gentiles who stirred up the great conqueror who would overrun their nations (vv.2-3). This is the promise of Cyrus who would come to power in Persia in 550 B.C. That was almost 150 years after God gave this message through Isaiah. "Who raised up Cyrus to march on Babylon and release God's people?" God required the pagans idolaters to answer that question. The answer is single. "I the LORD" have done this. It is true that when Isaiah gave this message to the people of God in Judah, those folks would not have any idea what he was talking about. However, the Gentiles in later generations would know from experience that Cyrus king who God ordained to do this thing. Indeed, later in this prophecy, Isaiah identified the king: "Thus says the LORD to his anointed, to Cyrus, whose right hand I have grasped, to subdue nations before him and to loose the belts of kings, to open doors before him that gates may not be closed" (Isaiah 45:1). The true God is not stretched to make such a promise because He is the beginning of all things. He is also the end of all things.

The defendants in this case have no hope in response to God's plan (vv.5-7). Everyone would see, yea experience, the evidence of Cyrus' unstoppable power (v.5). In that day, when the mighty king would march unimpeded throughout the land, each person would encourage his neighbor with empty words (v.6). The craftsmen would diligently mold and hammer together lifeless idols (v.7) And then all of the people would foolishly agree "It is good." Notice also that they would have to nail the lifeless thing to the floor so that it would not fall over! How utterly ridiculous it is for a person to put his trust in something like that.

God continued to prosecute His case and proved that the gods of man are powerless (vv.25-29). Conversely, the Mighty God raised up a particular king from a particular place to accomplish His preordained will (v.25). This promise is viewed from the future vantage point of Babylon where God's people would be languishing in captivity. God would raise up and send Cyrus from Persia which was modern Iran. God promised that this king would come from the rising of the sun, that is east of Babylon, which was near modern Bagdad (about 50 miles south). The king would march into Babylon from the north. Of course, people with the advantage of hindsight know that this is exactly how it happened.

"Who among the idols of the Gentiles prophesied this event?" God asks (v.26). God promised this victory and encouraged His people with the news 150 years before it happened (v.27). Why didn't the all-wise idols offer this same information? They could not because they are nothing. They are powerless. Gentile idols are a delusion. God forces the pagans to conclude that, "their metal images are empty wind."

Standing in stark contrast to the powerless, empty idols the pagan Gentiles served is the true God. This God comforted His people (vv.8-20). He was able to offer comfort because He determines what will be accomplished and then accomplishes it through His mighty power. He assured the captives that He would care for them. Why wouldn't He? These were God's special people (vv.8-9). He called them His servant, that is, the people who gladly and willingly do what pleases Him. In the next several chapters, God speaks of His servant, the nation of Israel, and His servant, Messiah. Sometimes it is challenging to decide which one He is speaking about. These servants are God's chosen ones. They are the promised offspring of Abraham. They are the ones God called from among everyone on earth. Are they special to God? Of course they are!

In the few verses of this part of the prophecy, God repeatedly encourages His chosen people who would be sitting in captivity in a foreign land. In three different verses God said something like, "Do not fear or be afraid" (vv.10,13, 14). Why should they not fear? God promised that He will provide food and water (vv.17-19). He promised to provide care for His own so that they will know and understand that He has done it (v.20).

But the most encouraging words to the ears of those captives would be God's assurance that He would make them a mighty nation. They must have wondered at this miracle of the poor and beggarly becoming more powerful than the mighty Babylonians who held their chains. Nevertheless, God promised that everyone who hates them will be put to shame (v.11). Indeed, God promised to make the "worm of Jacob" an irresistible force (vv.14-16). That term was not an insult but a reminder that God makes the lowly and powerless powerful. They who are captives will rise up and crush their enemies. Their Redeemer, the Holy One of Israel, will lead them (v.14).

While it is true that Judah's deliverance from the captivity of Babylon would reveal God's mighty power, it would not begin to fulfill the massive victory of this picture. It seems clear that verses fourteen through twenty are yet to be fulfilled when the Messiah Redeemer sets up His kingdom over all the earth. It was a great day when Israel's restoration was fulfilled in part. It will be an incredible day when Christ comes and completes the exaltation of the lowly nation.

God issued the verdict against the nations (vv.21-24). This is the second and final stage of the trial. The pagan gods are unable to effect history (vv.21-23). In the first stage, God addressed the challenge to the pagan nations; in this stage, God addressed the challenge to the pagan gods. The passage sounds reminiscent of Elijah's challenge to the Baal worshipers. They cried out, pled with, and worshiped extremely, gods who did not exist. In a similar way the pagans' proof is still empty (v.21). What can they say to God's evidence of might and power? Who or what among their idols could compete? God slams home the verdict one point after another. Are the idols able to accurately predict the future (v.22a)? No. Are the idols able to determine the history of humanity and then interpret it by telling their adherents what happened and why it happened (v.22b)? No. Why don't the idols do something, good or bad, to prove they have power (v.23)? They are incapable of promising anything, interpreting anything, or even doing anything!

In the final analysis, the pagans are guilty of worshiping the wrong god (v.24). The idols are nothing. What more does God need to say about them? Anyone who chooses to serve such powerless idols is an abomination to God. He really does not see it as freedom of choice. He does not assess it as just a wrong choice. God considers it an attack against Himself.

## APPLICATION OF THE TRUTH

Is it possible that God still offers the same kind of invitation? "World, bring your evidence to court against God!" Things have not changed much since God hauled the pagan Gentiles into court to sue them. The world is still guilty of serving idols. Idols that are still powerless to offer eternal life.

The world blatantly serves the idol of perverted religion. They have pressed down the truth about God and made up their own stories about Him. Their god is not offended by sin. Their god is not sovereign. Their god governs by majority rule. Their god weighs good works versus bad works in the end to determine eternal destiny. The people love it. They deem it far better to serve a god of their own imagination, a god for whom they can make up the rules, than to serve the God who reveals Himself in the Bible. The world thinks that God, the true God, is too demanding.

The real world where we all live runs mightily after the idol of power and popularity. People around you, people you know, sacrifice all they have in an attempt to gain this elusive god. This god is so tempting that young women sell their bodies and virtually their souls in an effort to please the god of popularity. Often they begin by selling themselves to one boy in order to be accepted or popular. But once they begin to serve this idol, it demands more and more. How many wrecked and impure women are there in this culture? How many have worshiped this god with all they have? In similar fashion, men sell their souls to gain power only to watch it evaporate in a matter of a few years. Parents offer their children on the altar of this false god seeking to enjoy power and popularity vicariously.

Who does not know someone, or several someones, who serve the idol of possessions. Yea, it would not be surprising if you were one of them. Materialism is one of America's chief gods. The whole system of the "American Way" is so intrinsically entwined with this god that it virtually governs the culture. The American dream is to own, own, own. What one owns doesn't matter as long as we own. By the way, where is that 1963 Chevy Belaire that your folks just had to have? And what about that ranch style house with the avocado green shag carpeting that your neighbor sacrificed his family to buy? And whatever happened to your eight track tape player? We live in a throw away culture because this god continually presents "new and improved _____."

The sad reality is that many professing Christians serve this god with all their might. "Then how can they be Christians?" one is forced to wonder. How sad that the goal of most professing Christian young adults is to serve and please this god—and they brashly admit it. In my generation, so-called Christians ran after this idol, but most of them were reluctant to admit it. They were closet worshipers of the god of materialism.

A near cousin to the idol of possessions is the idol of pleasures. This god is nearly as popular as the god of possessions and sometimes more popular. The worshipers of this god can worship it more vigorously when they have more possessions. This god governs Hollywood, and its doctrine is preached in almost every movie and television show. This god is so subtle that professing Christians serve it while pretending to serve the true God. Many professing Christians serve this god each Sunday when they think they are serving the true God. Many so-called Christian ministries arrange their services to accommodate and worship this god.

The above mentioned gods are only a small representation of the multitudes of gods men and women have worshiped in our culture. It is interesting to note that while there are numerous different gods in this generation, and throughout the history of humanity, many of them seem to have the same basic attributes. That is because the ultimate idol, the great idol is self. This is the idol above all idols. Unsaved people embrace all of the above gods because they actually serve and worship themselves. This is the god of Satan. He created it. He manifests its characteristics wholly. Eve chose to serve this god when she saw that the forbidden fruit was "good for food, a delight to the eyes, and to be desired to make one wise" (Genesis 3:6). Adam served this god and so did his son Cain and on goes the list. Which god or gods does your neighbor serve? Which god are you and I tempted to server?

The good news hasn't changed. Idols are still powerless against God. Which of the idols in the world can keep God from doing His will? In the end, all of the time, money, and energy expended in serving this nation's idols will come to naught. In the end, it is still an abomination to worship these idols. Serving idols is not a bad choice, not a mistake, but an attack against God. What will the idol server say to the true God after he has spent his life serving these idols?

The true God, the mighty God, will care for His people in a world that is opposed to Him. Because the world is opposed to God, it is opposed to God's people. It is easy to get discouraged when the success, growth, and prosperity of the idols is abundantly evident. It is difficult to stand against friends, family, and co-workers who embrace the idols. It is painful to be ridiculed and mocked for not joining in with the majority—especially when they are pretending to be Christians. But the truth remains unchanged. Jesus warned His disciples, "If the world hates you, know that it has hated me before it hated you. If you were of the world, the world would love you as its own; but because you are not of the world, but I chose you out of the world, therefore the world hates you" (John 15:18-19). He prayed to the Heavenly Father, "I have given them your word, and the world has hated them because they are not of the world, just as I am not of the world" (John 17:14). Later John encouraged followers of Christ to "see what kind of love the Father has given to us, that we should be called children of God; and so we are. The reason why the world does not know us is that it did not know him" (1 John 3:1). The world is not a friend of grace. Never has been—never will be.

Opposition not withstanding, God cares for His own. This is the true Christian's hope for eternity. This is our motivation for letting our good works shine in a dark world in order to glorify our heavenly Father. God still offers the invitation. Let the world bring their many gods. Yea, let the gods answer if they can. How great it is to know that the true God still stands supreme.

# 14

# TURN TO ME AND BE SAVED

ISAIAH 45:22-25

You planned a nice party or fellowship, sent out the invitations, anticipated a well-attended gathering, and then became very discouraged because only a few of the people you invited attended. At times like that, a person tends to wonder what caused the majority of the people to stay away. Do they have something against you? Do they not like you? Are they opposed to cookouts? At such times, human nature might even stoop so low as to conclude that the invited no-shows are just foolish and unable to identify a true benefit or blessing.

Sometimes it seems like people view the invitation to salvation like that. Imagine the only true God inviting sinners to spend eternity with Him. God, who is perfectly holy and altogether sinless, invites the very people who are by nature such awful sinners that they offend Him every moment of every day. But God invites those very people to come to Him so that He can fix them. The God of eternity offers incomprehensibly abundant life to sinners. This life stands in stark contrast to everlasting punishment which is the alternative of not accepting His invitation. To quickly embrace God's invitation of salvation seems like a logical thing to do. Why would anyone refuse? If a person has any ability to reason at all, any hint of thinking logically, he or she would not reject this invitation.

Add to this amazing invitation the reality of God's heart—that He desires for people to be saved—and the refusal of this invitation makes no sense at all. God, who has gone on eternal record as "not wishing that any should perish, but that all should reach repentance" (2 Peter 3:9), extends the invitation for salvation to the entire world. But even in the context of this invitation it is clear that not everyone in the world will take advantage of the invitation. In spite of God's tremendous mercy and grace there will be those who "were incensed against Him" (Isaiah 45:24b). That kind of response truly escapes even human comprehension. That people refuse God's offer of eternal salvation can only be explained in the realm of the infinite wisdom of God. God's people do not possess infinite wisdom yet.

This invitation falls in the context of God's message to people who were facing serious consequences because of sin. God's people had slowly but surely turned away from Him and had broken the covenant He made with them. The nation had split after Solomon's reign, and by the time God gave this message through Isaiah, the northern part of the nation was already scattered by the Assyrian kings. Now only the tribes of Judah and Benjamin remained, and things did not look too good for them. Assyria was still the powerhouse of the world, as illustrated by Sennacherib who was pounding on Jerusalem's door. But God's message looked into the future to a power that was hardly known at the time. God promised that Babylon was going to overrun Judah because of her sins and take the best and brightest of the people captive. But in this section of Isaiah (chapters 40-49), God looked beyond even the nation of Babylon to the next powerhouse that would rise on the world scene. God described in a certain amount of detail how Cyrus, king of the Persians, would overrun Babylon, free God's people from captivity, and send them back to restore Jerusalem.

One can understand why God's people would be confused by this message and why they would have mixed emotions when they heard this message. Underlying everything was the resident hatred for anyone who was not Hebrew. Only the children of Abraham were God's chosen. Therefore, by logical deduction, everyone else was un-chosen. The non-Israelites were condemned by default. People like Nebuchadnezzar and the Babylonians would prove their wicked, pagan condition by capturing God's people. That is understandable. But what would God's people think about Cyrus, who, also being a Gentile, would not only set God's people free, but would be called "God's servant"?

That thought must have really confused the people who heard Isaiah's message. However, while their minds were still reeling because of God's promise to call a pagan Gentile king His servant, God offered this amazing invitation. He invited the whole world to come to Him and be saved! What an amazing invitation. Surely God's chosen people struggled to understand how God could make that offer. Some of God's chosen people still struggle with this invitation. Some of the people whom God has chosen in salvation to be His own are so befuddled by this kind of invitation that they try to explain "the ends of the earth" as not really the ends of the earth. They conclude that God really meant to invite only the rest of the chosen, not the whole world. That is an example of creative interpreting. In fact, God invites the entire world to be saved and, therefore, the entire world is without excuse. Paul was careful to remind the sinners of the world, in his letter to the Christians in Rome, that they are without excuse. Indeed, this invitation leaves the whole world speechless before the eternal God.

## GOD INVITES EVERYONE TO TURN TO HIM AND BE SAVED (V.22)

The invitation requires change. When God said, "Turn to Me and be saved . . . ," He clearly indicated that repentance is necessary. To repent is to turn around and go a different direction. To repent is to change. The Gentiles in Isaiah's day needed to turn because they were sinners. They were sinners because they were born with the sin nature passed down from Adam. God's word teaches, "Just as sin came into the world through one man, and death through sin, and so death spread to all men because all sinned—" (Romans 5:12). No one escapes that principle of transmitted sin. Each person is born with it.

Could an ancient Gentile be tempted to argue that he did indeed have the sin nature from birth, but that he had disciplined himself throughout life and never committed sin? In such a case, one might think that he was not liable for judgment because the sin nature never came to bear. That is impossible. Because the Gentiles were born with a sin nature, they committed sin. It is almost the same as saying, "Because a person is born with lungs, he breaths." Almost without exception the one requires the other.

What kind of sin did the Gentiles do that required them to turn? Did they smoke, or drink, or play cards? Actually, common vices in that day, as well as this day, were minor compared to the deeper root of sin. The Gentiles needed to turn away from their old path because on that path they rejected God's self revelation. This is the universal condemnation God levels against all people. "For what can be known about God is plain to them, because God has shown it to them. For his invisible attributes, namely, his eternal power and divine nature, have been clearly perceived, ever since the creation of the world, in the things that have been made. So they are without excuse" (Romans 1:19-20). Sinners in every age are without excuse because they, like ancient Gentiles, have rejected God's self revelation. They need to turn.

Furthermore, because the Gentiles rejected God, they also rejected God's truth. "For although they knew God, they did not honor him as God or give thanks to him, but they became futile in their thinking, and their foolish hearts were darkened" (Romans 1:21).

When a person has a foolish heart that is darkened to the truth he has spurned, he will serve gods of his imagination just as did the Gentiles. "Claiming to be wise, they became fools, and exchanged the glory of the immortal God for images resembling mortal man and birds and animals and reptiles" (Romans 1:22-23). That is a very apt description of the Gentile sinners in Isaiah's day. They needed to turn away from this wickedness of serving idols and turn to worshiping the true God according to His self-revelation.

Lest we think that sin and sinfulness died out sometime in the Dark Ages, we must remember that all sinners in every age think like the ancient Gentiles and act like the ancient Gentiles. Sinners still need to turn to God at the bidding of His invitation. The basic principles of sin still exist in every person born. The basic manifestations of that sin principle are still the same. Modern idols might be more sophisticated, but they are still replacements of the true God. Therefore, it is imperative that sinners turn out of that way of life.

God invited the people of the entire world to turn to Him and be saved. The invitation to be saved implies a changed condition. "Be saved from what?" a person might ask. The person who is born with the sin nature is going to be trapped in slavery to sin. God invites him or her to be freed. Because sinners commit sin, they are guilty of the consequences of sin and must pay the wages of eternal punishment. God invites that person to be saved from those consequences. The person who is a sinner by nature is chained by the power of sin. God invites the enslaved sinner to be set free from that power.

Worst of all, sinners are captive to sin and Satan. That captivity is as real as the captivity a Hebrew man or woman felt while sitting in Babylon and longing to be free. The captivity to Satan and sin is as real as the bondage an alcoholic feels when he must have another drink, or the drug addict senses when he must have another fix, or the sex addict feels when she must have another sexual encounter. Ultimately, sinners are addicted to themselves and must be freed. God invites them to turn to Him and be saved.

To some people, the most astonishing part of this invitation is that God offers it to the entire world. Contextually, this would have been difficult to understand. The Jewish people who originally heard these words would have wondered why God would even want to save their persecutors. That would be senseless to them. Furthermore, if they were the chosen ones, how could God invite others to be chosen? Those wicked old Gentiles were not even born in Abraham's line, much less circumcised! Why would God invite them to turn from sin and be saved?

Sometimes it seems that a contemporary application of this invitation is as difficult to understand as was the original context. Thinking minds tend to wonder, "Why, if God offers such an amazing invitation to the whole world, isn't the whole world saved?" Or we wonder how a person could actually understand his sinful condition and not gladly embrace this invitation. Maybe God did not really mean that He offered this invitation to the whole world. Maybe He meant some of the whole world. The simple interpretation of the scope of this invitation is the best invitation. God offered salvation to the whole world, and then proved that He was serious about the invitation by backing it up with His own authority.

## God Offers the Invitation on His Own Authority (vv.22b-25)

God alone is the supreme authority of eternity (vv.22b-23). Therefore, God guarantees the invitation in Himself (vv.22b-23a). He does this because there is no other God. What other God could offer this invitation to turn and be saved and then back it up? It is as if God challenged both Jew and Gentile to name the god. There are certainly many from which they can choose. There are and have been multitudes of so-called gods. God acknowledged that fact many times in Scripture. It has always been a battle between the one true God and the multiplicity of false gods or non-gods.

Non-gods as they were—it is interesting that God even personifies them. For example, when Elijah pitted the worshipers of Baal against the true God, he pretended that they were crying out to real beings. "And at noon Elijah mocked them, saying, 'Cry aloud, for he is a god. Either he is musing, or he is relieving himself, or he is on a journey, or perhaps he is asleep and must be awakened'" (1 Kings 18:27). Nothing happened when they cried because their god was a figment of their imagination.

Since the non-gods are an imagination of man's heart, are they harmless? Not in the least. In reality when people worship the pretend gods, they worship demons. God warned, "They sacrificed to demons that were no gods, to gods they had never known, to new gods that had come recently, whom your fathers had never dreaded" (Deuteronomy 32:17). Therefore, when God appeals to the fact that He alone is God, wise people take heed. The world is full of pretend gods backed by demons. The true God, the only God who is able to do what He promises, invites the whole world to turn and be saved.

The invitation is powerful because God's Word is true. He is able to do what He promises. He speaks what is right and affirms it by His actions. This is exactly what Moses concluded when he was eyewitness to God's righteous act of judgment against Pharaoh's army. He exclaimed, "Who is like you, O LORD, among the gods? Who is like you, majestic in holiness, awesome in glorious deeds, doing wonders?" (Exodus 15:11). God backed up this marvelous invitation by the fact that He alone is the God who performs what He promises.

But not everyone is impressed by God's authority. They will be. This God guarantees that everyone will eventually acknowledge His authority (v.23b). This will come about as surely as God has acted according to His righteous Word in the past. Everyone will eventually bow in submission to God. Every tongue will eventually confess that He alone is God. The New Testament points out more specifically how this will be fulfilled in Christ. Paul argued that because God the Son laid aside His glory and willingly came to earth to be the sacrifice that pays the price to cover sin, "God has highly exalted him and bestowed on him the name that is above every name, so that at the name of Jesus every knee should bow, in heaven and on earth and under the earth" (Philippians 2:9-10).

Every saint acknowledges this truth about God's authority in life. Every sinner will acknowledge the truth in eternity. In eternity, which is never ending, sinners will cry out that God is the only true God. They will cry out forever that God's Word is righteous, dependable, and will come to pass. They will forever agonize over the fact that God is true. But doesn't the text say at this point that everyone will swear allegiance to God? That is one of a couple possible translations of the Hebrew word. "To swear allegiance" really does not fit the context of the passage nor the context of Scripture. Another, and more common, translation of the word means to take an oath, or as we would say, "tell the truth, the whole truth, and nothing but the truth." That is a better interpretation in this context. Every sinner will for eternity tell the whole truth about God—and it will not be a positive situation.

God affirmed His authority because in Him alone is righteousness and strength (vv.24-25). Just as everyone will eventually acknowledge God's authority, so too God promised that everyone who opposes His righteousness will be ashamed (v.24). Only in God does one find the source of true righteousness and full strength. Because God is the source of righteousness, He sets the standard, the measuring stick for what is right. We can accept it or reject it. Because God is the source of strength, He alone has the power to carry out what He calls right.

Many people refuse to acknowledge this fact (v.24b). They choose their own standard of right. They convince themselves that, if there is One God, He will not act according to His Word. Is this that big of a deal? The text teaches that sinners are not indifferent or unconcerned regarding their opinion about God. What they think matters a lot because their opinion about God goes more deeply than they can imagine. God said that they are incensed, burning with fire, against Him. Rejecting God's invitation is not just another expression of freedom of choice. God says that to reject this invitation is to show contempt, burning hatred for God. There is no gray area, no neutrality.

In contrast to the many who reject God in this life but will acknowledge for eternity that He is the only God are the justified ones. Everyone who is part of true Israel will be justified (v.25). This is obviously a reference to Israelites who are the genuine children of Abraham (and subsequently Jacob, that is Israel). Not everyone born in the line of Jacob is a true Israelite. Paul argued, "But it is not as though the word of God has failed. For not all who are descended from Israel belong to Israel, and not all are children of Abraham because they are his offspring, but 'Through Isaac shall your offspring be named.' This means that it is not the children of the flesh who are the children of God, but the children of the promise are counted as offspring" (Romans 9:6-8). Many Israelites were, and are, not spiritual children of Abraham, Isaac, and Jacob because they do not trust God as did those patriarchs. Some clearly rejected God to serve the gods of the world. Some claim to serve God but actually serve the gods of their own making. The Pharisees were like that. But all true Israelites will be justified.

This statement refers to more than the people who are racially born in the family of Abraham. It is also a reference to Gentiles who are children of Abraham. Paul calls Christians, people who have faith in Christ, the real people of God. They are the ones who were once marked out by spiritual circumcision. "For we are the real circumcision, who worship by the Spirit of God and glory in Christ Jesus and put no confidence in the flesh—" (Philippians 3:3). Faith is the distinguishing difference between those who have turned to God and are saved and those who will be ashamed in the end because they have hated God.

God said, "Is this blessing then only for the circumcised, or also for the uncircumcised? We say that faith was counted to Abraham as righteousness" (Romans 4:9). "That is why it depends on faith, in order that the promise may rest on grace and be guaranteed to all his offspring—not only to the adherent of the law but also to the one who shares the faith of Abraham, who is the father of us all" (Romans 4:16).

Faith in God, the only God who invites every sinner to turn and be saved, spells the difference. Do you believe that God alone is righteous and able to do what He promises? Have you turned from your gods to embrace this invitation? Without faith it is still impossible to please Him.

# 15

# COME TO THE WATERS

## Isaiah 55:1-5

God, the one true God, the creator of all, placed Adam and Eve in utopia. In that setting of perfection, Eve and Adam chose to exalt themselves against God and took what He in infinite wisdom had withheld from them. So sin entered God's perfect creation. The story from Eve's transgression to God's judgment in Noah's day is short and missing most of the details of a period that no doubt covers many years. One thing that can be said of that period of time is that, "The LORD saw that the wickedness of man was great in the earth, and that every intention of the thoughts of his heart was only evil continually" (Genesis 6:5). Because humanity had become so deeply entrenched in wickedness, God destroyed every living thing from the earth except for what He had placed in Noah's ark.

After Noah, the cycle began again. Within a few generations the people, as a whole, migrated to a plain in the land of Shinar. Nimrod, a son of Cush, who was a son of Noah's rebel son Ham, founded a city in that place. He spearheaded a movement to build a monument to humanity. "And they said to one another, 'Come, let us make bricks, and burn them thoroughly.' And they had brick for stone, and bitumen for mortar. Then they said, 'Come, let us build ourselves a city and a tower with its top in the heavens, and let us make a name for ourselves, lest we be dispersed over the face of the whole earth.'" (Genesis 11:3-4) The invitation was clear. "Come, let's build a monument to ourselves," they said. God, the true God, the creator of all, destroyed their work.

These Bible passages about the early history of humanity reveal a tendency for all humans to follow Eve's pattern of exalting self. It is still the world's way. It is still the natural way. One of the most obvious sins that accompany self-exaltation is the creation of gods. When the created being exalts himself above the Creator, he must replace the one true creator God with an invention of his own. The Bible is replete with such evidence. Human history is replete with such evidence. But in spite of the massive amounts of evidence proving that humans typically make their own gods to replace the true God, one bit of evidence is seldom reported. Manmade gods always disappoint. The gods of our imagination never satisfy. They always leave their designers looking for a new god, a better god, a god who can satisfy.

That is the story of God's people Israel. God created the nation for His own glory. He expected the nation to love Him and serve Him. They chose to follow in the line of Eve and Adam and exalt themselves. They rejected the true God and embraced the manmade gods of their pagan neighbors. God sent His messengers to His people warning of retribution if they continued in their sin. They rejected the messengers just like they rejected the One who sent the messengers. They wanted no part of humble repentance.

Isaiah was one of those messengers. God warned His people plainly as He sent message after message through Isaiah. Finally it was clear that the people would not concede, would not repent, would not humble themselves before God. Therefore, God would indeed send the Babylonians to destroy what was left of the nation after the Assyrians had scattered the northern tribes. But here is the amazing grace of God. Beginning with chapter forty of Isaiah's collection of messages, it is clear that God communicated His unfathomable mercy with promises that He would fulfil later.

While Isaiah's contemporaries probably had no idea what he was talking about, their posterity, who would read Isaiah's messages many years later while they were in bondage in Babylon, would be greatly encouraged. Here in chapter fifty-five, God offers a wonderful invitation for the thirsty and hungry people to turn to Him for satisfaction. God invites them who had run zealously after the gods of the heathens looking for satisfaction to turn to the one true God and find what they had forfeited their freedom hoping to find.

The promise transcends the bounds of time and ages. This is God's invitation for hungry and thirsty people in every age. It will be valid until the end of the age. As long as time stands this invitation stands. Sinners have opportunity to respond to this marvelous invitation until God finally says, "Time will be no more." Then the invitation ceases. But until then God kindly, patiently invites the needy sinner to come to Him to "eat what is good and delight [himself] in rich food."

## THE INVITATION (VV. 1-3A)

God's invitation for spiritually hungry, thirsty, needy people to come to Him for satisfaction is full of pathos. He pleads with the needy to come to His bounty. Notice the repetition of the invitation couched in the word "come" in the first three verses. God said, "Come, everyone who thirsts, come to the waters; and he who has no money, come, buy and eat! Come, buy wine and milk without money and without price" (v.1). He said, "come to me;" (v.3) As one would expect the word denotes movement from one place to another. When a parent tells her child to "Come here," the thought of the child moving from point "A" to point "B" is implicit. Here the Hebrew word is an imperative, which means that it is a command. But like the mother's command to her child, the command might also be a plea.

God invites the person who is thirsty to move from his place of need to the water He freely offers. God invites the hungry person to move away from his poverty and come to the banquet He has prepared. The bounty is ready, come and partake. This is not an invitation like a person might receive from a car dealer. One local dealer makes a phenomenal invitation to come to his place of business and buy a brand new vehicle for a fraction of the cost of new vehicles at other dealers. But when the excited customer shows up, that one particular vehicle is not available to that customer. God is more honest than car dealers like that. He does not offer something that He has yet to prepare. He offers satisfaction right now for those who are spiritually hungry and thirsty. Jesus taught the same principle about God's merciful invitation when He pictured the Kingdom of God like a king who invites people to come to a feast. "Again [the king] sent other servants, saying, 'Tell those who are invited, See, I have prepared my dinner, my oxen and my fat calves have been slaughtered, and everything is ready. Come to the wedding feast.'" (Matthew 22:4) In a similar story Jesus pointed out that, "at the time for the banquet he sent his servant to say to those who had been invited, 'Come, for everything is now ready.'" (Luke 14:17) The meal is ready, only the guests are needed to complete the banquet. The invitation is for now!

This is no insignificant invitation. God begs sinners to listen to His offer. The first word in the Hebrew text is little particle that is sometimes overlooked in English translations. In other English versions the little word is translated, "come" (see the English Standard Version). Sometimes this particle is used as an interjection to cry out, "alas" or "ah" when someone is grieving or lamenting. Here it is an interjection to say, "Ha!" or "Whoa, check this out!" The idea is, "Stop whatever you are doing and pay attention to this!"

The needy person must listen carefully to God's offer. Therefore God's message to people who are distracted by their world is, "Listen diligently." The Hebrew word shawmah is stated twice in the middle of verse two. The repeated word, "listen, listen" means just that— listen (v.2b) The same word shows up as an imperative again in verse three, "incline your ear." Interestingly this is a common Hebrew word to the English ear. It is the word that calls for God's people to pay attention. It is the Shema. We know that famous statement, "Hear, O Israel: The LORD our God, the LORD is one" (Deuteronomy 6:4) as the shema.

The "listen" idea shows up in a lot of Old Testament texts, when the message that follows is of extreme importance. For example when the nation was about to cross into the Promised Land God said, "Hear, O Israel: you are to cross over the Jordan today, to go in to dispossess nations greater and mightier than yourselves, cities great and fortified up to heaven," (Deuteronomy 9:1) The importance is not lessened in the New Testament. Though the words were written in Greek, the message is the same when Jesus told the young ruler that, "The most important is, 'Hear, O Israel: The Lord our God, the Lord is one" (Mark 12:29). The most important command is still the one we must listen to carefully. It will always be the shema. The most important invitation is God's invitation to find satisfaction in His provision.

Notice the promised result of listening according to the second verse. God promised that, "If you listen diligently to me, you will eat what is good, and delight yourselves in rich food." "Eat what is good . . ." is not a command but an expected result of properly responding to God's invitation.

This invitation reminds the reader that the true creator God is not an ogre or tyrant. The gods of man's imagination are temperamental, whimsical, and capricious. False gods demand obedience. The true God proves with His law that no one can obey Him and then stretches out His hand of mercy to us who have failed to disobey and offers us that which alone is able to satisfy the longing and aching in the sinner's heart. He pleads with sinners to come and be satisfied with Him. But often sinners respond that they are already satisfied. They love their sin, they love life without God, they love being free from perceived restrictions that they think are required in order to have fellowship with God. Nothing could be further from the truth. Redeemed sinners, those who have responded to God's invitation readily admit to the unsatisfying results of sin. When they were sinners, all alone, with only their thoughts to keep them company, they had to admit the deep dissatisfying taste sin leaves in the sinner's mouth.

God's invitation is not only full of pathos but it is also penetrating. It sinks into the conscience like a well aimed arrow and uncovers the sinner's natural dissatisfaction (v.2). God asks sinners, "Why do you waste your labors?" His question acknowledges that sinners work diligently to receive reward. Most of us go to work at least five days a week and labor at least eight hours each day. For what? A paycheck of course. At the end of the week we get paid for all our labors. But what does the laborer do with the money? We pay necessary bills like utilities, food, clothing, housing, auto, and on and on. Because necessary things are so many and so expensive some people grow weary working to get just enough to survive.

The laborer receives the wages for his labors and then what does he do? God pictures the weary laboring weighing out his silver for that which does not satisfy. Where does the sinner's paycheck check go each week? For necessary things like food, clothing, housing, transportation. But those necessary things keep changing, breaking, and wearing out. There is no end in sight until the grave. In an effort to ignore the monotony of the cycle, most people spend money on pleasures like vacations, toys, gadgets, and the fulfillment of fleshly desires. To what end? The result is always the same: NO SATISFACTION—just like God said.

Therefore, God asks the sinner caught in the dissatisfying cycle of work—earn—spend—work some more, "Why do you labor for 'no-bread?'" (v.2). "No-bread" is a substance that appears to be bread but does not satisfy like genuine bread does. "No-bread is everything you get in life in exchange for you much work and spending of money. "No-bread" is the reward for all religious labors outside of a relationship with Christ. When multitudes of religious sinners stand before the eternal Judge all they will have to offer Him is "no-bread." What good will it be? Will the fruits of their labors open heaven's door for them? Not an inch!

God's invitation is not for "no-bread" that costs all that a person can make. God offers real satisfaction freely (v.1). He invites the one who has no money to come and buy not just the basics, like water and bread, but even the delicacies of wine and milk. But how can they "buy" if they have no money? The money they spend on dissatisfying "no-bread" is of no value for gaining satisfying food. This offer highlights the free nature of God's gift. He invites thirsty and hungry sinners to come and feast freely on His provision. His provision cannot be purchased but will satisfy. He offers what is good. He offers rich food (v.2b). Have you heard His offer? Have you responded to it? What is the invitation really about?

## The Content of the Invitation (vv.3b-5)

God offers the everlasting covenant (v.3). The covenant is His agreement. The agreement God offers here is not a mutual agreement in which both parties come to the table. God does not offer a bi-lateral agreement which involves equal parties, but He offers a unilateral agreement in which He the superior offers benefit to the inferiors. We, the inferiors, can take it or leave it as it is stated. There is no negotiation of the terms.

The covenant God offers is established in the blood of Jesus Christ. Here are the simple points of the covenant:

1) You have offended God by your sinful nature and your acts of sin that flow from that nature.
2) The penalty for your offense is eternal punishment.
3) God the Son never sinned, but paid the price for all sin in His sacrifice on the cross.
4) God the Son rose from the dead to validate the acceptance of this price.
5) God invites all sinners to come and take this covering for sin that He offers through faith.
6) God promises to give eternal life to each sinner who accepts His offer by faith.

That is the agreement. Take it or leave it. God is able to offer it only because of the free sacrifice Jesus Christ made. Apart from the cross there is no offer.

The covenant is also established in the Seed of David. The covenant to which God invites sinners is an expression of His promised and sure love for David. While King David was still alive God promised him, "When your days are fulfilled and you lie down with your fathers, I will raise up your offspring after you, who shall come from your body, and I will establish his kingdom. He shall build a house for my name, and I will establish the throne of his kingdom forever" (2 Samuel 7:12-13). God began to fulfill that promise with the birth of Christ, and verified it as certain in the risen Christ. God will bring it to pass in every detail. God will fulfill His promise. Paul pointed out this fact when he told Jews in his day, "And we bring you the good news that what God promised to the fathers, this he has fulfilled to us their children by raising Jesus, as also it is written in the second Psalm, "'You are my Son, today I have begotten you.' And as for the fact that he raised him from the dead, no more to return to corruption, he has spoken in this way, "'I will give you the holy and sure blessings of David.'" (Acts 13:32-34 ). Why would an Israelite refuse such an invitation?

It is not only Israelites who have received God's invitation to enjoy His covenant. God offers the covenant to all people (vv.4-5). According to God's message through Isaiah, Christ, the Seed of David, calls a nation that Israel did not know to come and be satisfied. Christ is the leader of the people (v.4). He is the King, the leader and commander of His people. He is the Prophet, the one who testifies regarding God's message. As such He calls together an unknown nation. He draws sinners to Himself from every tribe, nation, and race. He has the authority to do this because He won the right through His sacrifice. God's invitation is fulfilled and validated through the Christ—and in Him alone. Remove Him from the equation and there is no invitation—no hope!

The good news is that there is hope. There is hope for Gentile sinners who were not privileged to be born into the chosen nation. The Gentiles are the unknown nation. God invites us to be satisfied in Christ. God invites people who have no other hope of satisfaction to be fully fed in Christ. What an invitation!

Christ accomplishes the work of redemption because He is glorified. He is the God-ordained channel of the invitation. There is no other way, no other offer, no other means. How foolish to reject Him. And yet not only do multitudes of Gentiles cast off God's invitation, so do the majority of those people who are born in the chosen nation. The Jews in Jesus' day illustrated the problem that knows no boundaries of time or geography. They labored for "no-bread." They ran zealously to get "no-bread." When Jesus offered the true satisfying bread from heaven, yea Himself, they were offended. One day multitudes followed Jesus from one side of the Sea of Galilee to the other side. They were determined to follow Jesus because He had fed more than 5,000 of them the day before by blessing a couple of loves of bread and a handful of little fish. This was their kind of leader!

But on that day Jesus talked about this covenant, this same invitation from God. He offered them the spiritual bread that alone brings satisfaction. He told them, "For the bread of God is he who comes down from heaven and gives life to the world" (John 6:33). Did they embrace the truth and say, "Give us this bread!"? No. When Jesus indicted that He was the bread that satisfies, "the Jews grumbled about him, because he said, 'I am the bread that came down from heaven'" (John 6:41). A little later in the conversation Jesus pointed out, "I am the living bread that came down from heaven. If anyone eats of this bread, he will live forever. And the bread that I will give for the life of the world is my flesh" (John 6:51). "After this many of his disciples turned back and no longer walked with him" (John 6:66).

They who thought of themselves as followers of the Seed of David preferred to labor for "no-bread." They preferred to spend their time and money chasing that which does not satisfy. Their tribe has not only continued but increased. How many people still reject God's invitation to come and feast on His provision of salvation in Christ, preferring instead the crumbs of "no-bread," the passing vision of "non-water?" Dead religion is the bane of society. A form of godliness without power is the norm for "Christian" America. Have you really embraced God's invitation for satisfying eternal life, or are you still trying to find satisfaction in your own, hand-crafted religion?

16

# SEEK THE LORD

ISAIAH 55:6-9

According to an old fable, a man made an unusual agreement with Death. He told the grim reaper that he would willingly accompany him when it came time to die, but only on one condition—that Death would send a messenger well in advance to warn him. The agreement was made. Weeks winged away into months, and months into years. Then one bitter winter evening, as the man sat alone thinking about all his material possessions, Death suddenly entered the room and tapped him on the shoulder. The man was startled and cried out in despair, "You're here so soon and without warning! I thought we had an agreement." Death replied, "I've more than kept my part. I've sent you many messengers. Look at yourself in the mirror and you'll see some of them." As the man complied, Death whispered, "Notice your hair! Once it was full and black, now it is thin and white. Look at the way you cock your head to listen to my voice because you can't hear very well. Observe how close you must get to the mirror in order to see yourself clearly. Yes, I've sent many messengers through the years. I've kept my part. It's too bad you didn't keep yours. I'm sorry you're not ready for me, but the time has come to leave."

What is sadder than a person who has been warned repeatedly, but still is not ready? It is not unusual for people to know that taxes are due on April 15, but not be ready. That happens to a lot of people. It is common for a student to know very well that a paper is due on the teacher's desk Monday morning, but he or she has no paper when the due date arrives. Things like that happen. But it is infinitely worse when a person has heard warning after warning to seek God while He may be found and then arrive at the portal of death unprepared.

Common sense wonders why a person ignores warnings about eternal condemnation. Logic is opposed to putting off getting right with God before it is too late. And yet most people who have ever lived are guilty of that very thing. One writer concluded that if a person hears God's invitation to seek Him but refuses to take advantage of God's offer, he or she deserves to go to hell. Words like that are shocking at first blush. Who would be so uncaring and unkind to think such thoughts, much less state them? But the fact remains: if a person hears God warning to turn to Him and not perish, and chooses to ignore His plea, he really does not deserve anything better than the promised eternal punishment.

God invited the people of Israel to turn to Him. He invited them to turn from their sin of serving lesser gods and to repent and trust Him. That was the message God gave Isaiah. However, the news is even greater in that God also promised through Isaiah that Messiah would call a nation to Himself from among the nations. In Isaiah 55:5, God promised that an unknown people would run to Christ. That "people" is the redeemed Gentiles. The Church, redeemed saints from every race and tongue, make up the nation of God's people. While it is true that God will in the future fulfill every promise He made to the nation of Israel, it is also true that He offers the invitation of eternal life to everyone.

Who is listening to the invitation? Who hears God invite the world to "seek Him while He may be found"? Surely, we hear. How have we responded to the offer?

## TURN TO GOD (vv.6-7)

Seek the LORD while He may be found (v.6). This invitation ranks among the greatest invitations God offers. It exceeds any invitation given among humans by humans. It is the promise of the Almighty Creator God who invites His created beings to pursue Him. He calls on everyone to seek Him. But do they? Do you? Have you?

To seek is more than look for, as one would typically translate the word. This Hebrew word means to resort to. But it means still more. Having resorted to God, the invitation to seek also requires that the seeker consult, investigate, study, and follow. One might wonder if the invitation implies that God is lost or absent. Nothing could be further from the truth. That is to see life and eternity from man's perspective alone. God is the everlasting Rock of salvation—He does not move. He cannot move! Humanity has moved. Because of sin each person is moved far from the Rock of eternal security. Sin has caused a great jungle of false gods, wrong thoughts, and sinful actions to grow up between the individual and God. We are hopelessly lost in a tangle of undergrowth spawned by our natural waywardness. God is not lost! He invites the lost sinners to resort to Him, to come to Him and investigate, study, and follow.

But God did not stop with inviting sinners to resort to Him and follow Him. He also invites sinners to call upon Him. To call can means to cry out as one who is in desperate need cries out for help. This cry would be heard from the lips and heart of the man who has fallen over a cliff and is hanging on to a root for dear life. So, too, the sinner who gets a vision of the enslaving nature of his sin will cry out to God for help. The sinner who understands the slightest pain of hell will cry out for God's mercy. The sinner who is gripped by the unfathomable mercy of God will cry to Him.

That picture of a needy person crying to the only One who can help ought to register in the listener's mind. We understand it. Yea, we identify with it. However, to call out to God also means to honor Him by responding to His invitation. He invites everyone to call to Him. For a needy sinner to do that very thing indicates that the sinner places trust in Him. Full trust displays honor and results in God's glory.

The invitation to resort to God, to call out to Him, comes with a very serious warning. Sinners should be motivated to cry out to God for help when they learn from this text that God implies that there is a time when He will not be found. He may, at His discretion, hide Himself, even from the sinner who needs help. This should not be a surprising revelation. In the early days of Israel's history, God promised to hide His face from them when the people chose to follow idols. "And I will surely hide my face in that day because of all the evil that they have done, because they have turned to other gods" (Deuteronomy 31:18). In the midst of his trials, Job felt like God was hidden and inaccessible. "Why do you hide your face and count me as your enemy?" (Job 13:24) he wondered. David feared that God would hide Himself. He pled with God, "Hide not your face from me. Turn not your servant away in anger, O you who have been my help. Cast me not off; forsake me not, O God of my salvation!" (Psalm 27:9). In light of the fact that God does indeed become inaccessible, the warning to call when He is near carries great weight.

Were these the musings of ignorant, uninitiated men of the Old Testament era? Did the problem lie in the fact that they knew nothing of the merciful God of the New Testament? No. Those ideas do not hold water when compared to the fact that God did the same thing in the New Testament settings. God the Son hid from Jews who rejected His deity. When Jesus told the religious people that He and God are one "they picked up stones to throw at him, but Jesus hid himself and went out of the temple" (John 8:59). God the Son also warned people who would not accept the truth that they were in danger. He told them, "'While you have the light, believe in the light, that you may become sons of light.' When Jesus had said these things, he departed and hid himself from them" (John 12:36). God the Son revealed that God hid truth from those who repeatedly rejected it. "At that time Jesus declared, 'I thank you, Father, Lord of heaven and earth, that you have hidden these things from the wise and understanding and revealed them to little children'" (Matthew 11:25). God does pull a veil over Himself. At such times, people can actually hear the preaching of the Bible but it has no effect whatsoever on them.

No doubt some people react to such an idea by declaring, "How dare God do that!" Who is the mere human to question God? God has the authority to conceal Himself whenever He deems it fitting. Humans are not God's authority though they presume that they can demand salvation whenever they want it. God the Creator is not servant to the creation to do as they demand. Because sinful humans perceive themselves to be superior, even though we hate to admit that, we actually think that we can tell God when we want His attention and when we do not. The person who puts off God's invitation until a more convenient time honestly believes that he or she has greater authority than God who extends the invitation.

The Almighty God who offers sinners the invitation to resort to Him also challenges the wicked to turn around (v.7). He admonished wicked people to abandon their way of thinking and acting. Who are these terrible, wicked people? That word is pregnant with meaning, isn't it? Wicked people are those who are guilty of stepping outside the law. One of the best uses of the word describes criminals. Be that as it may, the sad truth also is that the word describes every person by nature. Each person is born with the sin nature, the nature that causes us to be out of bounds with God who is holy. Not only do we have a tendency to be out of bounds, but we have the habit of being out of bounds! Because people own a sin nature, people sin. Folks step over the boundaries of God's law all the time. Every person is guilty of this!

That is why God calls for sinners to forsake their ways. They need to leave, or abandon, the path on which they march. We live according to habit because we walk the same path every day. That would be a good thing if a person walked the right path. But by nature people walk the wrong path. The path is trodden down and turned to dirt from our much walking on it. It is so obvious and so wrong.

But the warning here is that no one can change the path of life he walks on unless he first changes his thinking. A person lives the way he lives because he thinks the way he thinks. Jesus affirmed this fact when He taught, "The good person out of the good treasure of his heart produces good, and the evil person out of his evil treasure produces evil, for out of the abundance of the heart his mouth speaks" (Luke 6:45). That truth highlights a natural problem. How can a person think differently when it is so natural for him to think wrong thoughts that result in wrong actions?

The answer to that question is in the second part of the invitation in verse seven. Wicked people must return to God. The word return generally implies going back to a spot that one has left. Here the invitation is to return to God. It speaks of a right relationship with Him. Is that not a problem? What wicked person has ever had a right relationship with God? The invitation is for all humanity in all times. All humanity goes back to the same root. Therefore, in the Garden of Eden, represented in Adam, every person enjoyed fellowship with God. But also in the Garden of Eden, represented in Adam, every person broke that fellowship through sin. God invites everyone back into that fellowship.

God stands like the father of the prodigal son looking down the road of life longing for his children to take advantage of His invitation. He knows that His created beings have abandoned Him and rejected His kindness, and yet He still sends the invitation through His messengers. He still wants wicked sinners to resort to Him, to call out to Him, to return to Him from their wicked paths.

So what will the return cost the sinner? That is the question almost every sinner either asks or thinks about. There must be a cost. In fact, the cost for exchanging eternal condemnation for eternal life must be astronomical. Why must there be a cost? Common sense demands a price. Common sense will not even allow this reconciliation. Common sense demands that the holy God punish wicked people who have turned away from Him for eternity. Why should the faithful husband Hosea receive back into his arms his unfaithful, whoreish wife Gomer? She deserves the most severe punishment Hosea can offer.

That is the problem with human wisdom. It does not understand God's grace. The grace of God is truly incomprehensible. We understand it very slightly because we are not at all like God. His ways are not like our ways because His thoughts are not like our thoughts.

## ADMIT THAT YOU ARE NOT GOD (vv.8-9)

Having offered the invitation for sinners to abandon their paths and return to Him, God declares that our human thoughts are not at all like God's thoughts. Our thoughts are finite, but God's thoughts are infinite. Another way of putting the same truth is to conclude that God is the creator, and we are the creatures. Any time that reality is ignored, the one who ignores it thinks unrealistically. How could the truth be any simpler? In real life the designer determines the character of the project without consulting the project for a vote or an expression of the project's opinion. Generally, in such a scenario the project is inanimate and has no vote or opinion.

Likewise, God has drawn the picture showing that humans are the lump of clay and He is the potter. Paul shared that picture with the Christians in Rome when he asked, "But who are you, O man, to answer back to God? Will what is molded say to its molder, 'Why have you made me like this?'" (Romans 9:20). God the Creator creates from His resident wisdom. Honest assessments of His creation remind the creature that he cannot even fathom the first part of His wisdom. For example, brilliant scientists cannot even plumb the depths of space with all of modern technology at their disposal. But God's thoughts created the infinite space. The finite mind will never measure up to the lowest level of God's infinite wisdom. His thoughts are higher than the heavens compared to humanities earth-bound thinking.

Part of the reason for the vast disparity between human finiteness and Divine infiniteness is discovered in the fact that human thoughts are tainted by sin while God's thoughts remain perfectly pure. That truth helps to explain why people do not understand God's invitation. Sin has so dulled human comprehension that sinners really do not come to the right conclusions about God's invitation. Think about it. Who, in their right mind, would refuse an invitation for eternal life? it is tempting to think that such an invitation from God implies that everyone who thinks straight would naturally respond and be saved. But they don't. Do only people with massive amounts of human wisdom buy up the invitation? No. In fact, often it is not the humanly wise at all who God chooses to be saved (1 Corinthians 3:26-29). Or human wisdom requires that God must not really offer this invitation to everyone, because if He did everyone would be saved. But they are not. In the final analysis, human wisdom cannot explain how God is sovereign and the individual is responsible. Nevertheless, the invitation stands. And God guarantees the invitation! Truly our thoughts are minuscule compared to God's thoughts.

Furthermore, man's ways are not God's ways. Each person acts according to his thinking. There may be minor, short-lived exceptions to this rule, but the general rule is universal. How a person acts is determined by what he thinks. As a result, it is natural to think that the redeemed sinner must pay back God for His gift of salvation. People who think like that get very busy in their attempts to keep manmade rules that they mistakenly believe will please God. Or other sinners think that God could never love them and so they act very unlovely.

God's ways are higher than human ways because God acts according to His nature. He is perfect, and mere people don't even understand perfection. He is gracious and merciful beyond comprehension. Therefore, God's actions must bring Him glory. The great sin is for people to distrust God and try to force Him to think and act according to human wisdom. Great glory is piled on God when we take Him at His word, respond to His invitation, turn away from our natural evil ways, and resort to Him. That is God's plan. Any method or means of thinking that lessens God's glory cannot be His will. His invitation eclipses human wisdom. That is good. His grace is incomprehensible. That is good. Far better to embrace God's invitation than to reject it because we cannot explain it.

# 17

# GOD'S WORD IS ACTIVE

Isaiah 55:10-13

We enter a dark room, flip a little switch, and instantly the entire room is flooded with light. When was the last time you sat and contemplated all the details that had to work together to bring about the effect of light? Most people do not, maybe cannot, understand the intricacies of electricity that cause a light bulb to light. But almost everyone enjoys the results of electricity's vitality.

When a person turns the key on the steering column of his vehicle, he expects something to happen. If nothing happens, he is very surprised (unless he drives a clunker) and immediately attempts to diagnose the problem. Or, more likely, the poor fellow calls the towing company. Drivers naturally expect an expression of vitality when they turn the key in their vehicles. Not everyone understands the science of the internal combustion engine, but they recognize the sound of power, and they know that when that sound is missing something is definitely wrong.

Many people sit down at a computer, push a button, and are instantly flooded with information as it pours from a monitor. If they click on the internet, they can be overwhelmed with information. The computer is so powerful that some people suffer from information overload and become phobic about the computer's vitality. It has the ability to spew out unimaginable amounts of information.

In far greater ways, God's Word is powerful. It is full of vitality. When God sends out His Word, something happens—every time. There never has been a time, nor will there ever be a time, when God's Word does not accomplish something. It is so powerful that it must cause an effect each time He sends it forth.

That is the message of Isaiah chapter fifty-five. God began this message through the prophet Isaiah by inviting needy people to come to Him to

find satisfaction. His Word invites spiritually thirsty and hungry people
to come to Him and find wine and milk. His provision is free (v.1). He
wonders why people would spend their labors to buy that which does
not satisfy, when His provision satisfies for eternity (v.2). Therefore, God
invites sinners to listen carefully to His Word (vv.2b-3). His Word promises the Savior, the One who will call an unknown nation to Himself for
salvation (vv.4-5). That nation is made up of people who heed God' s invitation to seek Him while He may be found and to forsake their wicked
ways (v.v.6-7). While it is true that sinners do not always understand all
the details of God's mighty power displayed in this invitation, they must
trust Him (vv.8-9).

God assures the world in this invitation that His ways are not like
man's ways and His thoughts are not like human thoughts. His ways and
thoughts are high like the heavens in comparison to human thoughts
and ways (vv.8-9). God's thoughts are so high because He causes things
to happen just by thinking. God did not create the heavens and the earth
by putting dirt and water, and other things together. He spoke and it
happened. This is an astonishing truth! Since things happen when God
thinks or speaks, a person must be aware of His invitation and must
intentionally ignore it. When God issues an invitation, something will
happen. Either the person who hears the invitation will humble himself
or herself and yield to God (forsaking wrong thoughts and ways, v.7), or
the person will be hardened in his or her sins.

The wonderful promise of this text is that God's powerful Word makes
great things happen. He promised that His Word is like rain falling on
fertile soil. His Word causes an endless supply of sustenance. His Word
has vitality—it makes things happen. Indeed, not only is the history of
the human race governed by God's Word, but all of eternity is determined by it. Why then would a person resist His invitation?

## GOD PICTURES THE VITALITY OF HIS WORD (VV.10-11)

God pictured His Word like rain falling on fertile soil (v.10). Isaiah
pointed out the well-known fact that rain and snow do not return to
the sky from which they came. The rain and snow come down and water the earth, but then they dissipate without returning to the heavens
from which they came in the same form in which they came. One might

think it strange that God inspired Isaiah to talk about snow since it is as rare in Israel as it is in South Carolina. However, it snows frequently in the higher elevations of Mount Hermon. Rain on the other hand was a very familiar concept for the Jewish mind. It was and still is often scarce. Times of drought help people appreciate rain, and the ancient Israelites were even more susceptible to the ravages of drought. They depended heavily on the snow that fell in the high elevations of Mount Hermon to melt in the spring and water the crops in the Jordan Valley.

However, after the rain and snow fall, they do not return to the heavens from which they came. They return as vapor. Even in that day of relative scientific ignorance, it is clear that God's messengers were not ignorant of the hydrological cycle. However, unlike modern man's confidence in Super-Dopler radar, the people of God really did believe that God was responsible to send the rain. Why shouldn't they? Why shouldn't modern Christians agree with them? In the beginning God sent rain. The creation story in Genesis says, "When no bush of the field was yet in the land and no small plant of the field had yet sprung up—for the LORD God had not caused it to rain on the land, and there was no man to work the ground, and a mist was going up from the land and was watering the whole face of the ground " (Genesis 2:5-6). Things changed by Noah's time. God promised Noah that He would destroy the world by a flood. In His plan, the flood required rain. Therefore, God told Noah, "In seven days I will send rain on the earth forty days and forty nights, and every living thing that I have made I will blot out from the face of the ground" (Genesis 7:4). Whose plan was it? Who sent the rain? When did God get out of the rain business?

The same God who is responsible to send rain is also able to withhold rain as a form of judgment. This same God warned through Moses the messenger, "The LORD will open to you his good treasury, the heavens, to give the rain to your land in its season and to bless all the work of your hands. And you shall lend to many nations, but you shall not bor-row" (Deuteronomy 28:12). That would happen as long as God's people obeyed Him. However, if they chose to disobey and turn against the LORD in rebellion, they learned, "The LORD will make the rain of your land powder. From heaven dust shall come down on you until you are destroyed" (Deuteronomy 28:24). In light of these Bible truths, it is no wonder that God's people still believe God controls the rain in spite of the great scientific knowledge of the weather.

God sends His rain and snow according to His plan and promises that the rain and snow cause seeds to germinate and cycle. The rain causes the seed to sprout, which grows into grain, which provides bread, and which provides more seed to be sown for future crops. Therefore, in very practical ways, life depends on the rain that God sends. His rain causes germination. The Hebrew word used at this point actually means "to germinate."

Here an interesting concept is drawn together from other passages of God's Word. Without the "rain" of God's Word, the "seed" of God's Word will wither. In common practical ways, fruit production also depends on the seed which God provided originally. In the beginning days of creation, "God said, 'Let the earth sprout vegetation, plants yielding seed, and fruit trees bearing fruit in which is their seed, each according to its kind, on the earth.' And it was so" (Genesis 1:11). The human race has enjoyed the product of God's work ever since. Seed producing seed is still in effect. Scientists did not invent seeds ex nihilo. They develop some interesting and useful hybrids, but God made the first seeds.

This picture turns the mind to God's picture of eternal provision through His Word. Jesus taught the parable that explained how He, the sower, sows the seed of His Word on various kinds of soil (Matthew 13:18-23). Hard soil, thorn infested soil, rocky soil are ultimately unresponsive to God's Word. But fertile soil produces God-like fruit. The Word of God is both the seed and the rain that causes the seed to grow and produce. In both the parable and the picture of this text in Isaiah, the growth of spiritual thorns and briars is an indication that God's Word has been rejected. In fact, the writer to the Hebrew Christians drove this point home in a lesson that is almost shocking. He warned that it is impossible to turn people into good fruit producers if they have been familiar with God's Word but ultimately rejected it (Hebrews 6:4-5). Having established that truth, God said through the writer, "For land that has drunk the rain that often falls on it, and produces a crop useful to those for whose sake it is cultivated, receives a blessing from God. But if it bears thorns and thistles, it is worthless and near to being cursed, and its end is to be burned" (Hebrews 6:7-8). God warned that He sends His Word in the seed and the rain. If people reject what He sends, they are hopeless.

That is the same kind of promise God made to the nation of His people. He told them, "May my teaching drop as the rain, my speech distill as the dew, like gentle rain upon the tender grass, and like showers upon the herb" (Deuteronomy 32:2). They agreed with God—for a little while. But as a whole, the nation rejected the rain.

Whether people embrace God's Word or reject it, His Word is still effective (v.11). Isaiah promised that God's Word never returns empty. It goes out from His mouth with purpose and plan. The fact that the Word goes out from God's mouth reminds us that His Word is the expression of His being. People know God because His Word describes Him. That is God's plan. His Word is the statement of His will. God's people know what God desires and expects because He plainly explains those standards in His Word. Because God's Word comes from His own mouth, it obviously has the authority to accomplish His will. Anyone who argues with or rejects God's Word resists His authority. Everyone who treats God's Word lightly resists His will.

Everyone who resists God's will must face His judgment, because His Word is never useless. "What about the seed that landed on bad soil?" someone might ask. "Isn't that kind of useless?" And what about rain on rocks? What about God's Word that is scoffed or ignored by sinners? There is plenty of evidence of poor responses to God's Word. Does that mean that His Word is not useful? The false words, such as the Koran and the Book of Mormon, and the wrong interpretations of God's Words are a sign that God's Word has great power. Satan knows that God's Word is powerful and will not return to Him empty. That is why he produces so many counterfeits to it.

God's Word always accomplishes God's Will. God has a design and purpose in giving His Word to people. Therefore, on the one hand, the Word of God penetrated David's heart and he concluded, "I have stored up your word in my heart, that I might not sin against you" (Psalms 119:11). On the other hand, the Word of God hardened Pharaoh's heart. "Moses and Aaron did all these wonders before Pharaoh, and the LORD hardened Pharaoh's heart, and he did not let the people of Israel go out of his land" (Exodus 11:10). Does that mean that God's Word accomplished His will in David's life but not in Pharaoh's? Not at all. God's Word accomplished God's will in the life of both men. Paul taught that God raised up Pharaoh to show His power through him. He did that with the warnings and promises of His Word.

God's design for the Word of His gospel also penetrates or hardens hearts. No messenger of God ever speaks His gospel word in vain. Nor does God's gospel ever fail to produce the effect which He intends for it.

The gospel is no more preached in vain than the rain falls in vain. Is it a waste when the rain God sends falls on rocks, on the road ways of life, or out in the wilderness where no one lives? Is it a waste of good rain for God to allow it to fall in the peaks of mountains where no one dwells? Never. He sends His rain with purpose, and, eventually, everyone sees the purpose. So it seems in life that the "rain" of God's gospel is wasted on infidels, the sensual, the proud, the arrogant, the materialistic, the distracted, even the angry tyrant. They never listen. They never change. Many, yea, most of the people who have heard the gospel will perish for eternity. Was it wasted?

The rain of God's Word either softened the soil of the heart where it fell so that the soil accepted it, germinated the seed, and produced fruit, or it hardened the soil like South Carolina clay so that the soil of that heart became unresponsive altogether. At the judgment seat of Christ hardened hearts must acknowledge that they rejected the rain of God's Word. At that moment, the Judge of all the ages will respond with justice and condemn those people to eternal punishment. He is just because He sent the rain of His Word.

Israel, the nation of God's people, demonstrated the deadliness of rejecting God's Word. God referred to His own vineyard, Israel, when He warned, "I will make it a waste; it shall not be pruned or hoed, and briers and thorns shall grow up; I will also command the clouds that they rain no rain upon it" (Isaiah 5:6). When God stops sending His messengers with His message, people are hopeless. And yet often in that setting, the people clamor for false teaching, for teaching that tickles their lustful ears, and errantly convince themselves that it is raining.

## ULTIMATELY GOD'S WORD SHAPES HISTORY AND ETERNITY (vv. 12-13)

By God's Word He delivers His people in joy (v.12). Possibly this is a picture of the exiles leaving captivity in Babylon. This verse illustrates an important principle of interpretation: When it is possible to interpret a text literally, the reader should do so. When it is impossible for the text to be literal, the reader does well to let the statement be symbolic. The symbolism in this text is unmistakable. Isaiah said that when God's people go out from captivity (whether it be the captivity of Babylon or the captivity of sin), that the mountains will sing and the trees will clap their hands. Though the hills might be "alive with the sound of music," everyone knows that mountains really cannot sing and trees have no hands with which to clap. Those must be symbolic expressions of great joy because of God's deliverance.

The reality is that God's people can go out with joy. That certainly must have been true regarding the exiles who left Babylon for Jerusalem after nearly seventy years of captivity. Ezra and Nehemiah record how those people rejoiced when the temple and the city of Jerusalem were restored.

Probably this is a picture of God's people ultimately being delivered from the effects of sin. This truth applies to sinners throughout history. Sinners who understand the horrendous nature of the sin from which God has delivered them, feel like nature rejoices with them when they rejoice in salvation. Where there is no joy for deliverance from sin, there is apparently no deliverance or understanding of deliverance. But this also must picture the way saints will respond when they have the joy of entering the Millennial Kingdom. In light of verse thirteen, this is probably the most accurate interpretation. Imagine what a joy it will be for God's people, Israel, to come through the Great Tribulation, accept Messiah as their king, and enter His Kingdom. Exiting that great time of trial, the "going out" will definitely be a time of joy. This will come about only because of God's Word.

Also, by God's Word He provides for His people eternally (v.13). This verse taken as a literal interpretation must point to the Millennial Kingdom. The promise is regarding the blossoming of a barren place. Because this has not actually happened yet, some interpreters are tempted to view the scene as symbolic. Could something like this happen? Yes. Then it is probably best to interpret this as a literal promise of what God will do in the future. This is similar to other amazing promises about a special time and kingdom in this book. The eleventh chapter of Isaiah gives greater detail of that day when the lion will lie down with the lamb and all will dwell in peace.

The effect of God's Word will be an everlasting sign of His name. By His Word, according to His Word, Messiah's Kingdom will be established. By His Word, according to His Word, heaven and earth will pass away and the New Jerusalem will be inhabited forever. Is it therefore a good idea to listen to God's Word? With the whole heart. God's Word will do what God sends it to do. God's Word will either soften our hearts to produce His fruit, or it will harden our hearts to destruction. Listen to His Word with great care.

# 18

# LET US RETURN TO THE LORD — REALLY!

## Hosea 6:1-10

There is an old gospel song that was birthed in an evangelistic crusade in the late nineteenth century. William Sleeper penned the words to Ye Must Be Born Again in response to a sermon on John 3:3. According to that text Jesus told Nicodemus, "Ye must be born again." When I was in college, some of the fellows joked that when Arminians sang this song they sang, "Ye must be born again and again and again."

People like that populate the broader church scene. Many Christians remember the old altar calls in the church where they grew up. They, also remember how that particular fellow or woman would respond to the invitation for salvation almost every week. In a case like that, does the respondent receive salvation each time he or she responds? Of course not. Then what is the problem?

Sometimes a person confesses sin, repents, and trusts the promise of Christ's atonement for his sins, but then he falls into sin a few days later. When that happens, the new saint needs to learn the common lesson of how to live in sanctification. But sometimes the new believer is deeply troubled by the fact that he committed the same sin he just confessed on Sunday at the revival service. So the next Sunday when the pastor closes the service with an invitation to be saved, the man responds because he is quite sure that it didn't take last week. This man needs to learn that Christ's blood covers sin on a daily basis. He needs to learn to confess sin daily and forsake it. He needs to learn how to live victoriously over sin because the new birth Christ gave him also gives him the potential to live victoriously over that pesky sin.

Sometimes a person confesses sin, repents, and trusts the promise of Christ's atonement for his sins, but then doubts. In that case, it is possible that the person really does not trust Christ alone. It is possible that the person trusts his ability to believe. Ultimately, that person's faith in not in Christ's finished work, not in Christ's faithfulness to His promise. His faith is rooted in his own ability to hang on to something. That sinner needs to die to self, put himself on the altar of sacrifice, and receive new life by faith in Christ alone.

Sometimes a person grows up in a very religious environment. As far back as he remembers he has heard the gospel, the wonderful promise that God forgives sin. He knows all the jargon. He knows the principles of salvation well. He knows that each person has sinned, that sin brings the wage of eternal punishment, that sinners must confess sin, and that when God forgives that sin through Christ, He reconciles the penitent sinner to fellowship with him. Many people know these wonderful truths. However, knowing the truth and having that truth applied to the heart by the Holy Spirit through regeneration is not the same thing. Often people with this knowledge but without new birth treat forgiveness of sins flippantly. They sing, "Free from the law, oh happy condition; sin all you want with Jesus' permission." People like that are in a most danger-ous condition because they presume that they can demand that God save them when they are good and ready—and not before they are ready.

Those people will have a sad awakening one day. They are like the peo-ple of Israel and Judah in Hosea's day. They knew all the details about sin and forgiveness. They knew about God. They knew what God expected. But they wrongly assumed that they controlled their own destiny. They wrongly presumed that they controlled God. This text teaches the folly of a sinner thinking that he can offer himself an invitation to be saved from sin when it is convenient for him to do so.

### THE SINNERS SAID, "COME LET US RETURN TO THE LORD," (vv.1-3)

This is a great invitation. But why did the people of Israel and Judah declare this invitation among themselves? They invited themselves to re-turn to God because they recognized God's chastening (v.1). Like many of their modern counterparts, the religious Israelites were at least able to admit that God had something to do with their troubles.

Hosea began his forty-five year ministry during the reigns of King Jeroboam II in Israel and King Uzziah (or Azariah) in Judah. It was a great time to be living in Israel. Life was great. Jeroboam had recovered much of the land and the cities that his predecessors had lost to Syria (2 Kings 13). The land was producing abundantly (2 Chronicles 26:10). Many people lived in luxury, there was a building boom (Hosea 8:14), and national pride blossomed (Amos 3:15).

Down in the southern tribe of Judah, King Uzziah appeared to be God's blessing to the people. He restored much of the land lost in previous wars. He overthrew the Philistines and Ammorites. Maybe best of all, the king generally followed after God. This was true except in that glaring failure when he encroached on the priest's office. It is also true that he didn't remove the high places—but then again most of Judah's kings didn't. All in all he was a smashing success. The Chronicler recorded that Uzziah's "fame spread far, for he was marvelously helped, till he was strong" (2 Chronicles 26:15b).

No one wishes bad times on any nation or person. However, as a rule, people do not understand that God's goodness also leads to repentance. People are generally so satisfied with stuff, things, and pleasure that they don't have the time or the desire for a relationship with God. Even Jesus taught that it is difficult for wealthy people to get into heaven (Matthew 19:23). Riches and comfort distract mightily from the awareness that one needs to be right with God.

While it appears that everything was coming up roses in the land of God's people, things are not always as they appear. Hosea had to address the continual sin of idolatry. Baal worship still hung on in the form of Israel's worship at the calves in Bethel and Dan (2:8, 11:2) Sacred prostitution was still practiced (Hosea 4:10-18). Poverty existed alongside prosperity (Amos 8:4). Justice was perverted in the courts (Hosea 12:7). That is the stuff that was going on under the umbrella of success and prosperity.

Things deteriorated quickly after Jeroboam II's reign. In comparatively rapid succession, six different kings sat on Israel's throne. Jeroboam's son, Zechariah, reigned for only six months before Shallum murdered him. Shallum took the throne he coveted so much only to sit on it for one month before Menahem killed him. At about that time the mighty powerhouse of the north, Assyria, began to make multiple forays into the country wreaking havoc as they came. Finally Assyria under the command of Shalmaneser V would overthrow the nation in 722 B.C.

Hosea declared God's warnings first in the years of prosperity and now in the years of upheaval. Everyone knew that Israel, in particular, and Judah, subsequently, were in trouble. Society was a mess, and the enemy was causing pain. At this point, the people admitted that God had torn and struck down. They knew that their troubles were not a coincidence, an accident, or a series of strange and unfortunate events. Their forefathers had left them some training and background in God's law and history of dealing with His people. Therefore, they believed that God allowed this trouble.

Most religious people draw this same conclusion rather quickly—and rightly so. Sickness disrupts life and causes the person to think about his relationship with God. Financial trouble causes people to realize they should not trust in money. Relational problems make us turn to God and ask, "Why?" Several years ago a friend admitted to me that he never really learned how to pray until his son went into rebellion. He said that when the trouble came, he would spend hours on his knees before God begging for help. Humans tend to recognize that their God (god) is involved when trouble comes.

The people of Israel and Judah also knew they should return to God. Their very invitation reveals that they had left God. "Come, let us return to the LORD" is the acknowledgment that they had left God. They were aware enough of God's law to realize that their sin provided sufficient evidence that they had wandered away from God.

Most people are honest enough to admit that God's sphere and sin's sphere are separate and opposed. The hard part is getting sinners to be honest enough to identify sin as sin.

The Israelites didn't have a hard time admitting that they had sinned. Surely they drew a connection between God's judgment and their waywardness. However, notice that in their invitation and deliberations they did not confess particular sins. They owned the concept that they had drifted away from God, but there was no mention of their social injustices, their idolatry, or their fornication. Notice also that the people did not pray to God, confessing sin and repenting. They just talked to each other about true principles. Is what they said true? Yes, of course it is. Did they get to the root of the problem? No. In fact, they obviously did not understand the seriousness of their problem.

God had left them. In the verse just previous to this section of the prophecy, God said, "I will return again to my place, until they acknowledge their guilt and seek my face, and in their distress earnestly seek me" (Hosea 5:15). This is the horrible truth. The people talked as if they had left God standing on the corner of Fifth and Elm Streets when they wandered off into sin. Now they would just go back where they left Him and take up renewed fellowship. They could not have been more wrong. We err greatly to assume that God is always like the father of the prodigal son waiting for the rebel to come home. Rather, God is altogether sovereign and in control of all things. Yes, His heart is huge and His patience is superhuman. But in God's perfect wisdom, there are times when He withdraws. He withdrew from the Israelites, and they didn't know it. When will He stop convicting you and withdraw His hand of mercy?

These eighth century B.C. sinners were confident that they could contact God and get things right with Him because He was that kind of God. They acknowledged God's mercy (vv.2-3). They believed that He would heal the wounds He had caused (v.2). Their words indicate that they were very confident that God could heal their wounds. They admitted that they were wounded to the point of death. But that was not a great concern to them because, even after death has set in (2-3 days), God can still revive. The sad truth is that the people desired to have relief from the consequences of sin, rather than freedom from the grip of sin.

They also planned to return to God because they knew that He is faithful (v.3). In fact, like many religious people who get religion at revival services, they determined to know God better. These folks were very much like the people with itching ears that Paul warned Timothy about. They believe that more knowledge of God will make their problems go away. They were like modern religionists who go to seminars or start Bible studies because life is not going well. They wanted to experience God's faithfulness that comes out like the dawn. They expected God's kindness to refresh them like dependable spring rains.

But the sinners did not want to admit their sins and turn away from them! Any indication of that kind of heart or attitude is missing in this text. It does not appear. The people were able and willing to admit that they were suffering because God intervened. They certainly wanted God's blessing. But they failed to address the very thing that caused God's departure! How like modern sinners they were. Too many people know all of the details connected with the Savior. But they do not know the Savior because they refuse to come to grips with their sins—the very thing that keeps them from the Savior.

## GOD SAID, "WHAT SHALL I DO WITH YOU?" (vv.4-10)

God had actively worked to bring about change in the lives of these people (vv.4-6). God desires steadfast love, but from the Israelites (His chosen nation) He received only fickle expressions of love (vv.4,6). Sinners are prone to do that in any generation. God is not pleased with it. He expressed disappointment in their fickleness (v.4). When God recorded the words, "What shall I do. . .?" He did not express the kind of frustration that a haggard mother of a two-year-old feels. He was not at a loss but actually put the question to the sinners. "What do you think I should do with you? I have given you so much opportunity!"

God pointed out to the sinners that their so-called love for Him was as dependable as clouds without rain or the morning dew. Those things are disappointing. They bring no help or relief. So, too, the fickle, changing love of sinners for God is dependably undependable at best. They love God when times are bad, and then forsake God when times are good. They serve God when it is convenient, but they serve self when it is costly or inconvenient to serve God. They make all of their decisions in light of their own selfish desires, and only occasionally think about God's will. They are like clouds that promise rain to a parched land, only to dissipate at the rising of the morning sun.

Just in case the sinners had forgotten what God expects, He articulated His standard (v.6). He expects steadfast love from the people who name His name, not sacrifices. God is not impressed with meaningless sacrifices. But is this not the same God who used most of Leviticus and much of Numbers to define in detail all of the various sacrifices He required from His people? Yes, but the offerings God required were to flow out of a steadfast love and deep respect for Him. In modern terms this describes people who are quick to acknowledge that God loves to have His people meet together to praise Him and worship Him. But if our worship is not motivated by love and respect for Him, it is pointless. Bible reading, prayer, giving of offerings are pointless apart from love for God. Confidence in the practice of dead religious traditions will be the ball and chain that sink many good Baptists in eternal condemnation.

The difference between meaningless sacrifices and God-honoring service hinge on genuine love for Him. Steadfast love is begun only through a changed, regenerated heart. This love truly believes that God is the sum total of life and eternity. This love is evident in practical decision, in habits, yea, in the essence of life.

But what if sinners do not know what God expects? They are without excuse. God reminded the sinners in Hosea's day that He dissects them with His Word (v.5). His Word, unlike the writings of false gods that claim to come from God, are very plain. His standard is clear. Also, His Word reveals the individual's natural condition very clearly. That is often part of the problem. It is not the things of the Bible that we don't understand that bother us. It is the clear truth about God and about us that cause us to wince. The Bible clearly identifies our sinful condition. Therefore, the need to confess sin, repent of it, and be forgiven is obvious.

God's plan is for His messengers to keep declaring His standard. Through the prophets, God cut the sinners to pieces with His message. Through preachers who declare God's Word, God still opens up sinners to see themselves the way He sees them. Sinners do not like that. It is not uncommon to hear about people who are angry because a preacher said, in general or broad statements from the pulpit, that they are sinners. It is not unusual for me to hear sinners declare that they will never go to church again because one time a preacher accused them of being sinners. God's Word does that. Maybe the sinners are actually mad at God.

God put the final nail in the coffin when He decried the Israelites' failure to change (vv.7-10). At this point there was no doubt that their invitation to themselves was meaningless. God accused the sinners of transgressing the covenant (v.7). Instead of having steadfast love, the people stepped over the boundaries of God's covenant. All sinners, in every age, are like Adam who chose to ignore God's warning. It is not that a person is guilty before God of one accident. No, sinners by nature step outside the agreement over and over. God desires for His people to have steadfast love for Him. We prefer to love ourselves. That is the root sin. It is human nature to do this over and over.

The reason some people never quite get "saved" is because they, like the Israelites, never quite deal with the problem —their sin. It is one thing to say, "I am a sinner" and another thing to confess particular sins. Sinners are forced to deal with specifics because God gives evidence of the transgression (vv.8-10). God named the places and the kind of sin the people in this circumstance were committing. Gilead, Shechem, Ephraim (Israel) were defiled by sin. But they refused to acknowledge the problem. The sinners' invitation to themselves was pointless. Sure they understood that God allowed trouble in their lives. Sure God is the reviver of the dead and wounded. Sure God is faithful. But what were they going to do about their sins? God was faithful through His Word to point out their sins, but would they acknowledge them to God? Are you willing to agree with God that your sins are sins against Him?

# PART II

# GREAT INVITATIONS IN THE NEW TESTAMENT

# 19

# FOLLOW ME

## MATTHEW 4:18-22; 8:18-22; 9:9

Several years ago I was a delegate at a political convention. It was exciting to a point. There were brightly colored banners, flags, and placards. There was a band playing patriotic music. It seemed like everyone who was someone was there. A senator spoke. The governor addressed the jubilant crowd. Even the next president of the United States addressed the cheering delegates. No doubt the whole experience was an adrenaline rush. But when I thought about the nuts and bolts of politics, the daily grind of dealing with politicians, I decided that this was not the kind of place where I wanted to spend my life.

Some professing Christians are like that. As sinners, they found themselves in an exciting meeting. Maybe there was uplifting and inspiring music. Maybe a preacher gave a rousing "speech" about the Bible, complete with heart-touching stories. At the end, he asked for volunteers, and with adrenalin surging through his body the sinner gladly volunteered to be a follower of Christ. But what happened when the daily grind of being a Christ-follower actually came to bear in his life?

That same kind of "band wagon" volunteerism tends to sweep our culture during times of impending war. In the early days of the War Between the States, young and old men alike flocked to the recruiters' offices to join up. They watched the parades with smartly dressed soldiers marching vigorously down the streets. The band was playing, the soldiers' guns glistened in the sunlight, the caissons went rolling along with the cannons attached behind. All in all the army looked formidable. It was such an arousing sight that scores of men flooded the recruiters' offices begging for the chance to join up. However, after the First Battle of Manassas, the first battle of the war, 4,200 American soldiers lay dead on the battlefield, and a lot of fellows began to rethink the whole idea. By the time the conflict had dragged on for a couple of years, desertion became a real problem on both sides.

That picture is not too far from a description of the Army of the Lord. What did Jesus mean when He promised that "many are called but few are chosen" (Matthew 22:14)? What did Christ mean when He warned, "On that day many will say to me, 'Lord, Lord, did we not prophesy in your name, and cast out demons in your name, and do many mighty works in your name?' And then will I declare to them, 'I never knew you; depart from me, you workers of lawlessness.'" (Matthew 7:22-23)?

The word many in these sayings rings like an echo in my mind. It never goes away. How many professing Christians jumped on the bandwagon of Christianity in hyped-up circumstances, but then slowly, or quickly, returned to their old way of living? How many of those people who live just like their world honestly expect to get into heaven? How many of them would genuinely claim that they are followers of Christ? One simple matter must be acknowledged in all claims and professions: "Followers of Christ follow Christ." It is a simple truth with profound, eternal ramifications.

## SOME PEOPLE ACTUALLY FOLLOWED CHRIST

All of the Gospel records tell of people who volunteered to follow Christ. Matthew's account tells about two in particular who told Jesus that they wanted to be followers (Matthew 8:18-21). Were they kidding? Were they unrealistic? No. It seems quite certain that these were sincere people who claimed they wanted to be followers. One of the volunteers was a scribe (vv.18-19). As a scribe, he was part of the elite group of lawmakers and law protectors who were esteemed in Israel. People among this profession told God's people what God's law really required and what they needed to do in order to please God. While the men prided themselves in being the facilitators of God's law, in reality they were the formulators and teachers of the human traditions that superceded God's law.

The people in the crowd must have been astonished to hear a scribe confess that he wanted to follow Christ. Popular opinion dictated that having a scribe on board would certainly lend credibility to Jesus' ministry. For a scribe (an official teacher of Israel) to address the man from Nazareth as "Teacher" is even more astonishing. Should Jesus be delighted that this significant person wants to follow? He wasn't. The text indicates that Jesus and company were about to leave Capernaum by boat and travel to the barren region of the Gadarenes or Gergesenes. Was this man serious when he told Jesus that he would go anywhere, even to the wilderness of Gadara?

A couple of sons also volunteered to be Christ's followers (v.21, Luke 9:61-62). One really wanted to follow Jesus, but he explained how he needed to bury his father before he actually joined up. One should not presume at this point that the father had recently died. Not at all. The man meant that he needed to go home and wait for his father to die because he would forfeit his part of the inheritance if he was absent. Everyone in the culture knew that. That would be okay with Jesus, wouldn't it?

Another son really wanted to be a Christ-follower but explained to Jesus that it would be right for him to go first and tell his family "Good bye" (Luke 9:61-62). Of course this might take a few weeks, but that would be okay, wouldn't it? Normally that would be fine, but in these circumstances it raised a question of loyalty.

The would-be followers failed. When Jesus explained that it would not always be convenient for them to be identified with Him, they chose not to be identified with Him at all. Christ told the scribe that following Him can require sacrifice of comfort (v.20). Jesus did not own a house, nor have a place to call home. He was on earth temporarily. He was born in a borrowed manger and buried in a borrowed tomb. Did the scribe really want to identify intimately with that? The person who wants to feel at home in this world will not be comfortable following Christ.

Jesus explained to the son who wanted the family inheritance that following Him can require the sacrifice of an inheritance (v.22). That is not to say that there is something wrong with gaining an inheritance. In fact, God said through Solomon that it was the right thing to do. However, if the inheritance stands between the individual and faithfulness to Christ, it is eternally deadly.

Finally, according to Luke's account (9:62), Jesus told the son who wanted to say "Good bye" to his family that following Him can require sacrifice of family. It is good to love and honor family. But to put family before Christ has eternal ramifications.

In each case, Jesus, knowing the volunteers' hearts, exposed their real loyalty and desires. In each case, He uncovered the idol, the god, the most important thing in their lives. He revealed that He was not most important to these would-be followers. It was precisely the same thing Jesus did when He required the rich young ruler to sell his possessions before he attempted to become a Christ-follower. Jesus Christ cuts through the facade to expose real motives—real hearts.

The good news is that while some volunteers bombed out, some people followed Christ (Matthew 4:18-22, 9:9). Four disciples left everything to follow Christ (4:18-22). It is important to set the background and chronology of these stories. John the Baptizer was baptizing in the wilderness near Bethany. This was across the Jordan River several miles from Jerusalem. Jesus had gone out to John and been baptized by Him (Matthew 3:13). After Jesus' baptism, the Holy Spirit led Him into the wilderness where He was tempted for 40 days and nights (Matthew 4:1-11). This took place in the late fall of A.D. 26.

Jesus returned from the wilderness to where John was still preaching near the Jordan River. There John introduced a couple of his disciples to Jesus (John 1:35-42). The two disciples were John and Andrew. Andrew told his brother Simon that they had found the Messiah. Simon met Jesus who gave him the new name Peter (John 1:42). Then Jesus met Philip and Nathanael (John 1:43-51). These four followed Jesus somewhat loosely for several months. It appears that they were with Him at the wedding in Cana that took place in the early winter of A.D. 27 (January?). It is also clear that some followers were with Christ at the first temple cleansing in Jerusalem which took place in late winter A.D. 27 (March?). In late summer of that year, Jesus moved His headquarters to Capernaum. A few weeks later, in early autumn (September?), Jesus called these four disciples to follow Him for good. It was about a year after they had first met Him.

Now Jesus found these four men busy at their work. They were not at a revival meeting, a seminar, or camp. They were not even at the temple or a synagogue. According to Luke 5:1-11, Jesus had borrowed Peter's boat in order to preach to the crowds. The boat and Peter the boatman were available because Peter, Andrew, James, and John had worked all night and caught no fish. They were fishermen and business was horrible. After Jesus had taught the people, He advised the fishermen to go out and try again. This was like a philosopher telling professional fishermen how to do their business. How would they respond? These men knew Jesus. He was no stranger. They had met Him a year earlier, and now He was living in the same town with them. They obeyed, and Jesus provided an economic windfall for them.

Suddenly, business was great for the fishermen. Now they didn't need to worry. They had more than enough to pay their bills. No doubt, Peter's words at this point expressed the conclusions of all four fishermen: "But when Simon Peter saw it, he fell down at Jesus' knees, saying, 'Depart from me, for I am a sinful man, O Lord'" (Luke 5:8). The men were shocked into the reality of who Jesus of Nazareth really was. Immediately, Jesus commanded them to fall in behind Him (Matthew 4:19). To Peter and Andrew He gave the great invitation: "Follow Me." The three Greek words used here are important. Jesus told them to come, to follow after or behind. He told them to follow behind "Me." This was not an invitation to follow a system, or a doctrine. Nor was it an invitation to follow a movement. He certainly did not invite them to fall in with something exciting.

To be a Christ-follower means that we must come behind and follow the Person Christ. It is a command (an imperative). This is a command and invitation that Christ used often. He offered, "Come to me, all who labor and are heavy laden, and I will give you rest" (Matthew 11:28). He pictured God's invitation as that of a king who gave a banquet. He invited many saying, ". . . Everything is ready. Come to the wedding feast" (Matthew 22:4). It is the invitation His saints will hear in the last day when "the King will say to those on his right, 'Come, you who are blessed by my Father, inherit the kingdom prepared for you from the foundation of the world" (Matthew 25:34). Jesus offered that invitation, yea that command, to Simon and Andrew.

Jesus also offered the great invitation to James and John. In their case, the text says, "He called them." The word means to invite or summon. This is not a command but an offer to take up a different lifestyle.

All of the men—Peter, Andrew, James, and John—left their livelihood to follow Christ. Nothing was ever the same for them. For the next two-and-one-half years they were continually with Christ. They all lived for Christ from this time on. They all died for Christ.

Matthew's call was no different. He, too, like the four fishermen, forsook life to follow Christ (9:9). Jesus found him busy living life according to his own designs. Probably Jesus invited Matthew to follow Him in the winter of A.D. 28 (January) about four months after He had called the fishermen. Matthew was working an enviable job. Men vied to have such a position. Not only was it a government job, but it virtually guaranteed wealth. Matthew probably knew about Jesus since they both lived in Capernaum. But he was too busy living life to get involved with following a teacher. To follow Christ would require his total life, and life offered too much pleasure at this point. Suddenly Jesus interrupted Matthew's life. Jesus commanded the tax collector to join His ranks. Here Jesus used a different word than He used when He invited Peter and Andrew, and a different word than He used to invite James and John. Here the invitation is to come behind or to accompany as a follower. Again it is a command. Matthew heard, obeyed, left his livelihood, and his life changed forever. Notice that the text is clear to point out that Matthew obeyed immediately. He spend the next two-plus years with Christ. Because he lived for Christ, it is not surprising that he died for Christ. Tradition says that he was killed with a halberd (a long handled axe) in Ethiopia around A.D. 60.

Matthew and the four fishermen were certainly different than the three would-be followers. Notice that the three would-be followers came to Jesus and offered their meager services. But Jesus sought out the four fisherman and the tax collector and commanded them to follow Him.


## SOME PEOPLE STILL FOLLOW CHRIST

There are still people who, like the scribe and the brothers, volunteer to be in Christ's army. They vow to follow Christ. Why? Obviously, these people know something about Christ. Often they know a lot about Christ. They heard about him in Sunday School, church, home, and Christian school. They know about Christ's life and sacrifice. They seem to understand the problem of sin, and they certainly understand that Christ died to cover the penalty of sin and the power of sin.

On the basis of their intellectual understanding of Christ and His work, these people volunteer to follow Him. Often they make a decision like that at a revival service or camp. It all makes sense in their heads. And so they, like the would-be disciples, tell Christ that they want to follow Him.

These people could not be more sincere, but they are powerless. They were so sincere about their decision that they wrote the date in the front of their Bible. But for some unexplainable reason, life keeps getting in the way of Christ-honoring living. They want to live for Christ, but it seems so impossible. In reality, these folks would rather be popular than follow Christ. They would rather be comfortable than follow Christ. They would rather be rich than follow Christ. So they claim to follow Christ, but the fruit of their lives indicates otherwise. In reality, they follow Christ when it is convenient. Their lives are characterized by a spiritual roller coaster. Today they love Christ like crazy, but tomorrow following Him will be inconvenient. And so today they appear to be Christians, and tomorrow they appear to be no different than their world.

As a result, these people are content to compare themselves with other part-time followers and conclude that they are okay, in spite of what their conscience keeps telling them. They volunteered to follow Christ. What more could they do?

The really good news is that there are still people who Christ calls. Christ interrupts their lives. These people probably (at least often) knew something about Christ before they began following Him. Maybe they learned about Him in Sunday School or maybe through a friend, a tract, or a sermon they happened to hear. They understood the problem of sin and the work of Christ to forgive sin. It is possible that they even prayed at times in the past. Maybe they even followed Christ at a distance, having made some kind of "religious" decision.

However, the day came when they understood Christ's work of redemption, His invitation, His calling, and committed themselves to Him in faith. One day the redemptive work of Christ became a very personal issue to these people. One day this sinner could not shake the reality that Christ died for him in particular because it was his personal sin that killed Christ. One day genuine faith in Christ alone brought genuine regeneration. And typically, the redeemed sinner cannot even explain all that happened. He just knows that it happened.

As a result of Christ's invitation, Christ changed the lives of these people just like He changed life for Peter, Andrew, James, John, and Matthew. Now He is the essence of life, the sum total of all things. Now He is the reason for life. Now every decision involves Christ.

They persevere. When life is going well, they stand out as unique in a world the threatens to soften them to death. They stand in the face of trouble with a confidence fixed on another world. They really do follow Christ to the death, just like Peter, Andrew, James, John, and Matthew did. These people are different than the would-be disciples because Jesus commanded them to follow Him and they left everything. Which are you? Are you the volunteer who promises to follow Christ as long as it is convenient? Or are you the person whose life Christ interrupted and who must obey His command?

# 20

# COME TO ME AND FIND REST

MATTHEW 11:27-30

The other day I received an advertisement that invited me to enjoy a Caribbean cruise for a reduced price. The pictures of the cruise ship were impressive. According to the pictures, the food must be fabulous. The places where the cruise would stop probably offer some very interesting things to see. However, there was just one problem with this invitation. I am not interested in taking a cruise right now. Maybe I would like to do that when I am older—like retired. But right now, I am not interested in the benefits of floating on a nice boat, eating great food, and visiting exotic Caribbean islands.

Does that sound like the response of some people when they hear the good news of the gospel? A caring Christian has shared with a sinner the wonderful news that Jesus Christ was God incarnate—God in the flesh. He lived perfectly according to His own law and then allowed Himself to be killed in order to provide the price to pay for the sinner's sins. He rose from the dead to prove that He had the authority to provide this redemption price. The sinner listens politely to the invitation and then says, "I think that accepting this payment for sin by faith is probably a good idea. But I have a lot of life to live right now, and I don't want to be burdened with religious regulations." In the same way that I rejected the cruise invitation, the sinner rejects the invitation for salvation. It is not convenient right now.

Now suppose you meet that same sinner sitting on a bench in the park. It is obvious that the poor fellow is dejected. He looks like he is carrying the weight of the world on his shoulders. You sit down beside him and strike up a conversation. Soon you discover that he has just come from the doctor's office where he has learned that he has a terminal disease. As "fate" would have it, you happen to know a specialist who has had a one hundred percent success ratio in treating that disease. So you invite your friend to go to the specialist as your guest. How does the sinner respond to this invitation? Of course he is excited. Now he has hope. He thanks you profusely for the invitation.

What was the difference in the two hypothetical situations for this sinner? The man rejected the invitation to receive salvation because he could not see a compelling need for it. However, he gladly embraced the invitation for physical healing because the need was painfully obvious. So how do we get people to see their compelling need for salvation?

Any pastor who preaches the Bible and represents God fairly has struggled with this question. Every sincere evangelist has wondered how to make the gospel more compelling. Sincere Christians wonder if they should be more forceful, tell better stories, or share important and convincing facts. Surely there must be an argument that would be so clear, so watertight, so excellent that it would convince every sinner who hears it that he or she must accept the invitation for salvation immediately. Surely there is not! That is not encouraging news for people who would like to see every sinner whom they invite to salvation respond positively. However, it is good news to know that God, who invented salvation, the God who offers the invitation of salvation, is also responsible to reveal "these things" to baby-like people. There never has been or ever will be an argument compelling enough to cause a satisfied person to abandon his pleasure and ease for the cross of Christ. Only God can change that person's desires.

## Jesus Explained the Father's Gracious Will (vv. 25-26)

Jesus' public prayer in this case probably sounds a bit strange. In it He acknowledged that the Father hides "these things" from the wise. The text clear reveals that this was not private prayer. Rather it was in a public setting that Jesus thanked the Father for hiding these things. It is important first to observe that He addressed God as Father. This address revealed to the people who were listening that Jesus of Nazareth enjoyed an intimate relationship with the only true God. His address was certainly more than an admission of the universal "fatherhood" of God. That foolish idea has no basis in the Bible. God is indeed the creator of all things, and He is the Father of all who are redeemed. But some people are still of their father the devil.

Notice that Jesus of Nazareth also addressed the only true God as Lord of heaven and earth. That title is a reminder that God is rightfully the master over all things that He has created. It means that He rightfully sets the rules or boundaries. Who then has the authority to question God?

Jesus thanked His Father God for concealing "these things." That is a very important request. What are "these things" that God has concealed, and from whom has He concealed them? The context of the prayer would normally help, but no one can be exactly sure when this took place. Comparing Matthew and Luke (they are the only two evangelists who recorded it), one finds that it is possible that Jesus prayed this prayer after sending out the twelve disciples to preach the gospel (Matthew 10:1-42); after sending out the seventy (or 72) other preachers (Luke 10:1-24); and after He denounced the cities for not accepting Him after they had observed His many miraculous signs (Matthew 11:20; Luke 10:13-20).

If that is the setting, it is easier to understand this prayer. "These things" must be the truths that the people in the cities rejected even after observing the miracles of Jesus. "These things" then must be the truths the twelve and seventy preachers preached, truths that the people in the towns and villages rejected. The disciples preached the gospel. These things are the truths of the gospel: 1) Jesus is God; 2) Jesus will provide the atonement of sin; 3) Salvation is by grace through faith.

Would God actually hide such wonderful news? It is true that God hides truth from the self-sufficient person. Jesus called people like that the wise and understanding. They are intelligent people. Does that mean that no intelligent person can be saved? No. It means that it is very common for intelligent people to trust their ability to reason so much that they cannot accept the gospel. The idea of freely receiving salvation by grace through faith in the finished work of Christ is not reasonable to human intelligence. The cross makes no sense at all to human wisdom. That is why the Koran, from cover to cover, requires its followers to do good works in order to be rewarded with heaven. Indeed, all false religions demand good works. It is the way of human wisdom.

Experience bears out the truth of this statement. Time has proven that self-sufficient people reject the gospel. Isn't that the conclusion Paul drew for the Christians in Corinth? He told them to "consider your calling, brothers: not many of you were wise according to worldly standards, not many were powerful, not many were of noble birth" (1 Corinthians 1:26). The wise, the mighty, the intelligent are unable to see the truth of the gospel because God hides the truth behind their pride. Their pride and self-sufficiency keeps them from being able to see their need.

On the other hand, Jesus thanked the Father because He reveals "these things" to babes. While God hides the truth of the gospel behind the pride of the self-sufficient people, He shows truth to those who are dependent on Him. A babe in this prayer is the person who has spiritual humility. It is the person who has nothing to lean on or offer. It is the person who is wholly dependent on God for help. Only people who become that dependent on Christ will be saved. Jesus said that sinners must become wholly dependent like little children. He told the disciples on a few occasions, "Truly, I say to you, unless you turn and become like children, you will never enter the kingdom of heaven" (Matthew 18:3).

That is the character of a person who can be saved. In fact, in the Sermon on the Mount, Jesus pictured redeemed people as very needy. He taught, "Blessed are the poor in spirit, for theirs is the kingdom of heaven" (Matthew 5:3). The proud religionists of Jesus' day could not imagine such humility. To be a spiritual beggar was unacceptable to them. To be a spiritual beggar is the only way anyone can have hope in Christ.

Jesus acknowledged that this is the Father's gracious will. God chooses to open the eyes of people like that. It is the only way that a person will ever know the truth. It is the kind of thing that happened to Simon Peter when he was able to acknowledge that Jesus, the man from Nazareth, was indeed God's Son. When he acknowledged this astonishing truth, "Jesus answered him, 'Blessed are you, Simon Bar–Jonah! For flesh and blood has not revealed this to you, but my Father who is in heaven'" (Matthew 16:17). Other humans did not help Peter grasp the truth. Brilliant apologists did not convince him that Jesus was Messiah. God Himself showed Peter the truth. That is His plan. That is His gracious will. Therefore, the proud and self-sufficient are hopeless because they will not acknowledge their need.

## Jesus Explained His Authority to Offer the Invitation (v.27)

Jesus is able to offer this invitation because God the Father has given all authority to God the Son. The Father handed all things over to Christ.

Notice that on the one hand Jesus acknowledged the headship of God the Father, and on the other hand He points out that the Son is equal with the Father. Whatever authority the Father possesses, He already gave to the Son. Jesus proved that He possessed this authority over all power on earth by doing miracles that set aside the principles of physics. And still the people rejected Him. Jesus proved that He owned this authority in His teaching. It was so authoritative that the people were astonished at His authority. But they rejected Him anyway. Jesus proved that this authority was His by sending out preachers with the Good News (70 and 12). The people rejected them too. Jesus proved that the Father had given Him authority by promising power to the servants He sends to do His work. He told His servants in every generation, "Go therefore and make disciples of all nations, baptizing them in the name of the Father and of the Son and of the Holy Spirit" (Matthew 28:19). Most of all, Jesus proved this authority by forgiving sins and the religious leaders responded by calling it blasphemy. Jesus equated Himself with God, and it made the leaders so angry that they killed Him. Nevertheless, Jesus owned God the Father's authority.

Since God the Father gave God the Son all authority, it seems only right to conclude that God the Son is equal with God the Father. Indeed, Christ's divinity is the heart of the gospel. The sacrifice for sin required that a man live perfectly according to God's law. Only God can live perfectly. Therefore, only God can die in place of sinners to provide the acceptable sacrifice. The authorities crucified Jesus because He claimed to be God. Take away Christ's divinity and the poor sinner is left to do good works in a failing effort to gain salvation. If Jesus Christ is not God there is no one to provide salvation for the sinner.

It is also obvious that the Father and Son are equal because they know each other in perfect intimacy. Jesus said that no one knows the Son except the Father. This means that no one knows God the Son intimately, perfectly, like God the Father does. He also said that no one knows the Father except the Son. This truth follows with the truth Jesus spoke when He said that no one comes to God the Son unless God the Father draws him (John 6:44). At the same time, no one knows the Father except those to whom Christ gives the ability.

That is what Paul was driving at when he taught the Corinthians, "Now we have received not the spirit of the world, but the Spirit who is from God, that we might understand the things freely given us by God. And we impart this in words not taught by human wisdom but taught by the Spirit, interpreting spiritual truths to those who are spiritual. The natural person does not accept the things of the Spirit of God, for they are folly to him, and he is not able to understand them because they are spiritually discerned" (1 Corinthians 2:12-14). It is the gracious will of God to open the eyes of the understanding for sinners so that they can accept the truth that Jesus of Nazareth was God. Any conclusion short of that robs the gospel of its foundation and power. What could possibly be accomplished by a mere man dying on a cross like the martyr of a lost cause?

## JESUS OFFERED THE INVITATION OF REST TO THE WEARY (vv.28-30)

Jesus' invitation is for those who are weary and burdened to find rest (v.28). The invitation acknowledges a preexisting condition in sinners. Therefore, Jesus offered it to the ones who are tired. He said that the recipients of this great invitation are wearied. The word means that the people who hear and accept this invitation are exhausted from trying to "find" God. They have disciplined themselves and tried many different methods, programs, plans, or religions in an effort to find God. All of their efforts were futile. They expended their time and energy and gained nothing.

To make matters worse, the very people who have worn themselves out religious and gained nothing are still burdened. They sense the load of sin on their back that enslaves them. They live with the burden of guilt every day. They struggle under the burden of trying to keep rules in an effort to win God's favor. And they know that they fail every day. That is why Jesus condemned the Pharisees by saying, "Woe to you lawyers also! For you load people with burdens hard to bear, and you yourselves do not touch the burdens with one of your fingers" (Luke 11:46). The leaders of false religions load up the guilt on their followers by making them do religious works that do not alleviate their sin in the slightest.

But Jesus offers the invitation of hope to everyone who has this condition. The humble, dependent, childlike, spiritual beggar admits that he is burdened and wearied. He knows that he is a sinner. He knows that he is guilty before God. No one needs to argue him into that conclusion. He knows that there is nothing he can give to God in order to placate His wrath against sin. Therefore, the guilty, burdened, weary sinner cries out for mercy, and Jesus offers him this invitation. The self-sufficient do not understand that they are needy, that they have no hope. The invitation does not register with them.

The invitation requires turning around. The words "Come to Me" require the sinner to turn away from these things. He must turn away from trying to win God's favor by his works. He must turn away from his self-sufficiency. This is the nature of repentance. Repentance is turning and forsaking the old way of living under the burden of sin and trying to impress God with some kind of religious works.

Christ invites the wearied, burdened sinner to submit to Christ's yoke (vv.29-30). It sounds strange to hear an invitation that offers, "Come and take Christ's easy yoke." Yoke and easy seem to be contradictory. In reality, a yoke makes burden bearing easier. One of the most effective ways to train a young ox was to yoke him up with an experienced ox. In this way, the ox would learn how to work effectively. That is the essence of Jesus' invitation. He invites sinners to come and be yoked along with Him so that He can teach them. In that relationship, a person can learn facts about Christ that cannot be learned outside a relationship with Him. We only learn Christ by being yoked to Him in faith. In that close relationship, the Christian learns gentleness. There he learns meekness. This is where one learns rest of soul.

It is true that a yoke implies submission. But submission to Christ is true freedom. His yoke is easy. That is not to say that a Christian will not have burdens to bear. There are burdens in the Christian life. The daily sacrifice of self can be a great burden. Loving others above self is a burden. Being persecuted because of righteousness is definitely a burden. But all of these things are easier to bear when yoked with Christ.

In fact, the burdens a Christian must face are like rest and ease compared to the burden of sin and the burden of man's rules. Christ has paid the price. The penitent sinner's sins are covered by His blood. Therefore, submission to Christ is freedom. "For this is the love of God, that we keep his commandments. And his commandments are not burdensome" (1 John 5:3). Do you know this? Many have heard this invitation, but few embrace it. Better arguments will not force sinners to submit to Christ. Only God's work of grace will help a sinner embrace this wonderful invitation.

# 21

# INVITE THEM

## MATTHEW 22:1-14

J esus illustrated the heart of God very well when He told the parable of the king who gave invitations to His wonderful banquet. The story reminds the reader that God graciously invites people to enjoy His blessings. The story also reminds the reader that everyone who hears the invitation is not interesting in enjoying God's blessings. Many hear but few respond.

That story is very familiar to anyone who has attempted to tell the good news about God's invitation to salvation. More often than not the news is rejected. Too often the invitation is crumbled up and thrown away as it were by people who desperately need God's blessing of forgiven sins. Nevertheless, it is the joy and duty of God's people to continue to tell the good news that the King has invited people to come to His banquet. The story challenges God's people to be busy about the important work of inviting sinners to partake of God's bountiful provision.

### THE KING PATIENTLY INVITED GUESTS WHO WOULD NOT COME (VV.1-7)

Jesus introduced this parable with the common phrase, "The kingdom of heaven is compared to . . ." That is precisely what He taught the religious leaders. This story falls within the context of Jesus' last teaching to a stubborn religious culture. It was only a few days before the rulers would arrest Him and crucify Him. Jesus was teaching His final lessons to the rebellious nation while they gathered on the porches of the temple. Many people listened, but few learned. Especially the religious leaders listened. It is not that they wanted to learn something true from Jesus, but that they were looking for an opportunity to trap Him in something He said so that they would have a case against Him.

Jesus repeatedly illustrated the stubborn resistence of the religious leaders and the tragic results of their stubbornness by telling them stories. For example, in the parable of the two sons (21:28-32), He taught that Israel was stubborn against God and that God would open the kingdom to those who do not deserve it (i.e., tax collectors and prostitutes). In the parable of the tenants (21:33-43), Jesus taught that God will take the offer of the kingdom away from the Jews and give it to a people who will produce fruit for God's glory. The religious leaders were not ignorant. They understood that Jesus taught that they were failures, and the truth stirred their anger so mightily that they wanted to kill Him (21:45-46).

The first part of this story about a king throwing a banquet illustrates God's dealing with Israel. The picture shows how God invited Israel to participate in the kingdom of heaven. The kingdom of God has past, present, and future aspects. God's kingdom in the past was a literal nation. In the present, God's kingdom is where Christ the King reigns supreme in the hearts of His citizens. That means that in the present application, the kingdom of heaven is synonymous with salvation. It means that Christ is Lord. Then the kingdom of God will again have a physical expression in the Millennial reign of Christ in the future. The final expression of the kingdom will be the new heaven, new earth, and new Jerusalem. In this story Jesus revealed how Israel rejected Christ and, therefore, rejected the kingdom.

What does the story say? The king who invited guests to a supper pictures how God invited Israel to share in His kingdom (vv.1-6). That truth is illustrated by a king who gives a wedding feast for his son. This was an incredible feast. A typical wedding feast might last for weeks. The father of the groom invited many guests, and he entertained them throughout that time, generally at his own home. This particular supper was a royal wedding feast. A feast given by the king.

The feast is a picture of salvation. God offered salvation, based on faith in Christ's finished work, to Israel first. He invited the people of Israel to participate in the marriage supper of the Lamb. This is the supper John saw being celebrated in the future by all of those people who have been redeemed by the blood of Christ. He testified, "And the angel said to me, 'Write this: "Blessed are those who are invited to the marriage supper of the Lamb"'" (Revelation 19:9a).

The king invited people who should come, that is, people who one would naturally expect to respond positively to the invitation. It would have been a great honor to be invited to the king's supper. When the servants obeyed the king and went out to invite the proper people, they should have expected a positive response. The invited people already knew about the banquet and had most likely received a pre-invitation foretelling them of the upcoming event. This idea is clear from the use of a perfect tense, passive voice verb. People who already knew about the feast must have been very special people to the king. Only those who were in a special relationship with Him could expect to receive a pre-invitation. As citizens of the king's nation, they should have been overjoyed to attend. But the astonishing thing in this story is that they refused! (v.3) That is shameful. What were the people thinking?

The king tried a second time to invite the people. Through His servants, He pled with the people to come to the banquet that was already prepared and waiting for them. But instead of accepting the king's invitation some of the people went about their business as if their mundane tasks were more important than anything the king offered (v.5). Other of the people were even more offensive to the king. They assaulted his servants who brought them the invitation (v.6). As a whole, the privileged people rejected the king's kind invitation.

God is the offended king. Jesus revealed that God would destroy the religious but stubborn culture who rejected His offer to the banquet (v.7). This literally happened in A.D. 70 when Titus the Roman general destroyed Jerusalem. God the king had invited Israel, His chosen nation, to enjoy salvation through Christ. They rejected God's invitation.

## THE KING INVITED GUESTS WHO ATTENDED HIS FEAST (vv.8-14)

After the special people rejected his invitation, the king invited people from the highways (vv.8-10). These people were not worthy to be invited (v.8). The king sent his servants to invite the unworthy, the unexpected. He invited people like tax collectors and prostitutes (21:31). The story is a reminder that God still sends the invitation to receive salvation and enjoy the Lamb's banquet to all kinds of people. He still sends the invitation to people like us. We are all unworthy just like the tax collectors and prostitutes of Jesus' day. We are all unworthy because each one of us is guilty of sin, guilty of committing particular sins, guilty because we have fallen short of His glory, and guilty because we have turned to our own way. We are unworthy, but God ordered an invitation to be sent to us. In His amazing grace, the invitation for salvation is for us in spite of our unworthiness.

The servants obeyed the king (vv.9-10). He gave his servants orders to get his invitation out. They immediately went out to the road ways and invited everyone they could find. They invited bad and good. They invited people who were bad according to human opinion, and people who were good according to human opinion. Human opinion makes no difference to God. He invites everyone. As a result, the wedding hall was filled.

The king, satisfied that people had responded to his invitation, went into the banquet hall to see his guests. There he spied one guest who was improperly dressed (vv.11-14). The king punished the guest for wearing an unacceptable garment (vv.11-13). Why? Was this not harsh in light of the fact that he told the servants to invite the good, the bad, and the ugly? The king was right to be offended because he obviously had provided the acceptable wedding attire. He would not have expected everyone to be properly dressed if he had not made provision for that to be the case.

This is a picture of sinners, who accept God's invitation for salvation, being clothed in the righteousness of Christ. Paul confessed, "Indeed, I count everything as loss because of the surpassing worth of knowing Christ Jesus my Lord. For his sake I have suffered the loss of all things and count them as rubbish, in order that I may gain Christ and be found in him, not having a righteousness of my own that comes from the law, but that which comes through faith in Christ, the righteousness from God that depends on faith" (Philippians 3:8-9). Redeemed sinners must be dressed with that garment of Christ's righteousness if they would attend the wedding feast of the Lamb.

Redeemed sinners must be clothed in the garment of Christ's righteousness because God provides it for them. Scripture reveals that there will be some people who will attempt to get into the feast being clothed in their own righteous works. They will say, "Lord, Lord, have we not done many mighty works . . ." Christ the Judge will say, "I never knew you; depart from me, you workers of lawlessness" (Matthew 7:23).

Jesus ended the story by warning that many are invited, but few are chosen (v.14). The invitation goes to everyone. God is gracious to offer pardon to all. Those who have received and embraced God's invitation must be zealous to make the invitation known to all. But while we tell the good news we must remember that only a few receive the invitation. That is a revealed fact. We do not know who the recipients will be. We are not responsible to determine who they will be. We are responsible to invite and leave the "chosen" part with God. God has placed His invitation to the wedding feast in our hands. He has told us to go everywhere and invite. We must be busy at inviting. We must be satisfied to let God determine who will attend.

# 22

# ALL THINGS ARE
# POSSIBLE WITH GOD

## MARK 10:17-27

Throughout years of experience, I have observed many methods for presenting the invitation for eternal life. The one driving motivation in most presentations is the desire for the listening sinner to understand the gospel and to receive the gift of salvation by faith. To that end, many people have become creative and some have resorted to dishonesty. For example, there were the students I knew from a Bible college whose method was to drive along the city streets in the car on Friday night. When they spotted an unsuspecting person on the sidewalk, they would pull up beside the person and yell out the window, "Do you believe in Jesus?" If the person said, "Yes," the students marked that down as a conversion. How could they be so dishonest? Actually, they sincerely believed that such a confession was tantamount to "confess[ing] with the mouth that Jesus is Lord" (Romans 10:9). Most people conclude that this was mere foolishness.

Others are so desirous for sinners to embrace the message of salvation that they attempt to remove all impediments to faith. They even attempt to remove the offense of the cross. If the gospel message seems to be offensive because of words like "sin" or "blood" or "hell," they just remove the words, and often remove the ideas conveyed by those words. The result is that the sinner who hears this kind of invitation really does not understand that he or she is an ongoing offense to the Holy God and, therefore, really is not regenerated.

Still other witnessers of the gospel try to develop the foolproof, perfect argument. They believe that if they think hard enough and deep enough, they can come up with an argument that will be irrefutable. In that case, the sinner will have to accept Christ as Savior, whether or not he really wants to. The error of this reasoning is self-evident.

Finally, there are the soul winners who seek to remove any requirements that might seem to be attached to salvation. For example, it is common for sinners to resist the invitation for salvation because they do not want to be chained to the rules that accompany salvation. They like to party, they like to commit adultery, they like to covet, lie, or steal, just like their friends do. If they embrace the invitation for salvation, they will have to change. Therefore, some foolish soul winners tell such fearful sinners that they really won't have to change. They convince the sinner that God is so loving that He will take them just the way they are, and He will not expect them to change. Nothing could be further from the truth.

Jesus demonstrated true evangelism as He interacted with a successful young man who was very sincere about seeking eternal life. Jesus and the disciples had left Capernaum some days earlier on their way to Jerusalem where the authorities would arrest, torture, and kill the Christ (9:33-50). On the way they crossed over the Jordan River and, for several days, ministered on the east side of the river (10:1-12). In that setting, parents were bringing their children to Jesus in order for Him to bless them. The disciples attempted to put a stop to what they thought was foolishness (10:13). But Jesus used the situation as an opportunity to teach a very important lesson. He taught the adults that it is necessary for everyone to become dependant and trusting just like a child in order to gain eternal life. The key in that lesson is the necessity of humility and self-abnegation in order to be born again. In other words, no one will ever get into heaven due to his or her own efforts. No one!

With that lesson fresh on the disciples' minds, Jesus and the disciples left the house and continued on the journey toward Jerusalem and the eternal sacrifice for sins. As they traveled, a successful young man ran up to Jesus and, in no uncertain terms, expressed his desire to have eternal life. Jesus' response to the man is signal. He did not attempt to make the gospel palatable to the man's circumstances or chosen life-style. Jesus did not go out of His way to make eternal life irresistible. Rather, Jesus quickly identified the man's deficiency and shot the arrow of conviction right at that spot. No one embraces the invitation of salvation outside the realm of humility. Humility requires self-surrender—complete self-surrender. The person who will not let go of self will never accept the invitation for eternal life.

## A Sincere Man Sought Eternal Life (vv.17-20)

The scene opens with a successful man running to bow at Jesus' feet because he honestly wanted salvation. There is no doubt that this man, this young man, was also very successful. Verse twenty-two says that he had acquired much wealth (v.22). Generally that kind of acquisition is not a matter of luck, and the wording makes it clear that he did not inherit the money but earned it. Obviously, he was a pretty sharp fellow.

His success was also noticeable in the realm of religion. According to his personal testimony, in response to Jesus' requirement, the man had been extremely disciplined in keeping the law (vv.18-20). Jesus took for granted that the fellow knew the commands (v.19). Not only did he know the commands, but the guy claimed that he had kept all of the commands that applied to his relationship with fellow man (v.19). The examples of commands that Jesus picked out (it appears to be random, but it was not), came from the second section of the decalogue (the 10 commandments). The first section of the ten commandments deals with a persons relationship with God. The second section of the law deals with a person's relationship with others. This man confessed that he had kept all of those commands from the second section since he was a youth. Would his peers acknowledge the same truth about him? One can be almost certain that the man did not keep all of the commands perfectly. However it is also pretty certain that he probably kept the commands better than his peers. The man was obviously very disciplined and very successful.

Furthermore, this man revealed a deep desire for heaven. His desire is revealed in the way he ran to Jesus. Running in a long robe was not the best way for a man in that culture to command respect. Something drove him to Jesus. He was clearly concerned about this matter of eternal life. Who would not rejoice to experience such a desire for salvation from a sinner? Most soul winners would be astonished to have someone come and tell them they wanted to be saved, much less run to them and fall down before them. Modern Christians would  put this fellow on the church roll and make him a church officer based simply on his desire for the gospel.

In fact, it appears that the man had been trying to get into heaven all his life. Jesus told him that he needed to keep all the laws. This was a good way to help the man see that he had actually failed to keep God's law and was in need of salvation. But this successful young guy missed the point. He responded by claiming that he had been keeping these laws all his life. Literally he retorted, "I myself guarded these . . ." I myself indeed. "I" is quite important to this man. Maybe he was a type "A" personality, a controlling person who was driven to be sure that everything was just right. These people are common, especially in religious circles. They know the Bible, they know the rules for salvation, they have done everything in their power to make sure that they and their family members are all saved. That is the problem! People like this depend greatly on everything in their power.

The successful man ran to Jesus and showed Him great honor. He knelt before Him in an act which showed the most extreme honor of an underling to a superior. It was an outward sign of submission and honor. Truly this man believed that Jesus could help. One can tell by his responses that he honestly expected Jesus of Nazareth to answer his pressing question about eternal life. Jesus would do that because, as the man acknowledged, Jesus was good. He called Him, "Good Teacher." It was a title of respect and honor. But as soon as the expression of respect was out of the man's mouth, Jesus questioned his sincerity. "Jesus said to him, 'Why do you call me good? No one is good except God alone'" (Mark 10:18).

In this response, Jesus did not disavow His perfect goodness. He was indeed good. He had to be good because He was God in the flesh. That is just the point. Jesus forced this man to stop and think about what he was saying. He tried to get the man to see that he was talking to the One God. He had come to the only God who can open heaven for him. He asked God Himself about His rules! Did the man really want to know God's rule for getting into heaven?

While the story appears to be that of a sincere man who truly desired to be saved, it is really a story about the struggle between the Sovereign God and self-reliant man. This battle has been raging throughout the human race since Eve ate the fruit in the garden.

### Jesus Removed the Man's Facade (vv.21-22)

In clear words and loving tone, Jesus set forth the true issue that would keep this successful man out of heaven (v.21). It is not a picture of a wrathful teacher who is angry that a rich man is doing the wrong thing. The story indicates how much Jesus loved this sinner.

The verb in verse twenty-one virtually says that Jesus looked in him. It is a compound word that combines the common word for look or to see with a preposition that means by or in. Since the idea of "looking in" a person is not common and is difficult to comprehend, the word usually is defined as, gazing up, or in the spiritual sense to look at with the mind and comprehend.

Christ is able to do that. His gaze is penetrating. He knows every secret detail of every heart. Sometimes the Scripture pictures God the Son as looking with eyes of fire that penetrate the hearts of even the most stubborn people. He knows all, sees all. He instructed John, "And to the angel of the church in Thyatira write: 'The words of the Son of God, who has eyes like a flame of fire, and whose feet are like burnished bronze'" (Revelation 2:18). This is a reminder that Jesus knows the true condition of the heart of every sinner. Sincere messengers of God do not really know and must be careful not to presume that we do know the condition of a sinner's heart.

Jesus knew the condition of this man's heart and loved him in spite of it. He loves sinners enough to die for them. This man was one of the sinners whose sin would hang Christ on the cross. Within a few days of this conversation, Jesus Christ would hang on a rugged cross to pay the price to buy sinners out of sin. Surely He thought about the price He would pay to cover this man's sins. But He did not provide the covering for just this man's sins. He also paid for my sins because Jesus loves me.

Because Jesus loved this sinner, He revealed the problem. Human wisdom concludes that if you love the person, you will never do or say anything about the sinner's condition lest you cause embarrassment. Jesus knew that the man's view of wealth was standing between him and true humility. Therefore, He would point this problem out to the man. Notice that when Jesus rehearsed the basic laws of the ten commands, he left out the last one: "You shall not covet your neighbor's house; you shall not covet your neighbor's wife, or his male servant, or his female servant, or his ox, or his donkey, or anything that is your neighbor's" (Exodus

20:17). That was the man's problem. The man, who knew the law well, must have realized that Jesus left out that requirement. But he did not correct Jesus. Jesus intended even the rehearsing of the law to bring conviction of the man's sin.

The man loved possessions, so Jesus simply told the man to get rid of that which stood between him and full dependence on God. Money or riches is not the problem for everyone. Often it is personal pride that stands between the sinner and salvation. Sometimes it can be possessions, or position, or even power. It is possible that even a person (i.e., spouse, parent, friend) can stand between the sinner and humble dependence on God. Whatever stands between the sinner and complete dependence on God will keep him or her out of heaven.

Jesus loved the sinner, but in spite of His love He grieved the sincere seeker (v.22). The man became gloomy when he learned the truth. He heard Jesus' word (saying) and knew that it was true. Jesus didn't need to argue with the man. He didn't need to draw out exact and incriminating evidence. The simple word of Jesus was sufficient to strike the sinner with conviction. This is why some people leave out parts of God's Word when telling the gospel. The man would not have been helped if Jesus would have implied that he could trust wealth and still go to heaven. Sinners must hear the Word. If the Word makes a sinner gloomy that is God's indication that something needs changing.

Jesus loved the man, pulled the lid off the pot of seething maggots, let the man see what he really was, and the man went away grieved. He knew from Jesus' words that the requirement for entering heaven was complete humility—full dependence on God. He also knew that he could not bring himself to do it. The result was that he was sorrowful and distressed. He knew that he could not pay that price. He knew that he could not get into heaven. So the young successful man went away. That is the part that is hard to understand. Why did the man walk away? He walked away from his only hope because he could not accept the word of truth.

JESUS EXPLAINED THE GREAT TRUTH OF SALVATION    (vv.23-27)

The man walked away to be lost for eternity. The disciples were standing there watching the whole scene trying to comprehend what they had just witnessed. Jesus turned to them and explained how difficult it is for some people to enter heaven (vv.23-25). He said in plain words that it is difficult for a wealthy person to enter heaven (vv.23-24a). Notice that Jesus first scanned the disciples to see how they were responding to the foregoing situation (v.23). Then He explained to His bewildered followers that it is difficult for a wealthy person not to trust their wealth. The disciples were astonished to realize that something that is so common and so easy to trust can actually keep a person out of heaven (v.24b).

Just to make sure they got the point, Jesus repeated it more plainly. He said in even simpler words that it is impossible for anyone to enter heaven on their own terms (vv.24b-25). "Children, how difficult it is to enter the kingdom of God!" Jesus taught them. This statement teaches that it is not just the rich who find it difficult to depend wholly on God. An actual camel can actually go through the eye of an actual needle easier than a rich person can get into heaven by trusting his wealth. In other words, neither one is going to happen ever! Is the whole world full of sinners hopeless?

Jesus explained God's power (vv.26-27). This was necessary because disciples can be astonished at God's plan (v.26). At this point in the ongoing events, the disciples were exceedingly astonished. Did Christ really expect the guy to sell everything? Yes. Then does that mean that it is really impossible for people like the Pharisees, who were the master rule keepers, to get into heaven? Yes. Are all my efforts at winning God's favor actually pointless? Yes, that is precisely the case.

In light of the disciples' dumbfoundedness, it is not surprising that modern followers are still exceedingly astonished when they finally come to grips with the only means for entering heaven. We know from experience how easy it is to trust self and earthly accomplishments. We know how natural it is to try to convince human wisdom to "accept" Christ. We know how impossible it is for human wisdom to work up complete dependence on God. Therefore, it is common for us to watch the humanly wise sinners of the world reject God's plan out of hand because the truth is exceedingly astonishing. The Word of Christ still astonishes human wisdom.

The answer to this astonishment is for Christ's followers to comprehend God's power (v.27). Jesus told the disciples that if they put the problem of trusting wrong things alongside man and his ability, the end is hopeless. No man has the power to work up a right heart before God. No man has the ability to convince another to give it all up for God.

However, when we lay the problem of human desire for salvation alongside God, we discover His power. He has the power to change the heart. He has the power to do what no person can do. Sinners still walk away from the great invitation because it demands too much. God still delights to change sinners' hearts so that they embrace the invitation at all costs. When a sinner truly receives the invitation to be completely dependent on God, it is through God's work alone and for God's glory alone.

# 23

# YOU MUST BE
# BORN AGAIN

JOHN 3:1-10

At a time in the past, as a spirit floating around in oblivion, I decided it was a good idea to be born as a human. So I found a woman, implanted myself in her womb, and through a process taking nine months, I developed into a little human and was born. I chose to be born to this particular woman because I wanted to be six feet two inches tall, have dark hair and brown eyes. And, as you can see for yourself, everything worked out just the way I planned.

The person who believes that story is among the most naive and gullible of people. What could be more ridiculous? What could be more absurd? No one has a choice in the matters regarding their physical birth. No one gets to pick their gender, race, parents, or the location of their birth. People are born, and then live according to characteristics with which they were born.

Jesus used an analogy like this to help a brilliant teacher in Jerusalem grasp the true nature of salvation. Nicodemus thought much like the majority of people throughout history have thought about heaven, salvation, and the eternal state. Each religion other than Christianity has a laundry list of things the candidate for salvation must do in order to inherit heaven. There is virtually no exception to this rule. It is in keeping with human nature to expect one to do good works in order to please God. Since all religions other than Christianity and Judaism are the inventions of human wisdom, they all arrive at the same conclusion: No works—no salvation.

It is sad to admit that even many Christians fall into the same error. Most serious Bible students have wrestled with questions like, "Is belief a work?" God's Word promises that if you "believe in the Lord Jesus, . . . you will be saved . . ." (Acts 16:31). "But isn't belief a work of the flesh?" some sincere people wonder. Others go even further by insisting that the repentant sinner must walk down the aisle at a church service or camp meeting, shake the preacher's hand, and sign a card in order to be born again. Others expect sinners to pray a particular prayer, reciting precise words if they expect to be born again. Aren't those examples of human efforts expended in an attempt to be born again?

But coming back to Jesus' discussion with the teacher of Israel, one discovers that entering the kingdom of God is a matter of God doing a miraculous work that only He is able to do. True salvation is as simple as being born. True salvation is as impossible as deciding to be born.

## A Knowledgeable, but Inquisitive Man Approached Jesus (vv. 1-2)

Apparently while it was early in Jesus' ministry, probably while Jesus was in Jerusalem, Nicodemus searched Him out at night to ask Him a question. Nicodemus was not the average run-of-the-mill citizen of Jerusalem. He was an important ruler (v.1). The text points out the fact that the man was a Pharisee. As a Pharisee, he set the standard for all of the people to follow as they tried to keep God's law. The text also says that Nicodemus was a ruler of the Jews. This is a reference to the fact that he was a member of the Jewish ruling body, the Sanhedrin. That body of rulers was composed of only seventy of the most significant, most religious Pharisees and Sadducees.

Nicodemus respected Jesus, the man from the village of Nazareth who had recently come onto the religious scene (v.2). He graciously commended Jesus and called Him "Rabbi," which means teacher, a title of respect. For a teacher of the Jews to refer to another man as "Rabbi" was an expression of honor. Since this is what Nicodemus thought of Jesus, it is not surprising that he also admitted that God's signs through Jesus had attracted his and his peers' attention. While it was true that the other leaders had noticed Jesus, it is also obvious that this Pharisee and member of the Sanhedrin was unlike most of his peers. He concluded that, at the very least, Jesus was a unique prophet and teacher whom God sent. His peers, on the other hand, concluded that Satan sent Jesus.

## Jesus Answered the Question the Man Did Not Ask (vv.3-8)

A strange thing happened after this man introduced himself to Jesus and honored Him with his words. Jesus quickly introduced to the leader of the Jews the idea of the new birth (vv.3-4). He took the initiative even though the wise man had not even asked the question (v.3). Why did Jesus launch into this topic when Nicodemus had not asked about it? Some things about this scene are obvious. One is the fact that Nicodemus did not sneak out under cover of night to talk to Jesus about sports or politics. It is also obvious that the man was a religious teacher. Surely he wanted to discuss something religious in nature. But more than the obvious matters is the fact that Jesus, being God, knew what was on the teacher's heart. Therefore, He cut out all the small talk and went straight to the issue that brought the ruler of the Jews out at night for the meeting.

This simple act illustrates the established fact that God always takes the initiative in salvation. Sinners, whether they call themselves seekers or not, do not take the initiative to find God. To the contrary, God taught that naturally sinful people are content to keep denying the truth they know (Romans 1:19). Sinners do not even seek after God (Romans 3:11). Worse, sinners cannot take the initiative because they are spiritually dead (Ephesians 2:1). That was the condition of Nicodemus. So why was he there? God wanted the teacher to hear the truth about salvation in the same way that He wants all sinners to hear the Good News.

So Jesus, God the Son, laid out God's plan in clear terms to this intelligent man. He simply taught the man that if he wanted to go to heaven something had to happen to him. There was nothing for him to do. There is no room for human works in this explanation. Something or Someone needs to birth the sinner all over again or getting into heaven is out of the question!

Understandably the wise man was dumbfounded (v.4). He had always learned that the kingdom of God, that is salvation, is attained by the sinner doing things to please God. He knew from what teachers had taught him that one had to keep God's law in order to please God. But he also must have known from experience that neither he, nor anyone he knew, was actually keeping the law. Hence the meeting in the dark. He showed up, maybe at a prearranged spot and time. He honored Jesus by his opening remarks. And immediately, Jesus told the man he had to be born again or he would not get into the kingdom of God. It is not surprising to read that Nicodemus was very surprised. When Jesus proposed this remarkable thing, the guy was flabbergasted. Human wisdom has no room for such an idea as actual rebirth. Amazing discoveries by brilliant minds over the centuries not withstanding, being born a second time is still impossible.

In response to Nicodemus' incredulity, Jesus explained the idea of the new birth (v.5-8). By saying, "That which is born of flesh is flesh, and that which is born of the Spirit is spirit," Jesus pointed out that the work of the Holy Spirit cannot be repeated through the power of the flesh (vv.5-7). He drew a marked distinction. Having been birthed from flesh is different than having been birthed from the Spirit (v.6). These ideas stand in opposition to each other. To confuse the two ideas results in eternal disaster. Or to put it another way, the person who actually attempts to enter heaven through the efforts and accomplishments of the flesh will know for eternity in hell that it cannot be done.

Rather, Jesus taught that a sinner must be born of water and born of the Spirit in order to get into heaven. This is one of the most confusing statements in the Bible. What did Jesus mean? There are two fairly common interpretations of these words. One is that Jesus used the term water in a way equal to physical birth. That is, Jesus told Nicodemus that the only way for someone to get into heaven is to be born in the flesh first. At best that would be an unnecessary statement since only born people are the object of discussion. Furthermore, the argument contrasts the difference between flesh birth and Spirit birth. If water is the same as the natural birth process (i.e. amniotic fluid) this argument would make physical birth and spiritual birth equal parts of the process. That is the opposite of what Jesus wanted Nicodemus to see.

The second interpretation makes water equivalent to baptism. However, Jesus never taught that a person can only get into heaven by being baptized and by being reborn by the Holy Spirit. Scripture does not teach that baptism is a necessary part of salvation. In fact, Jesus admitted that He did not baptize anyone (John 4:2). He also promised the criminal on the cross that he would have eternal life apart from baptism (Luke 23:43). Paul baptized only about three people and he seemed to indicate that he wished he would not have baptized them (1 Corinthians 1:14-16). Since this whole argument centers on the fact that no one can get into heaven by doing works, baptism is pretty much out of the picture.

There is one alternative interpretation that is worthy of consideration. It is possible that Jesus used the term water to speak of the cleansing agent that the Holy Spirit uses in the new birth process. One can come to this conclusion by considering other symbolic uses of water in John's Gospel. Jesus promised the Samaritan woman at the well, "Whoever drinks of the water that I will give him will never be thirsty forever. The water that I will give him will become in him a spring of water welling up to eternal life" (John 4:14). He offered unending spiritual water in salvation. Jesus' invitation to the crowds at the Feast of Booths offered the same kind of spiritual water. "On the last day of the feast, the great day, Jesus stood up and cried out, 'If anyone thirsts, let him come to me and drink. Whoever believes in me, as the Scripture has said, "Out of his heart will flow rivers of living water"'" (John 7:37-38).

Consider also that, in this case, Jesus was talking to the teacher of Israel who knew the Old Testament. Surely Nicodemus was familiar with the promise in Ezekiel where God said, "I will take you from the nations and gather you from all the countries and bring you into your own land. I will sprinkle clean water on you, and you shall be clean from all your uncleannesses, and from all your idols I will cleanse you. And I will give you a new heart, and a new spirit I will put within you. And I will remove the heart of stone from your flesh and give you a heart of flesh. And I will put my Spirit within you, and cause you to walk in my statutes and be careful to obey my rules" (Ezekiel 36:24-27). This was the great promise of salvation. It is God's promise of the new birth for the people of Israel. It is accomplished when God sprinkles clean water on sinners through the work of the Holy Spirit. But what is that water?

Consider the cleansing nature of the Word. David asked, "How can a young man keep his way pure? By guarding it according to your word" (Psalm 119:9). Jesus reminded the disciples, "Already you are clean because of the word that I have spoken to you" (John 15:3). This is exactly what Jesus does for the Church "that he might sanctify her, having cleansed her by the washing of water with the word" (Ephesians 5:26). The Word of God is the water that the Holy Spirit uses to wash sinners and make them clean in salvation and sanctification.

Finally, consider the work of the Word in salvation. Peter admonished Christians to love one another from a pure heart "since you have been born again, not of perishable seed but of imperishable, through the living and abiding word of God" (1 Peter 1:23). James clearly demonstrated this truth when he wrote, "Of his own will he [God] brought us forth by the word of truth, that we should be a kind of firstfruits of his creatures" (James 1:18). No wonder Paul would conclude, "So faith comes from hearing, and hearing through the word of Christ" (Romans 10:17). The only way for sinners to enter heaven is to be born all over again as the Holy Spirit changes him with the Word of God.

Jesus explained to the teacher of Israel that when the Holy Spirit does this work others will know it. The work of the Holy Spirit is obvious, but the flesh is unable to control that work (v.8). It is like wind blowing in the trees. Everyone can see the result of the wind rustling the leaves, but no one can make wind show up and do its work at his pleasure. So, too, we can see the results of the Holy Spirit giving new birth to a sinner. But that sinner did not decide when and how the Holy Spirit would work.

## JESUS ALLOWED THE MAN TO REVEAL HIS DEFICIENCIES    (VV.9-10)

Nicodemus could not comprehend Jesus' teaching (v.9). Jesus' words did not make sense to the teacher's human wisdom. So he asked, "How can these things be?" To be honest, all humans should ask the same kind of question. Nicodemus concluded that being born again is impossible as far has human understanding is concerned. The teacher of Israel concluded that getting into heaven was impossible for human wisdom and understanding. He was right. Jesus taught that it is impossible. After the rich young man walked away from the invitation for salvation, the disciples were astonished that Jesus didn't do something to stop him. They wondered who could be saved. "Jesus looked at them and said, 'With man it is impossible, but not with God. For all things are possible with God'" (Mark 10:27).

The rich young man had the same problem Nicodemus had. This brilliant man could not see through the veil of sin. It is a common problem. All sinners suffer from spiritual blindness and, therefore, all sinners live in a sphere of spiritual darkness. God uses His Word to penetrate the darkness. God the Son was carefully, clearly, unfolding the eternal principles of salvation so that the teacher could realize how humanly impossible it is for a sinner to save himself. The teacher was honest and declared in frustration, "How can these things be?"

Jesus kindly, but plainly, pointed out the man's deficiency (v.10). Probably the world thought a guy like Nicodemus would not have deficiencies.

After all, as Jesus said, this man was the teacher in Israel. That means that Nicodemus was one of the most significant teachers of God's Scripture in Israel. Be that as it may, he did not know the mystery of eternal life. He was like many people who study the Bible for a lifetime and die without coming to grips with this wonderful truth. Church buildings around the world are overflowing with myriads of intelligent people who hope to earn their way into heaven by their works. They are just like Nicodemus.

The problem was that the man could not grasp the truth. Therefore, Jesus helped the man realize that he did not understand. He did not compute. His wisdom could not comprehend. He could not put the pieces of the puzzle together. Mark used this same Greek word a couple of times in ways that sheds understanding on what a sinner faces when he tries to grasp the reality of God's plan of salvation. For example, after Jesus taught the parable of the Tenants, the religious leaders (some of Nicodemus' peers) were furious. "And they were seeking to arrest him but feared the people, for they perceived that he had told the parable against them. So they left him and went away" (Mark 12:12). They saw the connection. They understood the parable, and it made perfect sense that they were the target. But Nicodemus could not come to the same obvious conclusions regarding new birth.

In the lesson of the fig tree Jesus taught, "From the fig tree learn its lesson: as soon as its branch becomes tender and puts out its leaves, you know that summer is near" (Mark 13:28). The disciples knew from experience that blossoming fig trees mean summer is coming. They fully expected a certain response based on what they had experienced in the past. But Nicodemus, being limited by human wisdom and experience, could not grasp the truth of the new birth.

This is why human wisdom creates man-made methods for being born again. Ask the professor of eternal life, "How were you born again?" and you are likely to hear things like: "I turned over a new leaf." "I started going to church." "I just decided it was time to get right with my Maker." "I heard a story at camp that scared me, and not wanting to go to hell, I walked the aisle and signed the card." That is the kind of thing Nicodemus would have to say.

The person who is truly born again might answer such a question (i.e. "How were you born again?") with an explanation similar to the confidence Philip Doddridge expressed in the song, Oh Happy Day. He wrote:

O happy day, that fixed my choice
On Thee, my Savior and my God!
Well may this glowing heart rejoice,
And tell its raptures all abroad.
'Tis done: the great transaction's done!
I am the Lord's and He is mine;
He drew me, and I followed on;
Charmed to confess the voice divine.

Or the true Christian might respond with the confident assurance expressed by John Newton in the famous song, Amazing Grace:

Amazing grace! How sweet the sound
That saved a wretch like me!
I once was lost, but now am found;
Was blind, but now I see.
'Twas grace that taught my heart to fear,
And grace my fears relieved;
How precious did that grace appear
The hour I first believed!

The person who is truly born again knows that God literally changed him through the miracle of the new birth. Can he explain it in terms of human wisdom? No. If he could explain it, it would cease to be a miracle. The wonderful nature of miracles is that they are God's work. God does His miracle of the new birth as the Holy Spirit applies His Word to sinners in need of salvation.

# 24

# THE SON OF MAN MUST BE LIFTED UP

## JOHN 3:11-15

God did a wonderful thing through Paul and Silas while they were visiting in the city of Philippi almost 2,000 years ago. A girl possessed by a demon pestered those evangelists until finally, through God's power, Paul released the poor girl from the demon's power. This angered her owners who had made much money from her supernatural, demonic powers. The charlatans rose up in unity and forced the town officials to throw Paul and Silas in jail.

One cannot say for certain how long it took for the jail keeper to figure out that he had a couple of religious fanatics in the house that night. But at some point, he drew a conclusion about these two guys who were singing hymns to God. That is why, when God sent an earthquake to destroy the prison, the jailer responded immediately with the question of eternity. He asked the evangelists, "What must I do to be saved?" (Acts 16:30).

The jail keeper's question is one that has, no doubt, been repeated millions of times. This is probably a question that lingers just below the surface in almost everyone's mind. Common sense tells sinners that they are sinners because they have offended the holy God, their Creator. Human wisdom also tells them that they need to do something in order to cover the offense and make friends with their Maker before they die. The big question is, "What?" What must a sinner do to be saved?

The answers to that question are as many as the religions that mankind has invented throughout history. An almost universal consensus is that sinners must do something religious in order to appease the angry Creator. "Something religious" can range from going to church on Sunday to making a once-in-a-lifetime pilgrimage to Mecca. Between those examples of human effort lies a quagmire of requirements and expectations.

Nicodemus was one of those religious kind of guys who wanted to go to heaven so much that he was willing to do whatever it took to get there. He was a Pharisee, the epitome of a law keeper. He was a member of the Sanhedrin, the body of rulers over Judaism. Certainly he had studied God's law for many years and probably had committed to memory many of the hundreds of man-made laws that explained how people should keep God's law. He was a man in the know. And yet this man came to Jesus with the same question on his heart that the Philippian jailer expressed. "What must I do to gain eternal life?"

Jesus knew Nicodemus' deepest thoughts and gave the teacher his answer before he even asked the question by telling him that he must be born again. The man was confused. What did Jesus mean by, "You must be born again"? Right away the intelligent man wondered how God could make being born again a "must" when he could not even understand the idea, much less do it. That was the point. This law keeping, proud, self-confident sinner needed to learn that what sinners "must do" is trust God. It seems too easy. But that is precisely what Jesus taught. When the world asks God, "What must I do to be saved?," God tells them, "Believe Me." Believe Me when I say that the Son of Man must be lifted up.

This idea really confused the teacher of Israel. This also explains why the man walked away from this conversation with Jesus unsaved. It appears in later references to Nicodemus that he eventually trusted Jesus Christ. However, after this conversation, he walked away no doubt discouraged because he was confused about what he must do. The answer is still astonishingly simple. What a sinner must do to be saved is believe that Jesus Christ, God the Son, did what God planned He must do. That is it!

## SINNERS DO NOT GRASP HEAVENLY TEACHING (VV.11-12)

Having laid down the principle of the new birth, Jesus continued to teach the teacher and uncovered his unbelief (v.11). The proposition that he was an unbeliever must have shocked Nicodemus because he was quite certain that he knew Jesus. At the opening of the conversation, Nicodemus, speaking on behalf of the Sanhedrin, confessed, "We know that you are a teacher come from God" (v.2). This statement implies that he and the rest of the religious rulers possessed a certain amount of knowledge about God. They must have been confident in their knowledge that God is the almighty, powerful, superintendent of the universe in order to connect Jesus' works with God. They had to admit that Jesus did signs and wonders. How did He do those things? Obviously, God the almighty Creator must have sent this special prophet/teacher/miracle worker into the world.

Who would know these things better than the spiritual leaders? The Sanhedrin was the ruling and teaching religious body in Israel. If anyone should understand God it would be those men who devoted their lives to knowing the law of God, interpreting it, and applying it to life.

Second, to conclude unequivocally that Jesus came from God also implies a full knowledge of Jesus. They must have concluded that He was more than a carpenter, the son of Joseph in Nazareth. They knew from experience that Jesus was a brilliant teacher who did miracles. Therefore, they had no other recourse than to conclude that God Himself must have empowered this special teacher.

By his confident assertion, Nicodemus illustrated the confidence of many sinners. Most people have at least some knowledge of Jesus. They can say with a certain amount of assurance, "We know that Jesus was a good man." Or they might affirm, "We know that He was a great teacher." Surely it is a well-known fact that Jesus of Nazareth was kind and loving. That He did miracles is also a well established fact. The world generally agrees with these conclusions about Jesus. So, too, with great confidence Nicodemus opened his

conversation with God the Son by declaring what he thought he understood. One of the major themes of this story is: "What human wisdom cannot comprehend about God's work through Jesus of Nazareth." Nicodemus might have been confident that he and his co-workers possessed a good understanding of who Jesus was. But he and they were wrong.

Jesus talked about things Nicodemus and his friends could not even comprehend. He explained the miracle of the new birth which completely escaped Nicodemus' understanding. Jesus explained why Nicodemus and his friends didn't really know Him. He said, "We speak what we know and bear witness to what we have seen, but you people do not receive our testimony" (v.11). The plural personal pronouns are significant. "We" refers to the Godhead. God the Son spoke what He knew from being in heaven with God the Father and Spirit. He explained the same truth to nay-sayers at the Feast of Booths. The complainers wondered how Jesus taught with such authority. "So Jesus answered them, 'My teaching is not mine, but his who sent me'" (John 7:16). Jesus simply taught what He knew in heaven where He lives for eternity with God the Father and God the Holy Spirit.

Likewise, Jesus declared, "We speak what we know," because God the Father speaks through God the Son. The writer to the Hebrew believers reminded them, "Long ago, at many times and in many ways, God spoke to our fathers by the prophets, but in these last days he has spoken to us by his Son, whom he appointed the heir of all things, through whom also he created the world" (Hebrews 1:1-2). God the Father is part of "We."

God the Spirit also speaks the Word of God. A couple of years after this conversation with Nicodemus, Jesus promised the disciples, "When the Spirit of truth comes, he will guide you into all the truth, for he will not speak on his own authority, but whatever he hears he will speak, and he will declare to you the things that are to come" (John 16:13). God the Father, God the Son, and God the Holy Spirit all speak the same message—the message they know. God the Father, Son, and Holy Spirit all testify to the same truth. The Godhead is eyewitness to God's plan. The Trinity knows and understands God's eternal plan of salvation.

"We" stands in contrast to "you." When Jesus said, "We speak ... but you do not receive our testimony," He referred to Nicodemus and his fellow Sanhedrin members. They did not receive God's message. This is the root to the whole problem. This is the problem. It is not that Nic and the Sanhedrin were unaware of God's person, nature or message. They had benefitted from God's general revelation of Himself just like the rest of the world has. God reveals Himself in nature, conscience, and the Bible so that everyone is without excuse. Beyond that revelation is the fact that Jesus taught about God's person, character, and gospel on many occasions. They have heard and know, but they choose not to believe what Jesus said.

Almost everyone in the greater Greenville, S.C. area knows something about God, something about Jesus. It is not that they are perishing for lack of knowledge. They perish because they will not believe what they have heard. Many of them are as religious as Nicodemus and his cohorts. They attend church regularly, hear sermons regularly, and read their Bible regularly. But they refuse to believe the simplicity of the gospel and seek to establish their own plan for salvation.

Jesus explained that Nicodemus could not grasp heavenly teaching (v.12). Since he failed to grasp earthly truths, how could he expect to understand heavenly truths? What earthly truth did Jesus refer to? Jesus taught earthly things like the need for new birth. While that is a miracle from heaven, it has to do with real people living in sin on earth. The activity of new birth takes place in bodies on earth. Nicodemus could not understand the concept. Furthermore, he could not grasp Jesus' illustration of the Spirit's work in new birth being like wind that blows on earth.

In fact, all of Jesus' parables were earthly stories. But typically the religious leaders seldom understood what Jesus taught just like Nicodemus failed to understand. However, while the brilliant, educated, religious leaders wandered in the darkness, the disciples understood exactly what Jesus meant by His teaching. At times, they even wondered why Jesus taught with parables. He explained to them, "To you it has been given to know the secrets of the kingdom of heaven, but to them it has not been given" (Matthew 13:11). In other words, it is God's plan to hide simple truth from self-sufficient people who think they can be reconciled with God on their own terms. As a result, sinners do not understand that Jesus' teaching explains Kingdom truths. They think He taught people how to be nice to people.

Because normal sinners like Nicodemus fail to grasp Christ's earthly teaching, how do they think they would be able to understand heavenly teaching. Jesus informed the teacher of Israel that he would also fail to grasp heavenly truths. Nicodemus and friends would never grasp the secrets of heaven. That explains why reasonably intelligent people refuse to believe that God gives sinners the ability to understand truth about God and His plan. It is a heavenly mystery. They do not get it. They cannot get it. Jesus explained to Nicodemus that he would not understand heavenly teaching and then proceeded to illustrate His point by teaching a couple of significant heavenly truths.

### Sinners Must Believe That God Had to be Lifted Up (vv.13-15)

The first heavenly lesson Jesus taught is that He is God (v.13). He couched this truth in the affirmation that no one has gone to heaven and come back to report about what they saw and heard. It is true that in the Old Testament some saints had gone to heaven. It seems that men like Enoch and Elijah went directly to heaven without dying. But they did not come back and report. Jesus knew that in the coming days some people would come back from the dead. For example, just before the crucifixion, He raised Lazarus from the dead. Apparently, Lazarus had been in heaven for four days. Also, some of the tombs of Old Testament saints opened at the crucifixion (Matthew 27:52). Paul would be caught up to heaven (2 Corinthians 12:2). But no one came back and told about the heavenly things they had heard or seen. Paul explained that this was because "he heard things that cannot be told, which man may not utter" (2 Corinthians 12:4).

Jesus alone came from heaven and declared the message of heaven. He taught Nicodemus the heavenly truth that the "Son of Man" is from heaven. This title is a significant reference to Messiah and well known to the religious teachers of Israel. Many years before Jesus, Daniel used the title "Son of Man" to describe the promised Messiah. He wrote, "I saw in the night visions, and behold, with the clouds of heaven there came one like a son of man, and he came to the Ancient of Days and was presented before him. And to him was given dominion and glory and a kingdom, that all peoples, nations, and languages should serve him; his dominion is an everlasting dominion, which shall not pass away, and his kingdom one that shall not be destroyed" (Daniel 7:13-14).

Religious leaders who knew the writings of the Prophets were looking for this deliverer—the Messiah. Nicodemus was one of them. Jesus spoke about a Deliverer for whom Nicodemus was looking. Religious sinners are still expecting "Jesus" to come again. They talk about His return glibly or almost mythically. But who is He? Who is the Son of Man? Who is the promised Deliverer?

The Son of Man is in heaven. In the Greek text, Jesus started this sentence: "But no one has ascended into heaven except . . . .the Son of Man" He laid down a contrast. No person can tell the absolute truth about heaven, but He who is by nature in heaven declares heavenly truths. He who is by nature in heaven must be God! Only God or His spirit ministers descend from heaven.

This is the rock in the river of life upon which many religious people get stuck. The religious leaders in Nic's day refused to believe that Jesus is God. Religious leaders still refuse to believe it. Consider for example this statement from the Koran, from a chapter called The Cattle [6.101] "Wonderful Originator of the heavens and the earth! How could He have a son when He has no consort, and He (Himself) created everything, and He is the Knower of all things." Devout Muslims reveal that religious leaders would still kill Jesus for claiming that He is God because they cannot understand heavenly teaching.

The second heavenly lesson Jesus taught Nicodemus is that God must be killed according to the curse (vv.14-15). This is more bazaar than the fact that Jesus of Nazareth is God of heaven! Bazaar to human wisdom or not, Jesus taught that the Son of Man must be lifted up like Moses' serpent (v.14). On the surface, Nicodemus agreed with this fact. He fully expected the Son of Man to be lifted up because the Greek verb can mean exalted. Jewish leaders fully expected God's Messiah to come to earth, be mighty (exalted) and deliver Israel. They knew that Isaiah had promised, "Behold, my servant shall act wisely; he shall be high and lifted up, and shall be exalted" (Isaiah 52:13).

However, in this truth Jesus promised that He, who claimed to be equal with God, would be lifted up like Moses lifted up the serpent in the wilderness. It was a story Nicodemus knew well (Numbers 21:4-9). One time while Moses was leading the wanderers in the wilderness, the people sinned. As judgment, God sent serpents into the camp that bit the people and caused them to die. The people cried to God for help. God told Moses to make a brass serpent and raise it up on a pole. God promised that everyone who looked at the serpent would live. The serpent was a figure of God's judgement against sin which He sent through serpents. The only people who were cured from sin's curse were those who believed God enough to look. That was it. No incantations, no medicine, no salves, no dancing or offering sacrifices. Just look and live!

Now Jesus taught the teacher in Israel that He would be lifted up in the same manner. He referred to His crucifixion on the cross which was a shameful death. God had already established that anyone who died on a tree was cursed (Deuteronomy 21:23). Nicodemus, the Old Testament scholar, knew that. So, in the crucifixion, Jesus Christ, God in the flesh, took the curse of all sin upon Himself when He was lifted up on the cross.

Sinners naturally cannot believe such a story. Again the Koran illustrates how bazaar human wisdom thinks truth is. In a chapter titled The Women [4.157] the text says, "And their saying: Surely we have killed the Messiah, Isa son of Marium, the apostle of Allah; and they did not kill him nor did they crucify him, but it appeared to them so (like Isa) and most surely those who differ therein are only in a doubt about it; they have no knowledge respecting it, but only follow a conjecture, and they killed him not for sure." Mohammed just dismissed out of hand the whole story of Jesus' crucifixion because sinners do not understand heavenly teaching.

Sinners like Nicodemus (religion not withstanding) cannot, will not believe heavenly teaching. However, the person who believes God has eternal life (v.15). The promise is for every sinner who places his complete trust in Jesus. It is not an invitation to believe certain facts about Jesus of Nazareth. Pharisees did that. It is an invitation to believe who He is, what He is, what He did. It is the command to fully trust that there is nothing for you to do but believe Him.

The promise is life of an eternal quality. God did not promise just never ending life. People in hell have that! Rather God promises life of the quality and character of the eternal God's life. Sinners like Nicodemus find this hard to believe. Indeed, they will not believe it. They prefer to focus on "What must I do?" The idea of looking at God the Son suffering with the curse of sin on Him on the cross, and believing, is absurd. If sinners had been Israelites in the desert with Moses, they would have died. Looking at the lifted up serpent did not require enough. Today, looking at the exalted Servant does not require enough. Multitudes of sinners perish for eternity because they will not look on the Son of Man who is lifted up and believe what He said about Himself. But many have believed. Many have looked at Christ's sacrifice and instead of trying to explain just accepted it with gratitude. The invitation to "look and live" is so simple. It is too simple for proud human wisdom to humble itself. But if you will look and believe, you too will have God-like life forever.

# 25

# GOD LOVED
# THE WORLD

JOHN 3:16-21

A young man meets an attractive young woman and they fall in love. It happens all the time. Over a period of time they get to know each other better and better, until one day he proposes to her and they get married. In their marriage the man's love grows deeper and deeper so that what he once thought was love now seems like a Junior High crush. Then one day, the man learns the shocking news that his wife, whom he loves so deeply, is seeing another man. Of course his heart is broken, and he confronts his wife. He lays down the ultimatum that this wrong relationship must cease immediately or there will be serious consequences. The wife responds, "I thought you said you love me." "I do love you," the husband assures her. "Then if you love me, why don't you let me do what I want to do?" the unreasonable wife wonders.

The wife's ridiculous argument is self-evident. It is because her husband loves her that he must insist on her loyalty in return. But this world has a perverted view of love. The standard of love in the world is complete self-love. Therefore, people interpret love in light of what they gain or how they feel.

That might help explain why the world concludes that since God is love, He will save everyone in the world from eternal punishment. Many people truly do not think that a loving God would ever be so cruel as to punish someone. This strange idea has been taught in seminaries in Europe and America for a hundred years. After three or four generations of such teaching, preachers have been brainwashed with error. Therefore, it is not surprising that a large portion of church-going people (which should never be confused with Christians) believe that a loving God will not condemn normal people to hell. Multitudes of people believe that if there is a hell, God has reserved it for people like Hitler, Saddam Hussein, their cantankerous neighbor, their ex-wife, or other such wicked and vile people. Surely, they think, God would not send nice people like Hollywood movie stars to hell.

John 3:16 is probably one of the most famous verses in the Bible. It ought to be. It lays out in simple, easy-to-understand language how incredible God's love is for the world. It presents to a world of needy sinners the solution to their sin problem. It promises everlasting life to every person who trusts God's promise. It is the consummate invitation. What more can one say about it? If this verse was the only communication the world had from God, it would be the sufficient invitation for salvation.

But while it is easy, yea pleasant, to focus on the wonderfully positive message of God's love, one must never forget that because God loves, He must set boundaries. Since it is true that the person who trusts God inherits eternal life, it must also be true that the person who refuses to trust God does not inherit eternal life. What does it mean to "not inherit eternal life"? Jesus explained to Nicodemus, the teacher in Israel, that refusal to trust God's promise does most certainly result in condemnation. Yes, the same God who loves supremely must punish supremely.

Nicodemus wrongly assumed that there must be some kind of work he could do in order to win salvation from God. Jesus taught him that there was nothing he could do. Jesus taught that sinners must be born again. Jesus taught that sinners can only be born again because God the Son must be raised up on a cross of condemnation for sin. The thought of God Himself dying a shameful death to pay the penalty for sin is atrocious to human wisdom. Human wisdom, of its own accord, cannot accept such an idea. Indeed, it will not! But whoever believes God's promise and plan will receive everlasting life. It is a marvelous plan and a marvelous promise. It is the product of God's love. Human wisdom will never accept it, but born again people believe the story, embrace the story, tell the story, and are willing to die for the story. The story of God's love displayed in Jesus of Nazareth is the greatest story ever told. It is also the most absurd story ever invented as far as unbelievers are concerned. Nevertheless, those who trust God's plan and work will live with Him forever and those who reject it will be condemned by God forever. That is the love of God.

## THE GREAT PROMISE (vv.16-18A)

God loves the world so much that He gave His Son (vv.16-17). There has never been a more encouraging, positive statement given to the human race. God gave His Son for us. More than that, Jesus explained to the teacher of Israel that God gave His unique Son (v.16). What kind of impact did that statement have on Nicodemus? What kind of impact does it have on people who hear it today? What kind of impact does it have on you?

God gave the Son. God is the Creator of all things who rightly expects His creation to honor Him. He is the holy and perfectly sinless God who is rightly offended by the creature's sin against Him. He is the righteous and sovereign God who rightly could condemn every person born to hell forever. But He does not. Instead, the Great Creator, Holy God, and Eternal Judge loved the world so much that He gave the ultimate gift.

What kind of love does God have that makes Him so compassionate and generous? His love must be unlike human love. Indeed, God's love eclipses human romance, infatuation, and lust so much that there is no comparison. God's love is sacrificial and intentional love for the benefit of the recipient. Unlike the world's love, God's love is not aimed at self fulfillment. It is love that was fixed in the past according to the verb tense and voice. God did not decide to start loving the human race because we, the creation, did something that caused Him to favor us. We are incapable of doing such a thing. Nor did God decide to love the world because we were so sorry that we needed His help. It is true that the whole lot of the human race are hopelessly sorry rascals. But that is not why God loves us. God loves because God is love. He is the essence and definition of love. Therefore, God has always loved.

More amazing than the fact of God's love is the object of His love. Jesus told the teacher of Israel that God loved the world. That does not mean that the inanimate objects of the planet were the focus of God's love, though it is true that He loves all of His creation. Rather in this case, the people who make up the world are the objects of God's love. Which people? Is it that God loves people who trust Him and hates people who don't trust Him? No. God loves the people and desires the very best for everyone. Paul expressed this wonderful truth by saying, "In Christ God was reconciling the world to himself, not counting their trespasses against them, and entrusting to us the message of reconciliation" (2 Cor. 5:19).

Only a God who is the very meaning of love could reconcile the world to Himself and refuse to take into account their trespasses against Him.

God's love is broader and deeper than human knowledge can comprehend. Jesus told Nicodemus that God so loved the world. He meant, "God loved like this . . ." God loved to an extreme. In truth one must admit that any love at all for offending, sinful, enemies is astonishing. Paul declared the immeasurable love of God when he wrote, "For if while we were enemies we were reconciled to God by the death of his Son, much more, now that we are reconciled, shall we be saved by his life" (Romans 5:10). He reminded Christians in Colassae, "You, who once were alienated and hostile in mind, doing evil deeds, he has now reconciled in his body of flesh by his death, in order to present you holy and blameless and above reproach before him" (Col. 1:21-22). To love the enemy and initiate reconciliation for him is extreme love.

In fact the measure of God's love is incomprehensible. We really cannot explain the "so" of God's love. It looks like this: "For our sake he made him to be sin who knew no sin, so that in him we might become the righteousness of God" (2 Cor. 5:21). No wonder the chief of sinners now redeemed cries out, "Thanks be to God for his inexpressible gift!" (2 Cor. 9:15). God loves the world soooooo much.

Jesus explained that God loves the world so much that He gave His unique Son. False religions stumble over the idea of God's son. They err to picture the Son in human terms—a son born through normal processes. Jesus referred to Himself as the monogeneis, the "one of a kind born." The word speaks of the only born one, the single one of its kind, the unique one. It is a word that would be used to describe Abraham's son Isaac as opposed to Abraham's son Ishmael. They were both Abraham's sons. But Isaac was the unique one. He alone was the one God promised and gave.

God also "gave" His own unique Son. It is interesting that the word for gave is also used to describe giving a sacrifice or an offering. God's gift of His unique Son is the demonstration of His immeasurable love. In giving God the Son, God gave Himself to the world. There is no greater expression of love than a man laying down His life for His friends. How much greater that He would lay down His life for His enemies?

God gave His Son to sinners like one would give an offering, and, at the same time, He sent His Son to save (v.17). Jesus told Nicodemus that God did not send Christ to condemn the world. There will be a day in the future when Jesus Christ will be the judge of every sinner, and He will condemn each sinner to hell. Jesus taught this fact when He told the fault-finding, Jewish leaders who wanted to kill Him, "The Father judges no one, but has given all judgment to the Son, that all may honor the Son, just as they honor the Father. Whoever does not honor the Son does not honor the Father who sent him" (John 5:22-23). Probably the leaders were not very happy to hear Jesus lay claim to that authority. He has that authority. He is the eternal Judge to whom everyone must give an answer.

But the time for final judgement is not yet. Rather God sent Christ that the world might be saved through Him. God, who determined in His infinite grace and wisdom to give the unique Son, sent Him on a mission. The verb Jesus used here gives us the English word apostle. It speaks of an authority sending someone as a delegate. Or the word means to send with a purpose, to send on a mission. The very nature of Jesus Christ is "the sent one." God the Father sent Him to save sinners. He did not send Christ to earth just to teach—though He was a great teacher. He did not send Him just to do miracles—though He was a great miracle worker. He did not send Him just to set an example—though His example is impeccable. Nor did God send the Son just to die. He sent God the Son to earth to die for a reason. God sent the Second Person of the Godhead on purpose.

The work of God is amazing. The promise connected with the work is even more amazing. Jesus taught Nicodemus that whoever believes God is not condemned (vv.16b, 18a). The important issue here is belief. Belief is full reliance and trust. To believe is to be convinced, to put full and active trust in something, someone, or some truth. Both of the times Jesus used this word (v.16b, 18a), He stated it in a verb form that describes a character of life. To believe something is to live it. If you don't live it, you don't believe it.

The object of belief is Jesus Himself. Jesus told Nicodemus that the real need is for sinners to put full and active trust in Jesus Christ. That means that people like the teacher of Israel need to be fully convinced that Jesus is who He said He is. He said that He was God in the flesh. It means that people need to be fully convinced that Jesus did what He said He did. He said that He died to provide the covering for sins. In other words, the person who really believes confesses that he or she has sinned because that is why Jesus died. The person who believes admits that his or her sin is an offense to God. The person who truly believes acknowledges that he or she can do nothing to cover that sin. The person who truly believes fully receives Christ's sacrifice as the offering for his or her sin.

Jesus said that the result of true belief is eternal life. It is true that eternal life is life that lasts forever. Everlasting life would be a tragic thought if it is a life of the quality that we have in this present world. But eternal life is more than everlasting life. It is life like the eternal God. It is life of God's quality that lasts forever. That is good.

## THE SAD REALITY (vv.18b-21)

Jesus assured Nicodemus that everyone who really trusts Christ will receive the fulfilled promise of eternal life. However, the other side of that coin is that everyone who does not believe is already condemned (v.18b). Belief in the unique Son is the critical issue again. Belief alone does not necessarily qualify. Most people have faith of some kind. There have been and still are millions of people who trust a church organization. Others blindly trust a religious organization's opinion about the Bible or even about Christ. Most people are not trusting in Christ. That is how Jesus described these people. It is their characteristic of living. They are not known as people who are trusting Christ every day. Do they have faith? Yes. However their faith is rooted in the fact that they trust their ability to believe. They might even admit that they "hope." But hoping to make it into heaven is not the same as trusting Christ alone for eternal life.

Again the unique Son of God is the object. To believe that Jesus simply existed will get the sinner condemnation, not eternal life. Most people believe that Jesus was a good man who set a good example. At the same time, most people refuse to believe that Jesus of Nazareth was God and that He alone provided the only means for salvation. The vast majority of people who have ever lived cannot—will not— fully trust this truth. It is too unbelievable to them. That is why Jesus warned people to, "Enter by the narrow gate. For the gate is wide and the way is easy that leads to destruction, and those who enter by it are many. For the gate is narrow and the way is hard that leads to life, and those who find it are few" (Matthew 7:13-14). The terms many and few are pregnant with meaning when one places the names of people they know in the categories.

Jesus explained to Nicodemus that He was God's Son, whom God sent to earth to provide salvation, because God loves the world. He also said that anyone who does not believe this truth is condemned already. Having laid that groundwork, Jesus succinctly said, "This is the judgment" (vv.19-21): Now Jesus laid out to Nicodemus the sad but certain truth of eternal judgment.

People naturally prefer darkness to light (vv.19-20). What makes this truth so ugly is the fact that the Light has come into the world (v.19). Where is it? Jesus is the Light. John began this Gospel account by saying, "In [Jesus Christ] was life, and the life was the light of men. The light shines in the darkness, and the darkness has not overcome it" (John 1:4-5).

Jesus agreed with John's conclusion and declared the same truth often. At the feast of booths Jesus told the people, "I am the light of the world. Whoever follows me will not walk in darkness, but will have the light of life" (John 8:12). He also declared, "I have come into the world as light, so that whoever believes in me may not remain in darkness" (John 12:46). He is the light because He is the perfect declaration and illustration of God's message to the sinful world. The light is God's Word. God speaks through Jesus Christ.

> Long ago, at many times and in many ways, God spoke to our fathers by the prophets, but in these last days he has spoken to us by his Son, whom he appointed the heir of all things, through whom also he created the world. He is the radiance of the glory of God and the exact imprint of his nature, and he upholds the universe by the word of his power. After making purification for sins, he sat down at the right hand of the Majesty on high (Hebrews 1:1-3).

God's declaration of light to the dark world is complete. The work is finished. The light has come. As a result, God's message through Christ is clear. John concluded, "This is the message we have heard from him and proclaim to you, that God is light, and in him is no darkness at all" (1 John 1:5).

But the sad truth is that in spite of the light of Christ, people love the darkness (vv.19-20). Every person does evil because of the sin nature. They know their deeds do not measure up to God's standard. They fear having God's standard (light) reveal their evil deeds. Therefore people avoid the light. They do not like God's Word. They do not like the preachers of God's Word. They twist the light of God's Word in an attempt to justify their sins. There has been and continues to be an ongoing warfare against the light (the Light). Societies deny the authority of God's Word.

Societies deny the application of God's Word and make laws prohibiting it. Scholars deny the truth about Christ. Every person by nature presses down this truth and refuses to embrace it. Nicodemus was no different. They are already condemned.

The good news is that people who do truth love light (v.21). What kind of person does truth? Christians. Born again people do truth. Christians are people who have come to the Light. Why does a person do that? Does he or she suddenly decide that light is better than darkness? No. God enlightened us, because we naturally prefer darkness. That is what Paul meant when he wrote, "For God, who said, 'Let light shine out of darkness,' has shone in our hearts to give the light of the knowledge of the glory of God in the face of Jesus Christ" (2 Corinthians 4:6).

Because God enlightened true believers, we brought our works to the Light and confessed them for what they are. True believers put full trust in Christ alone to cover their offenses with His blood. As a result of that faith, Christians continue to live in that light. As Paul put it, "At one time you were darkness, but now you are light in the Lord. Walk as children of light" (Ephesians 5:8). Rather then trying to justify their sins really born again people confess them. Christians are obviously different than the world. Nicodemus was not. Are you?

Jesus told Nicodemus that he must be born again. The very concept shook Nicodemus. He could not grasp it. Jesus explained that new birth comes from God. He explained that He was God in the flesh. He explained that the reason He was on earth was because God loves the world. He explained that He must die in order to provide the sacrifice for sin, like Moses' serpent on a pole. He explained that people naturally avoid the light of such teaching because it exposes their sins. But Jesus also explained that everyone who comes to the light lives uniquely. People who have eternal life embrace the light of God's Word. They and they alone understand God's love.

# 26

# "SIR, GIVE ME THIS WATER"

## JOHN 4:1-26

According to Acts 8:1, in the early days of the Church, a great persecution arose when Saul of Tarsus began to imprison and even kill the followers of Christ. As a result, the Christians in Jerusalem were scattered. They moved all over the Roman Empire, and as the went, they proclaimed Christ, preaching the Word. Would twenty-first century Christians respond the same way. Sadly, the norm for American Christians who face persecution would probably be to attempt to represent Christ silently so that they would not have to lose their homes and jobs and, as a result, have to move.

Modern Christians are notorious for wanting to stay in their comfort zones. As a whole, Christians in this culture try to avoid disruptions and discomforts at all costs. Who am I to talk? I minister in Greenville, the safest, most comfortable place in the world to be a pastor—according to some folks. Indeed, there are times when I wonder what it would be like to minister in the real world among pagans and false prophets. I personally make efforts to get among the unsaved people, even though it sometimes puts me in uncomfortable situations, because that is what Jesus did. Jesus never did much evangelistic work in Jerusalem. Most of His evangelism was in Galilee and the outlying regions. In Jerusalem, much of Jesus' ministry was confrontational and corrective.

One thing the is quite certain about Jesus' way of spreading the gospel is that He did not practice a "one size fits all" kind of evangelism. He met people where they were and dealt with them according to their particular needs. He could do that with perfect accuracy because He is God.

Nicodemus was a ruler of the Jews, a Pharisee, one of the strictest of the religious people. In contrast, the woman from Sychar was notoriously sinful. Nicodemus purposely came to meet with Jesus at night. The Samaritan woman did not plan to meet Jesus at all. But Jesus planned to meet with her. She would have called it an accident. Jesus knew that it was divinely arranged. Nicodemus wondered how he could enter the kingdom of God. That was the furthest thought from the woman's mind. Jesus responded to Nicodemus by laying out some pretty deep truths that one would have expected the teacher of Israel to understand (3:10-12). In His conversation with the woman at the well, Jesus also laid out a deep truth about living water. But then Jesus drove quickly to the practical matters of sin in her life.

Different hearts require different methods and different plans for presenting the gospel. While it is very important to have a desire to share the gospel, it is also important not to mistakenly think that the same testimony or same Roman's Road approach will be effective for everyone. It is imperative that Christians learn from Christ how to tailor the gospel invitation to the particular circumstances or needs of the person. Christ's representatives need to offer God's great invitation of salvation in a way that is fitting for the individual.

## PARTICULAR CIRCUMSTANCES PRECEDED JESUS' MEETING WITH THE SAMARITAN WOMAN (vv.1-6).

Jesus left Judea in order to go through Samaria (vv.1-5). John wrote that it was necessary for Him to leave Jerusalem (vv.1-3). Why? What happened in Jerusalem that made it necessary for Him to leave? And why did He need to go through Samaria of all places when He left?

Word was circulating about Jesus' popularity (v.1). Early in Jesus' ministry it became obvious that the people were astonished by His miracles. Why wouldn't they be? He was doing some pretty amazing things. More than that, the people were also amazed by His teaching. They concluded that this Jesus from Nazareth taught with authority, unlike the scribes who were normally considered to be the official teachers of the Israelites. Because of His amazing works and His authoritative teaching, Jesus gathered quite a following. Many people were identifying with His ministry through baptism.

Was that not a good thing? No, that was not a good thing. At this point in ministry, the attention would be detrimental. Probably Jesus had already cleansed the temple the first time (John 2:13-22) which stirred the religious leaders' ire. According to John's account in this passage, the Pharisees were aware of Jesus' following and were skeptical of His work. Action from the religious leaders to silence Jesus would be almost certain. One could count on it coming very soon. That was the problem. When the religious rulers silenced Jesus, it would be the grand culmination of His ministry on earth. He came to die on the cross to atone for sinners' sins. It was not yet the time for that action in God's plan. As Jesus explained to the people at the wedding some weeks earlier, His hour was not yet come (2:4).

Therefore, Jesus needed to leave the hot spot of the Jewish capital and go to the more remote, pastoral area of Galilee. That is easy enough to understand. However, John also wrote that it was necessary for Jesus to go through Samaria. Why? He could have taken one of three different routes to the northern region of Galilee.

First, Jesus could have traveled west from Jerusalem to the coast and then turned north into Galilee, traveling briefly through Syria. Second, Jesus could have traveled east from Jerusalem, passed through Jericho, crossed the Jordan River, turned north passing along the foot of the mountains in Perea, traveled past Samaria, and then turned west across the Jordan into Galilee, passing briefly through Decapolis. That was the normal route for devout Jews. It was by far the longest route, requiring at least a three day journey.

Third, the route that Jesus chose to take was the most direct. He chose to travel directly north through the hills, through Samaria, and into Galilee. But no sincere Jew would take this road. Jesus was a Jew. But more than that, He was the Savior who came to seek and to save those who are lost. Therefore, Jesus needed to pass through Samaria. That was an unusual response for a Jew. Why?

Samaria had been the capital city of the ten Tribes making up Israel after Jeroboam led them to break from Rehoboam, the son of Solomon, and king over Judah and Benjamin. Thereafter the two nations were known as Israel and Judah. Israel quickly departed from the true worship and service of God. After many years of rebellion, God allowed the nation of Assyria to overrun them in 720 B.C. and scatter the citizens to other nations (1 Kings 17:24-41). Assyria repopulated the land with Gentiles. Eventually the remaining Jewish people intermarried with the Gentiles, a practice that was unacceptable to devout Jews. Then a Jewish priest combined true worship with pagan worship (2 Kings 17:28-36), an act that was considered an abomination by God and true Jews.

About 130 years after these events, Babylon overran Judah and took the people captive. While they were in captivity, the Jewish people from Judah kept the race pure for the most part. After seventy years, Cyrus, king of Persia, set the people of Judah free and they returned to Jerusalem. Once they were reestablished in the land, the Jews rebuilt the temple and city walls under the leadership of Ezra and Nehemiah. The Samaritans (the mixed race from the remnant of the northern ten tribes) were very angry because the pure Jews would not let them help build the temple. So in response, the Samaritans built their own temple on Mt. Gerizim. The Maccabeans destroyed that temple in 129 B.C. because they considered it to be an abomination to God. Since that time the Samaritans had no place to worship, and they did not have the full Old Testament Scriptures like their counterparts in Judah. They only had the Torah for their Scripture.

One can understand the feelings of animosity between the two groups of people in Jesus' day. That is why no devout Jew would pass through that region on the way to the northern region of pure Judaism. But Jesus is God, and He knew that He had a meeting with a Samaritan woman in Sychar. John MacArthur observed, "He was keeping a divine appointment that He Himself made before the foundation of the world." Jesus taught a very important lesson here. We must submit to God's leading and direction in matters of offering the great invitation. He knows, He arranges, He ordains. He even accomplishes His will in circumstances that seem to be abnormal or even unacceptable to the traditional norm. It is critical for God's people to be in such close fellowship with Him who leads His servants to do His work. We must always be alert to the fact that God puts His messengers in particular places at particular times in order to tell His gospel to particular people. There are no accidents with God!

Jesus arrived outside the city of Sychar and sat down at Jacob's well (v.6). The text says that He was tired and thirsty, which is a good reminder that Jesus was altogether God and also altogether man. Being fully man, He was tested like we are. It was 12:00 noon, the sixth hour. If John would have calculated the event according to Roman time, it would have been 6:00 p.m. when the women of the town would be likely to gather water. However, it is clear from the story that there were no other women at the well. Just Jesus and this one outcast woman who, no doubt, was unaccepted by the others. Therefore, it is better to conclude that John reasoned according to Jewish time which finds Jesus sitting at the well in the heat of the day.

He was tired and thirsty. The journey from Jerusalem had been long. It was about thirty miles from Jerusalem to this spot. That means that this was probably the second day of the journey. He sat down at a well Jacob had dug on property he purchased from Hamor (Genesis 33:19). The well would have been much like any well of that day. In fact, it is quite certain that this well is extant today near the modern city of Nablus. Unfortunately, like many true Biblical sites, it is enclosed by a church at a monastery. The well is 100 feet deep and probably is built over a flowing spring. It is located at the foot of Mount Gerizim about one-half mile south, southwest of ancient Sychar.

While Jesus rested at the well, the disciples had gone into Sychar to buy lunch. Lunch was a necessary evil. Would they buy from people who despised them?

### Jesus Told a Woman Wonderful News (vv.7-15)

This woman showed up at the well, and Jesus asked her for a drink of water (vv.7-9). Twenty-first century Americans would not think that anything about this picture was strange. First century Israelites would. This was a very unusual request (v.7). First, it was a general practice for travelers to carry their own leather water bottle on a cord in order to dip it into a well and get a drink. Why didn't this traveler have a leather water bottle?

Furthermore, this picture was not typical for more serious reasons. A Jew would not ask a Samaritan for a favor—period! Not only that, but generally men did not talk to unfamiliar women. A sincere Jew would not want to be found in the presence of a woman of ill repute (if he knew she was that kind of woman, which Jesus did). Most important, a rabbi's career would be ruined if sincere Jews found him in this circumstance. No wonder the woman was surprised (v.9). She understood that this was an unacceptable situation. She understood that "Jews have no dealings with Samaritans" (v.9b).

But Jesus used the unexpected to open the door for the great invitation of the gospel. He told the woman about living water (vv.10-12). Jesus explained to this woman that living water was a gift from God (v.10). The story reveals that this poor woman did not understand Christ's offer of living water any better than most modern Christians do. Actually "living water" speaks of a fresh running stream as opposed to stagnate water in a cistern. The term referred to fresh, cool, pure water. If there was any "living water" in Jacob's well, it was way at the bottom where the spring fed into the well.

Jesus wasn't talking about H2O. He was telling the spiritually parched woman about eternal life. Readers of the Old Testament might have picked up on Jesus' line of reasoning. God promised in the Old Testament that He would give refreshing, living water. That is the kind of water David thought about when he wrote, "As a deer pants for flowing streams, so pants my soul for you, O God" (Psalm 42:1). It is what he meant when he confidently asserted that the man who is right with God "is like a tree planted by streams of water that yields its fruit in its season, and its leaf does not wither. In all that he does, he prospers" (Psalm 1:3). This is the eternal life God meant when He said through Isaiah, "With joy you will draw water from the wells of salvation" (Isaiah 12:3).

Because the woman's only Scripture was the Torah, she was not aware of these promises. Therefore, Jesus explained that if the woman understood what He meant, she would gladly ask for the gift. That was the problem. She did not perceive the truth. Still the darkness of sin keeps sinners from understanding God's truth. Paul explained. "God, who said, 'Let light shine out of darkness,' has shone in our hearts to give the light of the knowledge of the glory of God in the face of Jesus Christ" (2 Corinthians 4:6). If God does not shine that light into the sinner's heart, the sinner is hopeless.

How sad that this woman heard the wonderful news about God's gift of eternal life, and she didn't ask for it. Why didn't she? The woman thought according to human wisdom (vv.11-12). She countered Jesus' offer with human reason. "You can't offer living water, fresh water, because the well is deep and you have no bucket" (v.11). She remembered that "Jacob, our forefather, gave us water." Did Jesus imply that He was as good as Jacob (v.12)? Jesus didn't argue about forefathers, human ability, or the natural logistics of getting a drink of water from a well that was 100 feet deep. That wasn't the issue!

Instead of reasoning with the woman on human terms, Jesus explained the advantage of THE living water (vv.13-15). He taught her that living water is eternal life (vv.13-14). He explained that the person who drinks of Christ will be satisfied. In fact, satisfaction with Christ is eternally self-perpetuating. But all of this went right over the woman's head. She could not escape human wisdom because she was concerned with only temporal needs (v.15). She desired only physical relief. The important issue in this woman's mind was that if she could get everlasting water, she would not have to travel one-half mile every day to get water from this well. She could not grasp her eternal need, could not understand that her sin separated her from God which left her with unquenchable thirst. Why not?

### Jesus Revealed The Truth (vv.16-26)

In no uncertain terms, Jesus uncovered the woman's real need (vv.16-18). The woman was a sinner (vv.16-18). Out of the blue, Jesus focused the bright light of truth on the woman's problem. For apparently no good reason He said, "Go get your husband." Why did He say that? The woman was trying to conceal her deep need. She tried to hide her sin. Jesus pointed out how much of a sinner she was. In comparison, we remember that Jesus didn't have to tell Nicodemus that he was a sinner—that's why he came to Jesus. Sometimes you must pull the cover back on sin to help a person understand how thirsty he really is. The woman did not deny Jesus' focus on her sin. She faced the fact of her sinful condition with a brief reply (v.17a). She admitted that she did not have a husband, which was another feeble attempt to cover the extent of her sin.

Jesus directed the conversation so that He could reveal the nature of true worship (vv.19-24). The woman tried to deflect attention from her needy condition by confessing that she had figured out that He was a prophet (vv.19-20). She realized that a prophet could tell the truth about her. Since prophets are religious people (like preachers are), she thought it best to talk about religion and the differences between Jews and Samaritans. Did she try to change the subject (v.20)? It appears that this was a calculated attempt to move the discussion away from her sin to traditions of worship. It was the kind of thing God's messengers hear often. When people find out that I am a Baptist preacher, they immediately flee to the fact that they are Methodists, or Presbyterians, or Catholics. Maybe this was the woman's admission that she, like Nicodemus, was looking for an answer to her sinful condition. Maybe not.

Jesus taught the woman that true worship takes place in the heart. The place of worship is not the key (v.21). The nature of worship is. True worship acknowledges God's nature. Since God is true, He must be worshiped in truth (vv.23-24). Since God is spirit, He must be worshiped in spirit. (vv.23-24). Religion is content with external forms. Dead religion is not concerned with God's character because its worship is not about God. However, regeneration creates a new heart that desires to worship God. That is the difference between mere religious worship and the worship that pours from a true Christian's heart. True worship begins with salvation (v.22).

Jesus revealed this woman's only hope (vv.25-26). How strange that this woman would bring up the issue of Messiah. She wondered about Messiah (v.25). Maybe when Jesus mentioned that salvation came through Jews, she remembered hearing about Messiah. Maybe she actually understood that Messiah is the anointed One sent from God. She confessed the belief that Messiah would have the answers. She was right! Finally, it appears that the woman was making headway. Now maybe she could understand truth.

Jesus introduced the woman to Messiah (v.26). How did she respond when Jesus replied to her musings about Messiah by saying, "That's Me! I'm Him!" Why didn't she know that already? He had told her about eternal life, and she didn't get it. He had revealed her deepest secret sins, and she didn't get it. He had explained the nature of true worship, and she didn't get it. Would she finally realize that this One talking to her was her only hope of eternity?

Part of the Christian's duty is to shine the light of Christ on sinners. Help them understand that they are thirsty. Help them understand that Christ offers eternal satisfaction. Help them understand that their sinful life leaves them thirsty. Tell them about God's nature and how He longs for their worship. Introduce them to Christ. Offer the great invitation. God will use His truth to do His work for His glory. Good arguments might change a sinner's mind, but only God can change a person's heart. Shed the light of God's word on the sinner's heart and pray that God will change the person.

# 27

# BELIEVE IN CHRIST — HAVE ETERNAL LIFE

## JOHN 6:22-40

Recently I read one man's opinion of Christianity in America. He described America's Christianity as being "a mile wide and an inch deep." New statistics from religious pollster George Barna actually confirm this shallow, meaningless condition of Christian testimonies in America. Barna concluded that eighty per cent of the people who responded to his most recent survey identified themselves as Christians. Of those eighty percent, only twenty-seven percent believe that salvation is by grace and without works. Maybe that is why only twenty-five percent of the people who claim to be Christians attend church, read their Bible, and pray. Maybe Christianity is not even an inch deep in America.

Some people conclude that the reason there is not much commitment among Christians is because the very foundation of Christianity, the doctrine of salvation, does not require anything except belief. Hindus often go to unbelievable extremes in order to win salvation from their gods. They have been known to make personal sacrifices that cause red-blooded Americans to wince. They must do this, because, according to some interpretations of Hindu doctrine, sacrificial works are the only means to receive salvation.

Serious Mormons do a number of good works throughout life in order to obtain heaven in the end. Those who aspire to reach the highest level of heaven must dedicate two years of their life to a supposedly austere missionary endeavor. While they acknowledge the atoning sacrifice of Jesus Christ, they also teach that people cannot appropriate Christ's expiation of sin apart from individual efforts manifested through faith, repentance, and continued works of righteousness.

The Jehovah's Witnesses teach similar doctrines. They, too, accept the fact that the prefect man, Jesus of Nazareth, gave His life as a ransom for sin. However, according to their teaching, only those who are "recovered from blindness have a full chance to prove, by obedience or disobedience, their worthiness of eternal life" (J.K. VanBaalen. The Chaos of Cults. Grand Rapids: Eerdman' Publishing Co., 1979, p.271.). Again, obedience to prescribed laws is the prerequisite to salvation.

The Roman Catholic Church teaches their adherents that acceptable works are essential if a person would go directly to heaven at the point of death. They teach that a sinner must first respond to God's grace, then confess faith, which of course is the firm acceptance of all of the traditions of the Catholic Church. Keeping the traditions coupled with other good works and baptism in the Holy Catholic Church prove a person's worthiness to be justified.

A strict Armenian theology among Protestants requires sinners to do good works in order to gain salvation, and then continue to do good works in order to maintain salvation. Not to do good works is to risk losing salvation. The good works begin with believing in Jesus Christ and continue thereafter.

Before long it becomes obvious to the researcher that essentially every religion or sect in the world today that does not hold to the clear teaching of the Bible on salvation departs at this point of good works versus faith in Christ alone. The Jews struggled with that issue in Jesus' day. They still do. They still are like the Pharisees who became proud of their ability to accomplish a manmade list of good works. They assumed that this would be sufficient to win God's favor and salvation. They became angry with Jesus because He taught otherwise.

Jesus had miraculously fed 5,000 men, plus women and children. The next day the crowd gathered around Jesus again. He confronted them about their earthly, fleshly motivation for following Him. He told them that they needed to take of the heavenly bread in order to assuage their spiritual hunger. He told them that He was that heavenly bread. They couldn't understand what Jesus taught. The crowd was sure that they needed to do some kind of good work in order to receive eternal life. Jesus told them they needed to trust Him. They did not. They could not. They demonstrated the human inability to accomplish spiritual salvation.

## The Multitude Sought Jesus (vv.22-27)

This scene opens with a crowd surrounding Jesus. They had stayed over from the previous day. They asked Him a very practical question (vv.22-25). Their question stemmed from confusion that was caused by the recent circumstances (vv.22-24). Just the day before Jesus had fed 5,000 men, plus women and children, at a spot somewhere near the foot of Mount Arbela. This was about five miles north of the ancient and modern city of Tiberias (6:1-15). In the  evening, after the people had eaten, they saw Jesus send the disciples in a boat across the northwest tip of the Sea of Galilee toward the village of Capernaum (6:17). What the people didn't realize is that during the night a storm overtook the disciples in their journey, and Jesus walked across the water to be with the disciples and encourage them (6:20). The disciples docked the boat at Gennesaret, which is about three miles west of Capernaum and five miles northeast of Mount Arbela — their starting point the previous evening. Apparently they gave up on the idea of getting to Capernaum.

The people in the multitude didn't know that. They assumed, based on what they had heard, that the disciples were in Capernaum, and probably Jesus was still hanging out near the base of Mount Arbela. When they got to the place where they had eaten the previous day, they discovered that Jesus was no longer there. So the people naturally thought that Jesus must have walked during the night up to Capernaum. That is why the text shows the crowd gathered at that fishing village the next morning (6:24). John recorded that many of the people came to Capernaum in boats from Tiberias in an attempt to find Jesus (v.23). They did find Him, but not where they expected. In fact, it is possible that Jesus was not in Capernaum either, but probably in Gennesaret where the boat landed after the storm (v.25).

At any rate, the people wondered how Jesus got there (v.25). The first question they asked when they found Him was, "Rabbi, when (or how) to you get here?" They knew that He did not get into the boat with the disciples. They saw no other boats on the shore. This great and perplexing question was a very practical matter of life. Consider the picture drawn by God's pen. The multitude of people stood in the presence of the Creator and Eternal Judge who will send people to hell for eternity or usher them into Heaven through His grace, and all they are concerned about is how He got from point "A" to point "B." That is amazing!

Actually, one should not be too hard on the people in the crowd that day because they simply demonstrated human nature. It is just like human nature to be so consumed with temporary and passing matters that we do stop to think on the eternal plane. Folks typically interpret everything in light of human wisdom and the sphere of human existence. To suggest a super-natural action or divine cause in any particular situation is unacceptable even to people who call themselves Christians.

The people wondered aloud how Jesus got to that place. Jesus answered them. But He did not address their question (vv.26-27). The person who reads the Gospel narratives realizes that it was not unusual for Jesus to skip the expected answer and drive to something more important. In this case, Jesus' answer uncovered the people's real motivation (v.26). The fact that He chose not to answer their question is a good indication that He did not deem it to be the important issue of the moment. One must wonder how many of our questions God brushes aside because we are missing the point. Generally, we miss the point because we are focused on the wrong thing.

Jesus skipped the obvious answer in order to reveal that the people were not really following Him because they saw signs. Obviously, He knew that they thought they understood what motivated them. However, God always knows what drives the people better than the people know what drives them. There is no doubt that Jesus accomplished signs. These were miracles that God the Son did with the purpose of affirming His divinity. These particular people had seen a sign and drew a conclusion based on it. The sign was undeniable. Less than twenty-four hours before, they witnessed Jesus breaking a couple of loaves of bread and a few little fish into enough food to feed 5,000 plus people. "When the people saw the sign that he had done, they said, 'This is indeed the Prophet who is to come into the world!'" (John 6:14). Their response proved God's plan for signs. The sign accomplished God's will by affirming in the minds of the people that Jesus was special. They acknowledged that Jesus, the man from Nazareth, was indeed the Prophet . . ."

That is not a hint or indication that the whole multitude collectively was born again. That would be rare indeed. They simply admitted that Jesus was the promised prophet. That could amount to nothing more than the admission by modern Muslims that Jesus was a great prophet. Almost all false religions esteem the man Jesus. Millions of unsaved people admit that Jesus is the promised Messiah. That is not the point. The question is,

"Do they believe what Jesus taught about Himself, what He taught about them, and what He accomplished for them?" Apparently the people did not connect the dots any better than modern seekers do.

Therefore, Jesus accused the people of following Him for the wrong reason (v.26b). He pointed out that they actually pursued His company for fleshly reasons. They were interested only in what their flesh could gain. Do you follow Christ because He is your ticket out of hell or because you love Him? Maybe there is not much difference between ancient Israelites and modern Americans.

Jesus challenged the people to follow for more noble reasons (v.27). He warned them that they sought that which would not ultimately satisfy. They wanted bread, or ordinary food, every day. They were sure, based on human wisdom, that their flesh needed food to be satisfied. Who would disagree with that conclusion? In reality though, the flesh is never satisfied with earthly provision. Feed it today, and it will still want to be fed tomorrow. Fleshly desires of any kind will not be quenched.

That is why Jesus taught the people that they needed to labor for everlasting food. But if Jesus was talking about eternal matters here, if He meant salvation, why did He tell the people to labor for salvation? Are the false religions actually correct about this? Well, it is true that in a sense a sinner needs to pursue salvation diligently. Jesus referred to this intense labor when He said, "From the days of John the Baptist until now the kingdom of heaven has suffered violence, and the violent take it by force" (Matthew 11:12). It is not likely that a person is going to accidently stumble into eternal life. Jesus illustrated the nature of the seeker's search when He taught, "The kingdom of heaven is like a merchant in search of fine pearls, who, on finding one pearl of great value, went and sold all that he had and bought it" (Matthew 13:45-46).

Since one is expected to labor to find salvation, it was altogether fitting for Peter to challenge those who inquired about how to make the guilt in their souls go away, "Repent therefore, and turn again, that your sins may be blotted out" (Acts 3:19). The sinner should chase after salvation with all his might. He or she should cry out to God for it. Indeed the sinner must plead with God to do His work because only His work will change a sinner's heart. The beauty of the whole story, as it is told in the entirety of chapter six, is that a sinner will only cry out to God, or labor for eternal food, when God is drawing him to Himself.

### The Multitude Thought They Understood Jesus   (vv.28-40)

Jesus told the people to labor for eternal bread, but they still asked for physical bread (vv.28-34). Like many people who have a head knowledge of Bible truths, they truly wanted to do the works of God (vv.28-29). Jesus had challenged them to labor for eternal food (v.27). They responded positively. They essentially said, "We want to do that. Tell us what to do." Shouldn't a godly person rejoice that they wanted to get on board? Their response was very much like the response of other people who heard the good news of salvation. They were like Nicodemus who came to Jesus to learn how to get eternal life. He was interested. They were like the rich young ruler who ran to Jesus to hear about eternal life. They were like the crowd at Pentecost who cried out in the middle of Peter's sermon, "Brothers, what shall we do?" (Acts 2:37). Their response was like that of the Philippian jailer who pleaded with Paul and Silas, "Sirs, what must I do to be saved?" (Acts 16:30). Their response was much like that of millions of Americans who respond to invitations at camp, revival services, or to other public appeals. The preacher says, "You must be born again!" The sinner responds, "Tell me what to do." True Christians rejoice to hear about genuine desires to do God's will.

Jesus explained what kind of work (labor) God approves (v.29). He told the people to "work hard to believe in Jesus." That sounds rather strange for a couple of reasons. First, to believe generally is not considered to be the same as work. Second, it seems strange for Jesus to explain that the work of God is to believe in Him, because these folks already confessed that He was the Prophet (v.14). Okay, they believed that Jesus was the promised Prophet, but could they embrace God's kind of Messiah? Could they embrace the reality that Jesus, the man from Nazareth, was God. As God, He died for the sinner's sins. Because of sin, the person, no matter how kind or religious, is still just a sinner. Those sins offend God, which means that the individual is an offense to the holy God. Worse is the fact that there is not one thing, not one work the sinner can do to cover his own sins. He is in a real difficult spot. Therefore, the sinners in the crowd in Jesus day, like all sinners in this day, must trust Jesus' work alone in order to be born again. In short, the sinner must believe that faith in Christ's work is sufficient for God to call him "justified." Like the people of this age, the people in the crowd that day had a better idea. They didn't mind concluding that

Jesus was the Prophet, but to acknowledge all that the concept "Promised Prophet" entails was asking too much.

As a result of the wrong view of Christ, the people admitted that they exalted Moses over Jesus (vv.30-34). They decided that since Moses gave them signs, they should also expect signs from Jesus to affirm that He was who He said He was (vv.30-31). Does that mean that they concluded that Jesus' feeding 5,000-plus wasn't sufficient? They were contradicting themselves. They already admitted on the basis of that one sign that Jesus was the promised Messiah (v.14). Yes, but Moses fed people for forty years; Jesus fed them only once. Why this fixation with Moses? Obviously, they couldn't get their minds off human ability.

In order to help the people understand truth, Jesus explained the real source of Moses' miracle (vv.32-34). It wasn't Moses who fed the people, but God the Father who provided bread from heaven. The same God provides everlasting bread. However, everlasting bread is Christ (v.33). In this simple lesson, Jesus invites the sinner to partake of the Everlasting Bread that promises to assuage spiritual hunger (v.34). What an incredible invitation. Now that they understood better what God offers in Jesus Christ, how did they respond? The people said, "Give us this bread all the time. . ." What was wrong with them? The phrase, "all the time" means that they wanted plain, old bread every day. This was their response to the offer of eternal life? They could not think outside human wisdom. People still want God's promised salvation within the terms of human work, ability, and wisdom.

Finally Jesus explained to the people that He is the bread of life (vv.35-40). He tried to help the people understand why so many of them continued to hunger spiritually (vv.35-36). They partake of the ordinary things of life and continue to hunger. Jesus invites sinners to eat of the bread of life and promises them that everyone who trusts Him will be satisfied. He promises that they will have no more spiritual hunger or thirst (v.35). But people can't believe it! (v.36).

They see the sign, the see the truth, but they don't believe. Why not? They cannot believe that they are so spiritually dead that there is not something they can do. They cannot believe that faith in Christ's blood alone is sufficient to cover sin. They cannot believe that all they can do is believe. They see all the facts. They contain in their brains all the truth that the Bible reveals about Christ. But they cannot thrust themselves in complete faith on Christ alone! So is the plight of the typical religious person.

The good news is that some do see and believe. Jesus taught the people that God's will is for people to see and believe Him (vv.37-40). Jesus came to do only the Father's will (vv.37-38). Part of the Father's will is to give people to God the Son for salvation. Jesus knew that the Father gives people to Him (v.37). He knew that every single person the Father gives will come to Him (v.37). Therefore, He freely promises to give life to every person who comes to Him in faith (v.37).

We know the Father's will because Jesus revealed it to the whole world (vv.39-40). The Father's will is that Jesus Christ will raise from the dead every person who the Father gives to Him (v.39). The ones the Father gives are the same ones who look on the Son and believe (v.40). To look is to observe or perceive. It means that the sinner understands who Jesus Christ is, what He accomplished, and why He accomplishes it. The ones the Father gives to the Son are the ones who believe (v.40).

Almost everyone has an opinion about Christ. The only right opinion about Him is that He is who He says He is. Since that is true, no one has the ability to do any work good enough to accomplish what Christ already accomplished. Only Christ can save from sin. He who would do the work of God must humbly embrace Jesus Christ alone as Savior.

# 28

# THE LIVING BREAD

JOHN 6:41-51

Several years ago, I was in a setting where a friend introduced me to some of his acquaintances. The group had already been conversing for several minutes, during which time the other fellows carried on like fellows would be expected to do. So when the friend introduced me as a pastor, one of the fellows apologized because he had repeatedly referred to me by my first name and had not shown respect that he thought a minister deserved. Frankly, it didn't make any difference at all to me, but it did reveal that somewhere in this man's training someone taught him to regard ministers with high esteem. He was embarrassed to suddenly realize that he had been ignorant of my station in life.

One day millions of people are going to be more than just embarrassed when they discover that Jesus, the man from Nazareth, is actually the King of kings and Lord of lords. No doubt there are many people who think that they are being kind and complimentary to acknowledge that Jesus of Nazareth was a good man who went about doing good deeds. They think that they are condescending to say that Jesus was a great teacher who influenced world religion in an unusual way. In fact, it is possible that many people take pride in their toleration and gracious acceptance of One who has been so controversial over the centuries. There are multitudes of people who believe that Jesus, Mohammed, and Confucius are all up there on the same high level of respect.

People are going to be shocked one day when they discover who Jesus really is. They will be without excuse just as the people will be who were eyewitnesses to Jesus' ministry. Many of Jesus' peers believed that He was special. Maybe He was even as special as Moses. Moses gave the manna (or so they errantly reasoned), and Jesus gave them bread on a couple of occasions. Moses was a prophet, and Jesus appeared to be a prophet. But who understood Jesus' teaching about Himself?

In this text, Jesus plainly instructed the religious people of Galilee about His deity, God's plan for eternal life, and their personal responsibility to God. They didn't get it. Most people don't. But rejection of truth or even denial of truth never changes the reality of truth. In these few verses, there is a brief explanation for three of the most important doctrines in the Bible. Jesus taught that He is divine, that God draws sinners to salvation, and that salvation is by faith. To reject any of these truths is to deny salvation. Jesus graciously invited the people gathered near the Sea of Galilee to put their trust in Him. They, like multitudes of people who Christ invites today, prefer to interpret all things according to human wisdom.

## JESUS IS DIVINE (vv.41-42)

Jesus declared that He came from heaven. Those who heard His teaching did not doubt the intent of His words. In this context, He indicated that He was the bread from heaven. Though the immediate context of Jesus' discussion with the people does not record Him saying the exact words, "I am the bread which came down from heaven," the Jews were able to put this truth together from what He did say. For example, Jesus said, "My Father gives the true bread from heaven" (v.32). Then Jesus said, "The bread of God is He who comes down from heaven and gives life. . ." (v.33). Jesus also said, "I am the bread of life" (v.34). Finally, Jesus said, "I have come down from heaven. . ." (v.38). Therefore, the Jews' conclusion was exactly right. Jesus did say that He was the bread which came down from heaven.

Christ presented Himself as the heaven-sent bread in contrast to the manna that the Jews vaunted. They looked back to the miracle bread that God provided hundreds of years earlier while their forefathers wandered in the wilderness (v.31). According to their arguments, the Jews gloried in Moses' provision of bread for forty years, failing to acknowledge that the bread came from God through the hand of Moses (v.32). They held Moses' provision of manna as a wonderful miracle; but even as they reveled in that miracle, they ignored their forefathers' attitude about the heaven-sent manna. Moses recorded their response with these words,

"But now our strength is dried up, and there is nothing at all but this manna to look at" (Numbers 11:6). The forefathers did not esteem that bread too highly. Jesus taught that He was the real, life-giving bread that came from heaven.

In this affirmation, Jesus laid claim to deity. He said that He came from heaven. He said that the Father sent Him (v.38). If, indeed, He is the Son of God whom the Heavenly Father sent from heaven, He could not be only human. Furthermore, if He can impart eternal life, which He affirmed in verses thirty-five and thirty-nine, He must be God. If He is really God, He could not have been born through natural processes. That means that He must have been born of a virgin. That controversy raged from the day Jesus was born until the present day. Controversy or not, Jesus did not waver at all in this claim. He knew that He was God in the flesh fully divine, fully human.

The religious leaders complained about Jesus' claim. They understood exactly what Jesus affirmed. These Jews were leaders. In the beginning of this discourse, one finds  Jesus conversing with the multitude that was gathered by the seashore looking at the boats (vv.22-40). Now, at this point in the story, Jesus was saying things in the synagogue which was in Capernaum (v.59). It seems most reasonable, therefore, that the responses were arguments from leaders who would have been gathered around Jesus in the synagogue.

John recorded that the leaders were complaining about Jesus' statements. The verb tense means that they kept on complaining; they were doing it regularly. These fellows opposed Jesus in a lot of ways, but this was a new reason to complain. Why? What was the issue? The leaders were complaining because they could not see beyond temporal bounds. The idea that this man standing in their presence was the bread of life sent from heaven transcended all human reason. It did not fit in the common interpretations and understandings of the day. In their thinking, this man could not be Messiah who God would send to Israel. Why not?

They were convinced that the Messiah would be mighty, powerful, a warrior who came to set the nation free. They looked for a national Savior, not a Savior from sin. They like their sins. Freedom from sin wasn't important to them. This man named Jesus was born in obscurity under questionable circumstances. He was not a mighty warrior nor did He appear to have any potential as a great general. In fact, it appeared that this man did not even like war! Jesus from Nazareth suffered humiliation because the religious leaders did not accept Him. Therefore, this man could not be divine. Surely the religious leaders, of all people, would recognize a divine being. But Jesus? The people in Capernaum knew about Jesus' family. They knew Joseph the carpenter and assumed that he was Jesus' father. They knew Mary and were convinced that she could not have been a virgin and given birth to Jesus. That old story was well known in Capernaum.

Therefore, human wisdom prevented the men in the synagogue from accepting Jesus as the Christ sent from God to give eternal life. Human wisdom still rejects the idea of God coming in the flesh. Human wisdom rejects the possibility of God dying for an individual's sins. Human wisdom rejects the requirement that a person is not able to do any work of any kind in order to gain salvation. Evidence of such limitations of human wisdom abounds. False religions that require adherents to work diligently for their salvation abound. Agnostics are multiplying and many people who live in this very religious modern culture claim to be atheists. That is where human wisdom leaves the sinner. But what else does the sinner have? If human wisdom rejects Christ's divinity, how can anyone be saved?

### THE FATHER DRAWS SINNERS TO JESUS (vv.43-46)

Jesus taught that because of human limitations no one comes to Jesus through his own strength (vv.43-44). Sinners come to Christ only when God the Father draws them. It is God and only God Himself who draws sinners to Christ. The word that John used here means to pull along against resistance. Therefore, other uses of the word in the New Testament show fishermen who dragged the net full of fishes to shore (John. 21:6,11); or that the Philippian merchants dragged Paul and Silas to th authorities (Acts 16:19); and that the Jewish leaders dragged Paul out of the temple (Acts 21:30). One can easily see the natural resistance in each of these cases. Fallen human nature requires that God drag sinners to Christ. A couple of other examples reveal further ideas about the act of drawing. For example, Peter drew his sword from its scabbard (John 18:10). Surely the sword did not resist, but neither did it come out of the scabbard of its own accord. One of the most instructive uses of the word is when Jesus said, "And I, when I am lifted up from the earth, will draw all people to myself" (John 12:32).

The drawing of sinners to Jesus Christ is God's supernatural work in the hearts of people. He draws sinners through the witness of Himself in nature. He draws sinners through conviction in their consciences. He draws sinners primarily through the revelation in His Word. Everyone God draws will come to Christ. Jesus established this truth in a couple of statements in the context of this discussion. According to verse thirty-seven Jesus promised, "All that the Father gives me will come to me, and whoever comes to me I will never cast out" (John 6:37). Two verses later Jesus said, "And this is the will of him who sent me, that I should lose nothing of all that he has given me, but raise it up on the last day" (John 6:39). When God draws a sinner to Christ, that sinner becomes a forgiven, redeemed saint.

God must draw us sinners to the Savior because the sinner's natural will is inclined against it. It is not that people are physically incapable of coming to Christ, rather people have a will that is predisposed against it. We don't want to come to Christ. Paul expressed the problem like this: "And you were dead in the trespasses and sins" (Ephesians 2:1). To be dead in trespasses is not the same as being literally, physically dead. It means that every person is born in a condition of sin against God; and in that condition, not one person has any desire to please God, to delight in Him, or to be right in our relationship with Him.

It is true that God gave people a conscience that tells them when they are wrong. It is also true that sinners normally have enough intellectual capacity to collect data that indicates that there is a God to whom they must answer. But the desire to empty oneself of self and trust God alone for their eternal state escapes human ability. God does that for us. He draws us to Christ, and sinners who are drawn to Christ will be resurrected. This is the end result of the promise of eternal life. It is such a significant truth that Jesus repeated it three times in the context (vv.40,44,54).

Jesus went on to teach that those who learn from the Father come to Christ (vv.45-46). This fact requires that God teaches sinners (v.45). Here Jesus quoted an Old Testament principle that is found in several places in the Scriptures. It is a general statement pointing to the fact that God will teach all people in the Millennial kingdom. In this case, Jesus employed the statement to say that, while God is drawing sinners to the Christ, He is also teaching sinners. Therefore, one must conclude that every sinner who listens and learns from God will come to Christ. That is an explanation of the principle that genuine faith in Christ is rooted in hearing God's Word. Paul put it like this, "So faith comes from hearing, and hearing through the word of Christ" (Romans 10:17). God teaches through His completed Word, the Bible.

God draws sinners and He teaches them, but no one comprehends God apart from Christ (v.46). Thus, the writer to the Hebrews wrote, "Long ago, at many times and in many ways, God spoke to our fathers by the prophets, but in these last days he has spoken to us by his Son, whom he appointed the heir of all things, through whom also he created the world" (Hebrews 1:1-2). Because the Father speaks to the world through His Son, He must draw all sinners to Christ. That being true, Pilate's question to the Jews is still the eternal question which we all must answer: "What will you do with Christ?" Many people still reject the Christ just like Pilate and the Jewish leaders did because they cannot accept the fact that the Savior of the world could be of such humble beginnings and life. That is why God must draw sinners along to Christ by teaching them. We have no natural will to accept Him.

## Sinners Gain Eternal Life Through Faith (vv.47-51)

Having explained His divinity and the Father's work of drawing sinners, Christ offered Himself to the Jews as the bread of life (vv.48-51). He reminded them that their forefathers ate the miraculous manna, but they also died (v.49). Jesus pointed out this grim fact because of the Jew's habit of looking back to their forefathers' experience as the perfect example. They failed to acknowledge that the miraculous manna did not give eternal life. Maybe they didn't care about eternal life since they were wholly focused on temporal life.

Jesus Christ presented Himself to the temporally minded Jews as a contrast. He said that He is the living bread (vv.48, 50-51). He is the living bread that came down from heaven. This fact reiterated the present argument regarding His divinity (v.50). Since He is the living bread, and since He came from heaven, He is also the bread that imparts life. Only the Divine Savior can impart eternal life. He must be God. And because He is God, anyone who partakes of Him will live forever (vv.50-51). Indeed, He taught the Jewish leaders that He came from heaven for that express purpose that others may eat (v.50). Those who eat of this living bread will never die (v.51a). Of course at this point, Jesus was speaking about eternal death or eternal separation from God the Father. Those who partake of Jesus Christ, the living bread, may very well experience physical death. But at the point of physical death, the living souls of those partakers ascend directly to God in heaven (2 Corinthians 5:8). At the rapture during the last days, the bodies of those believers will be resurrected and changed into everlasting bodies.

Jesus continued by teaching that His flesh is the bread He offers. How can that be? This was a reference to His literal, bodily sacrifice on the cross. But the Lord was not suggesting that His people literally eat His body. That would be impossible. Rather, He used the picture of eating to describe how believers are intimately identified with Him and His sacrifice.

At this point, Jesus taught one of the most amazing truths in the Bible. Jesus offered this living bread, His sacrifice, to the world. That does not mean that He offered eternal life just to the elect, but that He offered it to the entire world. Christ's sacrifice was sufficient to cover all of the sins of the entire world. Therefore, He is able to offer salvation to the whole world. However, while Christ's sacrifice was sufficient for all sins, it is not efficient for the whole world because many will not have it.

But Christ promised eternal life to all who believe (v.47). Notice that it is the individual who believes. What is included in the idea of "belief"? Faith is more than mental assent. Many people acknowledge the facts about Christ. But their lives don't change since they really don't have faith. To believe requires that the believer have full confidence that God is in Christ reconciling sinners to Himself. It means that I must have full confidence that I am a sinner and have nothing at all to offer God for reconciliation. It demands full confidence that God has accomplished all that is necessary for me to be saved according to His plan.

Christ promised that He gives everlasting life to every person who has that confidence. Eternal life is a matter of quality of life now in this world, and the promise of quality of life forever in God's presence. It is available for all who will believe. It is presented freely by Christ who offered Himself as the bread of life. Why do people insist on trying to find satisfaction in the experiences of their ancient forefathers when Christ offers eternal satisfaction?

# 29

# JESUS' WORDS ARE
# SPIRIT AND LIFE

## JOHN 6:52-71

I magine the classic scenario where a man is shipwrecked and marooned on what a appears to be a deserted island in the Pacific. It's a classic Robinson Crusoe picture. This marooned sailor happened to be the chef on the ship that sunk in the raging storm. Unlike the movies and the novels, the chef discovers that there are very few  food resources on the island. Every day he goes deeper and deeper into the jungle looking for something to sustain him for another day. The coconuts are not ripe, there are few berries, and it seems that the fish have disappeared.

One day, after repeating the search-and-eat sequence for over a week, the now famished man hears what sounds like a crowd of  people in the distance. He stumbles through the thick foliage and walks into a beautiful resort where people are enjoying all kinds of food, drink, and delicacies. The cook sees the man and, taking pity on him, invites him to sit down and feast sumptuously on what he has prepared. Now imagine that famished man thanking the cook for his kindness but refusing to eat because he will eat only food he has prepared himself. The famished man walks back into the jungle searching for food, while the cook and all the people watch him with disbelief. How could he be so foolish?

That really sounds like an impossible story. Surely something that bizarre would never happen! But something that bizarre happened in Jesus' day with regularity. In the case of this text, Jesus had fed 5,000 men plus women and children. The next day the crowd came back to get more food. Jesus warned them that they needed to search for heavenly bread, food that satisfies for eternity (6:27). They countered Jesus' challenge by rehearsing how Moses fed their forefathers the temporary bread in the desert (6:30-31). Again Jesus offered them everlasting bread from heaven (6:33). Furthermore, Jesus explained that He Himself is the eternal, everlasting, satisfying bread that came from heaven (6:35-40).

The religious Jews who heard Jesus say these things grumbled (6:41). They knew Jesus' lineage. They knew that He was from Nazareth. They knew His mother and father. If it had anything to do with experiences and events that took place in the human realm on earth, they knew! But Jesus wasn't talking about human events that are accomplished by the flesh. Jesus offered eternal life which is a miracle of the Holy Spirit. Jesus offered life that cannot be gained by any human work. And just when the religious people thought they had heard the most extreme things, Jesus said, "I am the living bread that came down from heaven. If anyone eats of this bread, he will live forever. And the bread that I will give for the life of the world is my flesh" (John 6:51). Eating the flesh of a man from Nazareth? That was absurd! No decent human would consent to that!

Jesus still offers that which must be the miracle of God. Spiritual truth is still grasped only by people who God is drawing to Christ. Human wisdom alone will never understand the miracle of eternal life. The mind can be impressed with the facts about eternal life. The human conscience can and does desire eternal life. But the words that Jesus speaks continue to be spirit and life. The sin-marred flesh cannot contain them. Human nature rejects such wonderful truth out of hand. Jesus still invites famished, spiritually destitute sinners to eat His flesh and drink His blood. Our friends and neighbors still recoil at such an idea because the words that Jesus speaks are spirit and life. Rejoice and thank God if you understand Him. Plead with God to open your eyes if you don't.

## JESUS EXPLAINED THE BREAD OF LIFE CONCEPT TO RELIGIOUS PEOPLE (vv. 52-58)

The religious people disputed about the saying Jesus had just uttered (v.52). What saying? Jesus offered His flesh as the eternally satisfying bread of life (v.51). That statement must have hit the religious listeners like someone clapping their hands on their ears. It certainly set their religious senses tingling. In this part of the discourse, Jesus had explained how He was the bread sent from heaven to assuage spiritual hunger (vv.35-40). That claim was pretty difficult for the people to digest. But then, Jesus went on to explain that every person who the Father draws to the Son understands this truth (vv.41-51).

Surely the people who heard this teaching struggled with it. They still do. Jesus taught in very plain words that each person who the Father draws understands this amazing truth and comes to Christ (vv.44-45). Everyone who comes to Christ believes Him completely (vv.46-47). Everyone who believes lives forever (vv.48-50). What a triad of amazing statements this was. No wonder the people staggered in their thinking. These things taxed human wisdom beyond its capability to comprehend.

Indeed, the religious mind could not contain such truth (v.52). These are the people who grumbled when Jesus said that He was the Bread of Life come down from heaven (v.41). Now they were really upset. In their thinking Jesus just compounded the problem by saying that eternal life is found only by eating His flesh (v.51). As one might expect, the next thing stated in the record is that the people were disputing angrily among themselves. That they could not comprehend what He offered is clear from the question the asked themselves: "How can this man give us His flesh?" It is significant that God often recorded human response to the invitation for salvation in His Bible. For example, Nicodemus responded to Jesus by asking, "How can a man be born when he is old?" (3:4). The Samaritan woman responded, "Where do you get that living water?" (4:11). Human nature is always left in a quandary. How can these things be? That is why God requires sinners to simply trust Him.

Jesus didn't give up on the grumbling, disputing, religious people. He offered five promises through the Bread of Life (vv.53-58). First, He offered eternal life (vv.53, 54a, 58). Notice how Jesus refused to argue on their level. They disputed, "How can this man give us His flesh to eat?" Jesus didn't argue about His ability or His authority, He simply reiterated what He had already proposed in verse fifty-one. "Unless you eat the flesh of the Son of Man . . . you have no life in you." Because the people evidenced the fact that they were struggling to understand, Jesus stated the offer two ways. First, he taught that if a person does not eat of His flesh, that person does not have life (v.53). Second, Jesus taught that the person who does eat of His flesh also has the guarantee of eternal life (v.54a).

It is important to point out that Jesus did not use the same word for "eat" consistently in this lesson. One word, translated in this case "to eat" means to consume, devour, or eat something like a meal. That word is used in the verses that talk about eating real food, manna, bread, and such (vv. 23 , 26, 31, 49, 50,51,52,53). All of those verbs occur in the same past (aorist) tense form. People eat actual bread and that is the end of it. But, when Jesus zeroed in on the important lesson about eating His flesh, He used a different word that is translated " feeds on my flesh." This word means to gnaw, nibble, or crunch. More important it is a symbol of comradeship. Jesus used this word in verses 54, 56 and 57. Most significant is the fact that these verbs that talk about comradeship or fellowship are all present tense verbs. It is an ongoing activity.

Furthermore, Jesus added drinking His blood to the requirement for salvation. What was He talking about? It's no wonder the people were baffled. Sacrificed flesh and blood speaks of the complete, vicarious, substitutionary, sacrifice of Himself. Jesus Christ offered His entire physical being as a sacrifice. Therefore, the eating and drinking of Christ's sacrifice has to be a continual, spiritual feeding.

Human wisdom attempts to make the drinking and eating literal and physical because that is the extent of human experience. Life is lived in the physical, actual realm. It is like the religious Jews who understood Moses' manna but could not comprehend what Jesus taught. It is like Roman Catholics who conclude that in some magical way Christ's body and blood must be actually present at the Eucharist. They believe that is what Jesus taught even though Jesus taught this lesson months before He gave the Church the pattern for Communion at the Last Supper. Confusion is also demonstrated by many proclaimed "Christians" who are sure that they must gain salvation through works of the flesh. It is all about this life. It is all about what a person experiences and what he can do. This led Bishop Ryle to conclude: "Fallen man, in interpreting the Bible, has an unhappy aptitude for turning meat into poison. The things that were written for his benefit, he often makes an occasion for falling" (J.C. Ryle).

But what did Jesus mean? The offering of Christ's blood and flesh is the literal sacrifice of His body and blood on the cross. He offered it as a substitution for sinners in order to provide a covering for their sin. Eating and drinking is the sinner's identification with, embracing of, reception of that sacrifice in his heart, by faith. This is no different than how the ancient Israelites related to the Passover Lamb. They slew the Passover Lamb as a substitute for their own deaths. They showed full identification with that slain lamb by applying its blood on their door post. Furthermore, they demonstrated identification with the lamb by eating its flesh. Why did they do this? Because they believed God. They intimately identified with the blood and flesh of the lamb because of faith. If they had no faith, they enjoyed no deliverance. The lamb's blood and flesh was not the real issue. Faith in God's prescribed salvation was. How many Egyptians ate lamb for supper that evening and yet died when the death angel came? Literal flesh and literal blood wasn't the issue. Faith resulting in obedience was.

Also feeding on Christ's flesh and drinking Christ's blood is parallel to looking on the Son and believing in Him (v.40). The results are the same also. No exceptions! When Jesus told the people, " . . . unless you eat . . ." He meant that there are no other options, no debates, no alternatives. Not to eat the flesh and drink the blood revealed the absence of continuing, enduring life (present tense verb). There are no exceptions to this rule. In contrast Jesus taught that feeding on Christ results in "having eternal life" (also a present tense verb). This was Jesus' offer. It still is.

Second, Jesus offered resurrection (v.54b). Jesus promised that He will raise up the person who has eternal life. The promise itself might cause one to wonder why, if the promise is eternal life, does Christ also promise resurrection? Doesn't eternal life make resurrection unnecessary? The soul is eternal and goes into God's presence at death. The body must be glorified and join with the soul at the last day. This is interesting in light of the fact that the body is the object of human wisdom's attention. Everyone would like a perfect body that lasts forever. That is an earth bound kind of desire. But only those who feast on Christ's sacrifice will actually have a perfect body for all of eternity.

Third, Jesus offered true satisfaction (v.55). His sacrifice (flesh and blood) is the only thing that offers true satisfaction. The human sphere, the world, offers an endless buffet of food that never satisfies. The sinner keeps searching, trying new ideas often, but always ending with dissatisfaction. Conversely, the person who truly trusts Christ and His finished work has a deep abiding satisfaction.

Fourth, Jesus offered fellowship (v.56). The one who feeds on the reality of Christ's sacrifice dwells in Christ. At the same time, the one who is continually feeding on the certainty of Christ's sacrifices enjoys the privilege of Christ dwelling in him in the person of the Holy Spirit.

Fifth, Jesus offered the source of life (v.57). Christ, God the Son, taught the people that His source of living is in His relationship with the Father. In a similar way, the soul who keeps feeding on the sacrifice of Christ finds Him to be the true source of life now and forever. What a contrast that is to life as human wisdom knows it: "The fathers ate manna and died" (v.58). How do people respond when they hear such an invitation? Surely people we know, work with, and love have heard this good news. Do they respond like the people who heard Jesus responded?

## MANY DISCIPLES WERE OFFENDED BY JESUS' WORDS (vv.60-71)

The people who heard Jesus did not respond very well. Many of them grumbled (vv.60-65). Why? Because Jesus' teaching escaped human comprehension (vv.60-62). The disciples, the very people who had decided to follow Christ, concluded that this was a hard saying (vv.60-61). In plain English terms, they concluded that this was a fierce, tough, harsh word. One might agree with their conclusion when we also discover that no natural person has the ability to attend to it, to perceive it, or consider it. It is hard. It is worse than hard. It is impossible! As a result, the learners who had followed and listened to Jesus now responded the same way the religious leaders responded to Him. The people described in verse forty-one murmured with discontented complaining. Now it is plain that the disciples had the same opinion about Jesus' fivefold offer of eternal life that the religious leaders had.

They grumbled because they were scandalized. They were scandalized because no normal person would be able to accept this kind of teaching. What was Jesus thinking? How could He expect them to believe what He said? About the time the people concluded that Jesus' words were hard and incomprehensible, He presented something that really blew them away (v.62). He asked them, "What if you saw the man from Nazareth ascend to the throne of God in heaven?" This was blasphemy if Jesus wasn't God the Son. So again Jesus established the major building block in the entire argument. The man from Nazareth is God in the flesh come to gain eternal life for sinners who believe in Him.

The people's response opened the way for Jesus to explain again the principle of regeneration (vv.63-65). He reminded them that it is the Spirit that gives life (v.63). The flesh can accomplish amazing amounts of religious work, but to what end? In the power of the flesh, religious people can do good to the needy. They can keep rules and traditions like baptism and Eucharist (also called Communion) in human strength alone. They can read the Bible, memorize Scripture, pray, go to church, give an offering, and do any number of acceptable church things by human strength. But it is all pointless, useless, valueless. Only the unseen, all powerful, Holy Spirit of God gives life. The sinner cannot tell Him what to do. The sinner cannot tell Him when to do it. The sinner is not in charge of his new birth.

Therefore, Jesus pointed out that some followers didn't really believe (v.64). They concluded in their minds that Jesus was "the prophet" (v.14). Isn't that the same as belief? They left family and work (at least temporarily) to follow Him. They truly wanted to benefit from His miracles and blessings. But they did not believe! They believed a lot of facts about Jesus, the man from Nazareth. But they did not believe the whole person and work of Jesus. None of that surprises God.

Therefore, no one comes to Christ apart from God's drawing (v.65). When God draws the sinner, he must respond. Here are two sides of the same coin. On the lost side of salvation, the sinner must be challenged to respond to God's drawing. On the saved side of salvation, the saint realizes that he had to respond to God's drawing.

Jesus taught, "The Spirit gives life, some of you don't believer, and anyone who comes to Me is drawn by the Father." That is the same kind of message we must teach and declare. How did the people respond to Jesus' message? About the same way they respond to us when we tell the good news. Many turned back (vv. 66-71). The many disciples, unlike the eleven, did not believe (vv.66-69). That is why they could just walk away. Because Jesus demanded something they did not have or could not produce, they had no choice but to leave. Jesus requires of those who would follow Him that the miraculous work of the Holy Spirit take place in a person's heart as God draws and the Holy Spirit regenerates. No human can reproduce that!

Jesus reminded the believers that He is sovereign (vv.70-71). He sovereignly picked the twelve. There were no job applications. He purposely picked Judas to do His bidding. Human wisdom cannot explain it. We must accept it through faith.

No wonder people turn away and stop following Christ. They have no other choice. It is foolish to attempt to force non-followers to be followers. Only God can change their hearts. We must, as Jesus did, make the message very plain. Like Jesus did, we will need to repeat it over and over, showing every facet of salvation. But when the listener concludes that the words that appeal to the spirit and result in eternal life are too hard, and they walk away, we cannot mollify the message. We must present the gospel clearly. We must appeal to the sinners over and over. But we must never attempt to do what God is not doing at the moment. The words Jesus gave to the people were spirit and life; but when the people discovered that God's plan excluded their efforts, many of them chose to walk away. Jesus let them walk!

# 30

# RIVERS OF LIVING WATER

One beautiful fall day a local hiker went for a hike in a nearby national park and got lost. That evening he was able to make limited contact with rescuers on his cell phone during which he told them he was okay, but thirsty. The rescuers found him about four days later. He confessed that he believed he was alive because of divine providence and a bottle of water he found in the woods. Divine providence is a wonderful thing when you are lost and don't know which way to turn. A bottle of water is a wonderful thing when you are thirsty—yea, dangerously thirsty.

Experts reveal that a person can exist for several days without food. But after three days without water thirst becomes a critical situation. In fact, if a person does not experience thirst, it is a symptom of sickness. Belladonna, a form of heatstroke or sunstroke, is accompanied by a burning dry heat that alternates with chills and also a fever with no thirst. One of the symptoms of a particular strain of malaria is a fever without thirst. It is good to be thirsty because the human body must have liquids in order to function or even to survive.

It is good to have spiritual thirst too. Spiritual thirst is an indication that the soul is dissatisfied. However, a quick review of the human race indicates that it is natural for people to turn to the wrong sources in order to assuage their thirst. Fallen nature thirsts for pleasure. It thirsts for power, prestige, and possessions. Fallen humanity runs vigorously after things that will satisfy immediate needs but leave the soul unfulfilled. The person who has a craving thirst for alcohol does his body much damage. Likewise people who have a thirst for the passing things of this world, but no thirst for eternal satisfaction, are in grave trouble.

For what do you thirst? Jesus invited people who understood and acknowledged the spiritual thirst in their souls to come to Him and drink freely. He promised that people who drink the water that He offers will be eternally satisfied and will be able to point other thirsty people to the same abundant spring of spiritual satisfaction. Most of the people rejected His offer. Most of them still do. Most people still clamor for the passing fancies of temporal life that leave them thirsting for more. Most people are like the people who heard Jesus' amazing invitation. Instead of coming to Him to find satisfaction, they argue about who Jesus is. Those are people with no thirst. They are spiritually sick. They are in the throes of spiritual death.

Are rivers of living water flowing from your heart? Do you know spiritual satisfaction? Can you tell others where to find spiritual satisfaction? Jesus invites thirsty people to come to Him and get this river of water.

## JESUS OFFERED A GREAT INVITATION (vv.37-39)

Jesus offered the great invitation on the "great day" of the feast (v.37). Which day was the great day? According to the text, it was also the last day of the feast. Which feast? This was the last day of the Feast of Tabernacles. This feast was one of the three most important celebrations of the year for God's people, the Jews. It began on the fifteenth day of the seventh month, which would be equivalent to October 15. Originally, according to God's instruction in the law, the feast lasted seven days. By Jesus' time the leaders had added an eighth day. No one is exactly sure why the extra day was added or what the people did in that day that differed from activities in the previous seven days.

The Feast of Tabernacles was one of three feasts that God required all adult males living within fifteen miles of Jerusalem to attend. The Passover and Pentecost were the other two feasts that had compulsory attendance. Probably this feast was the most popular of all the feasts because it was a time of rejoicing and thanksgiving. God intended for this feast to remind the people of His provision not only during the foregoing year but throughout the history of Israel. In order to foster these memories, God instructed the people to set up temporary booths made of boughs and branches with thatched roofs. The lodging places had to be temporary in order for them to recall Israel's temporary wanderings in the desert. God's requirement was: "You shall dwell in booths for seven days. All native Israelites shall dwell in booths, that your generations may know that I made the people of Israel dwell in booths when I brought them out of the land of Egypt: I am the LORD your God" (Leviticus 23:42-43).

The feast was celebrated at the end of all harvests in order to remind the people of God's provision. It's not surprising that the feast was sometimes referred to as the Feast of Ingathering (Exodus 23:16). It was a joyous and happy time. Josephus, the Jewish historian, called the Feast of Tabernacles the "holiest and the greatest festival among the Jews" (Josephus. Antiquities of the Jews.).

The symbol of water figured greatly in this feast. It was a celebration that emphasized the refreshment of water. Each day the people gathered at the temple waving palms and willow branches in their hands. The priests worked their way through the crowds and trekked down to the Pool of Siloam where they filled a golden pitcher with water. Then the priests returned to the Temple through the Water Gate carrying the sacred vessel of water. They poured the water from the pitcher on the altar while the choir of Levites sang the Hallel (Psalms 113-118). On the last day they marched around the altar seven times to recall the battle of Jericho. It was a sight of grandeur, thanksgiving, and rejoicing as the throng waved their palm branches and thanked God for the manna, the quail, and the water that gushed from the rock.

The people of Israel had been doing this for centuries. At times there had been long periods of spiritual rebellion when the people did not keep the feasts consistently. But as a rule, they did the feasts even if they were in a state of rebellion against God.

Against that backdrop, in that setting, Jesus stood up and boldly declared the great invitation. John recorded that Jesus did this on the last day of the feast. Was it the seventh day after all of the pomp and circumstance had taken place? Was it the eighth day? Whichever day it was, it was at the end of the feast when everyone had symbolized God's provision of food to assuage hunger and God's provision of water to assuage thirst. They had been symbolizing God's provision for at least seven days in a row.

Then Jesus stood in a prominent place and announced the great invitation. His action had to strike the crowd as odd because Rabbis always sat down to teach. But Jesus wanted everyone to hear His offer. Therefore, He probably stood up in a prominent place where people would notice Him. From that place Jesus cried out so that all could hear. The word

John used here means to cry out, shriek, or scream. Jesus declared the invitation with passion. How many people were jammed into the temple courtyards that day? How many heard the Lord's offer? Every person who heard Him was without excuse.

Jesus simply demonstrated the truth that God has always cried out like wisdom at the head of the street. God continues to reveal Himself to all men. This is especially true regarding the people in America. All are without excuse because God's message is on the radio, the television, and in thousands of churches all the time. Not a soul in Greenville has an excuse for not hearing the invitation. The message is on billboards, church signs, television, internet, radio, and the newspaper. How many Christian bookstores are in this town? The invitation is lived out by neighbors and co-workers, as well as articulated clearly. God declares His nature and authority in nature, the conscience, and His Word. No one in this town has an excuse for not hearing! Few people in this nation have an excuse for not hearing the great invitation.

But what does Jesus offer in this great invitation? He offered an abundance of living water (vv.37b-39). He promised that people who experience spiritual thirst can find satisfaction in Christ (vv.37b-38). Obviously, Jesus addressed people who were spiritually thirsty. These were the same people who had just demonstrated God's provision. They had even offered a sacrifice to cover sins. Josephus wrote, "On the eighth day all work was laid aside, and then, as we said before, they sacrificed to God a bullock, a ram, and seven lambs, with a kid of the goats, for an expiation of sin" (Josephus. Antiquities of the Jews. 3.10.4.). What people could possibly do more good religious works? They had done all that God required for the feast.

But how was it with their souls? Were they spiritually thirsty? Many people still do many religious things, but they continue to realize that there is something missing. They are spiritually parched. All of their good works do not quench the thirst. A new book reveals that Mother Theresa confessed to having no spiritual satisfaction, no real trust in God, no faith in prayer. In short, she confessed that she hated her hypocrisy. When she experienced spiritual thirst, she turned to a religious organization called the Roman Catholic Church. She believed in the organization. She had faith in the traditions. She committed her life and eternal state to the church and died without hope. Why didn't she come to Christ who alone promises the satisfaction this poor woman longed for so desperately?

Jesus invited thirsty people to come to Him and drink. "Who was this man?" the people must have wondered. His invitation really sounds like He has God's authority. Indeed, that is the root issue. The sinner who comes to Christ for salvation from sin, the spiritually parched sinner, must believe in Him. He or she must continually put all trust in the person of Christ. He or she must fully trust that He is God, that He has provided salvation, that He will carry out the promise of eternal life. To rest in Christ's work and promise alone is to believe in Him.

Jesus promised that the person who believes in Him will have rivers of living water flowing out of His heart. This is not a reference to one particular verse of Scripture but is a reference to various Old Testament principles. For example, Solomon concluded, "Whoever brings blessing will be enriched, and one who waters will himself be watered" (Proverbs 11:25). God revealed to Zechariah the prophet, "On that day there shall be a fountain opened for the house of David and the inhabitants of Jerusalem, to cleanse them from sin and uncleanness" (Zechariah 13:1). God spoke through Isaiah, "And the LORD will guide you continually and satisfy your desire in scorched places and make your bones strong; and you shall be like a watered garden, like a spring of water, whose waters do not fail" (Isaiah 58:11). The principle of refreshing water from God was well known in the Scriptures.

Jesus promised the multitude that the thirsty sinner who comes to Him will experience complete satisfaction. That is the meaning of rivers of living water. The longing deep within the repentant sinner will disappear. The desire to be right with God will be assuaged. The guilt of sin will disappear. All of the fear and doubt in the inner man will be replaced by God's continual refreshing. Why would a spiritually thirsty person look elsewhere for satisfaction?

More than that, the promise also states that satisfied saints will reveal to others the source of satisfaction. The confidence and peace in the inner man will become obvious. The person who has the rivers of living water flowing from the inner most being will invite others to come to the same fountain and drink freely. This is the story John Peterson wrote about in his gospel song, Springs of Living Water:

> I thirsted in the barren land of sin and shame,
> And nothing satisfying there I found;
> But to the blessed cross of Christ one day I came,
> Where springs of living water did abound.

Drinking at the springs of living water,
Happy now am I; my soul they satisfy.
Drinking at the springs of living water,
O wonderful and bountiful supply.

O sinner, won't you come today to Calvary?
A fountain there is flowing deep and wide.
The Savior now invites you to the water free,
Where thirsting spirits can be satisfied.
(Springs of Living Water, John W. Peterson)

John added an explanatory note to Jesus' offer teaching that the living water is experienced through the indwelling Holy Spirit (v.39). He explained that at the point when Jesus made this offer, the Holy Spirit was present and worked in hearts and lives, but the Holy Spirit was not indwelling believers yet. At the last supper, Jesus promised the disciples that this would take place at a later time. He said, "And I will ask the Father, and he will give you another Helper, to be with you forever, even the Spirit of truth, whom the world cannot receive, because it neither sees him nor knows him. You know him, for he dwells with you and will be in you" (John 14:16-17). Though the Holy Spirit was already with the disciples, the day was coming when the Holy Spirit would be in the disciples.

Christians in this age enjoy the very thing Jesus promised. He said that this miracle would begin to occur after He was glorified. He was glorified when He rose into heaven and was seated at the right hand of the Father. That event is recorded in Acts 1:9. After Jesus ascended into heaven, the disciples went back to wait in Jerusalem just like Jesus had instructed them. They met together daily. They took care of business like voting for a disciple to take the place of Judas. Then during the Feast of Pentecost when the disciples were gathered together in a room, God fulfilled His promise (Acts 2:1-4). He sent the Holy Spirit who indwelt each of the disciples, the men and women who followed Jesus and believed in Him.

Now, in this age, each person who trusts Christ has the indwelling Holy Spirit ministering to and reminding him or her that he or she belongs to God. He is like an ever-flowing river of refreshing water. Paul explained that miracle when he told the Christians in Rome, "For if you live according to the flesh you will die, but if by the Spirit you put to death the deeds of the body, you will live. For all who are led by the Spirit of God are sons of God. For you did not receive the spirit of slavery to fall back into fear, but you have received the Spirit of adoption as sons, by whom we cry, 'Abba! Father!' The Spirit himself bears witness with our spirit that we are children of God" (Romans 8:13-16). What an amazing reality this is. Evidence of Christ's regenerating work is like rivers of satisfying water flowing from our innermost being.

### Jesus' Invitation Caused Varied Responses (vv.40-44)

In response to Jesus' invitation, some people concluded that He was the Prophet or the Christ (vv.40-41a). Which prophet? They could not deny that Jesus was a special prophet (Matthew 21:11). Maybe He was a forerunner of the Messiah, either the figurative or the resurrected Elijah, as the people asserted according to Mark 6:15.

Others concluded that maybe Jesus was the Prophet. This is what many of the 5,000-plus people who ate free bread and fish concluded (John 6:14). Which prophet is the prophet? These people thought about God's promise in Moses' day when Moses told the people, "The LORD your God will raise up for you a prophet like me from among you, from your brothers—it is to him you shall listen—" (Deuteronomy 18:15). Was Jesus of Nazareth that Prophet? Multitudes of people still agree that Jesus of Nazareth was special. But like people in Jesus' day, they conclude that He was not God. If He was not God, He cannot be the Savior from sin. Therefore, the thirst continues.

Based on His invitation, some people concluded that Jesus is the Christ (v.41a). Some people draw the same conclusion today. Believers who come to Jesus must acknowledge that He is the anointed One sent from God to save people from sin. Those who do experience spiritual their thirst assuaged. Some draw all the right conclusions but do not trust Christ. They are no better off than the demons according to James who wrote, "You believe that God is one; you do well. Even the demons believe—and shudder!" (James 2:19).

Some people concluded that Jesus was just another man (vv.41b-44). They think they understand the Scriptures (vv.41b-42). The worldly-wise people at the feast argued that Christ must not come from Galilee! That is common sense if nothing else. The Messiah would not be a hillbilly from the back woods hills of Galilee. Apparently, these folks did not read

Isaiah 9:1 that promised that Messiah would come from, " . . . beyond the Jordan, Galilee of the Gentiles . . ." Jesus quoted that exact reference regarding Himself in Matthew 4:12-16. Others of those wise people argued that Christ must be the offspring of David. He was. The genealogies of Matthew 1:1-16 and Luke 3:23-38 prove that. Finally, some people argued that Jesus could not be Messiah because Christ must come from Bethlehem. He did. That is why Herod killed the babies in that village (Matthew 2:3-6).

Actually the root problem here was lack of thirst. Where there is no thirst, there will be confusion and disdain for Jesus (vv.43-44). There is still division because of Christ. Families, nations, schools, and churches, are divided because of Him. The United States Supreme Court has attempted to arrest Him and silence Him. But He does not cease to be Christ just because the world wants to arrest Him.

Jesus still offers the invitation. People who are willing to acknowledge their thirst are still invited to come to Him and find everlasting satisfaction. Some people are either unable to know they are thirsty or live in denial about it. Many people are very thirsty, admit they are thirsty, but refuse to come to Jesus. They do not believe Him and, therefore, He cannot satisfy them. Thirsty sinners must come to Christ and believe Him wholly, or they will never be satisfied.

# I AM THE LIGHT–
# FOLLOW ME

JOHN 8:12-20

J esus offered this invitation while a crowd was milling around in the temple treasury. It appears that the setting was immediately after the Feast of Tabernacles. It is possible that this teaching followed soon after the Lord's teaching about rivers of living water as it is recorded in chapter seven.

There were three courts surrounding the temple. The furthest court out where everyone, even Gentiles, was allowed to congregate was called the Court of the Gentiles. The second court, the Court of the Women, was within the walls and prohibited to Gentiles. All Jewish people, men and women alike, were allowed in this area. The inner court was off limits for everyone except the priests and any Jew who took an offering for the priest to offer on the altar of sacrifice.

The temple treasury was located within the precincts of the Court of the Women. Porches surrounded the court and within the porches were thirteen offering boxes called The Trumpets. No doubt they were called this because they were shaped like trumpets, small at the top, large at the bottom. Seven of the offering boxes were for designated offerings while the remaining six served to collect any offerings that were not designated. The first trumpet was for the _ shekel temple tax which every Jew paid. The second trumpet was for offerings for the upkeep of the temple. The third and fourth trumpets was where women put their money for the purchase of doves which they had to offer for purification after childbirth. Into the fifth trumpet people placed contributions to pay for the wood that was necessary to keep the fire burning on the altar. The sixth trumpet was for money for the incense. The seventh box collected money for the upkeep of the golden vessels and utensils used in temple service.

During the Feast of Tabernacles this would have been a very busy place. Surely Jesus had attracted much attention when He stood and cried out that He was the water of life (7:37). That invitation was especially pointed in light of the ritual of the priests pouring water at the base of the altar each day. Jesus gave that invitation on the last day of the feast. Probably on the same day, Jesus also offered the invitation that He is the Light of the World. He directed that invitation primarily to the Pharisees. The "light" invitation would have stood in vivid contrast to another important ceremony during the Feast of Tabernacles. On the first day of the feast, the priests lit four giant candelabra that stood in the middle of the Court of the Women. This ceremony, called The Illumination of the Temple, took place when darkness fell on the first night of the feast. It was accompanied with much rejoicing and dancing and reminded the Israelites of the pillar of fire their forefathers had followed through the wilderness. Some say the ritual was followed each night during the feast.

Now, at the end of the festival, possibly with the candelabra just being lit for the last time, Jesus spoke out and said, "I am the light of the world!" Imagine what kind of impact that would have had on the people. Surely there were many devout Jews in the courtyard that day who wondered who this crazy man was. Why did He say such a thing? Who did He think He was? Just the day before, the religious leaders had met to discuss arresting Him. Everyone seemed to be curious about this man.

The world is still curious about Jesus who is called the Christ. Many very religious people reject Him out of hand. Sadder yet is the fact that many people who claim to be followers of Jesus Christ, who claim His name as Christians, who profess to be saved by His sacrifice, really don't believe that Jesus is the light of the world. What does it mean that Jesus is the light of the world? What are the ramifications of His claim?

## JESUS INVITED RELIGIOUS PEOPLE TO FOLLOW HIM (V.12)

At some time near the end of the festivities at the Feast of Tabernacles, Jesus invited some of the most religious men in the world to follow Him because He is the Light of the World. His claim had to be astonishing to that august body of religious leaders. He offered this invitation in the context of a festival in which the people remembered the light of the fiery pillar. Against that backdrop, Jesus' words spoke volumes. For a week the devout people of Yahweh had been remembering God's provision for His people in the wilderness. They had danced and rejoiced at the lighting of the candelabra. Maybe they actually thought about the miracle of the pillar of fire moving, staying, guarding, and enlightening. Now, Jesus essentially told the religious leaders, "That's me!"

Also, in light of the Old Testament concept of the Light of the World, Jesus' words must have hit like a sledge hammer. Especially the Pharisees were familiar with the key Old Testament passages that taught this concept. David said, "The LORD is my light and my salvation; whom shall I fear? The LORD is the stronghold of my life; of whom shall I be afraid?" (Psalm 27:1). He also wrote, "For with you is the fountain of life; in your light do we see light" (Psalm 36:9). Isaiah promised God's people, "The sun shall be no more your light by day, nor for brightness shall the moon give you light; but the LORD will be your everlasting light, and your God will be your glory" (Isaiah 60:19). Job knew that "when his lamp shone upon my head, and by his light I walked through darkness" (Job 29:3). Micah looked ahead to God's work for Israel in the future and concluded, "Rejoice not over me, O my enemy; when I fall, I shall rise; when I sit in darkness, the LORD will be a light to me" (Micah 7:8).

All of these passages reveal that God alone is the Light of the World. What did the Pharisees think when Jesus told them that He was that Light? They were already angry at Jesus. Probably their blood pressure skyrocketed!

Jesus' invitation was not a minor issue. It is still not the kind of invitation that one should treat like an insignificant e-mail that stays in their files for months without being answered. Jesus told the religious leaders that, because He is the Light of the World, they needed to follow Him. His invitation to follow was demanding.

To follow requires more than an acquaintance with. Many people in Jesus' day claimed to follow Him—to a point. There were zealous people who latched on to this new and exciting teacher until they learned from Him what it would cost them to follow Him. One time, "a scribe came up and said to him, 'Teacher, I will follow you wherever you go.' And Jesus said to him, 'Foxes have holes, and birds of the air have nests, but the Son of Man has nowhere to lay his head.' Another of the disciples said to him, 'Lord, let me first go and bury my father.' And Jesus said to him, 'Follow me, and leave the dead to bury their own dead'" (Matthew 8:19-22). To follow the Light would cost those fellows more than they were willing to pay. They went back to their comfortable darkness.

Multitudes thought it was kind of neat to follow this miracle worker who provided free food, until He explained that no one follows Him as a result of their own volition. When Jesus explained the need for intimate fellowship, the need for followers to eat His flesh and drink His blood, most of them changed their minds and turned back. Even the disciples complained that Jesus was making the requirements too stiff. Jesus said, "'This is why I told you that no one can come to me unless it is granted him by the Father.' After this many of his disciples turned back and no longer walked with him" (John 6:65-66). High expectations are not a difficult issue for people whose hearts God has changed. Those expectations are impossible for people who have unchanged hearts.

Many who claim to be Christians in this day do not understand what it means to follow Christ. The Greek word is used in various ways. It means to come after or to follow behind like the crowds that followed Jesus. It also means to accompany or go along with which is something a little more difficult than the peripheral members of the crowd did. The word means to obey like a soldier who does the commander's bidding. It means to learn and heed instruction like a student who follows a teacher. In the Christian's case, to follow requires all of the foregoing ideas plus, it means to be a disciple, to abandon all in order to be like the Master.

Imagine Jesus, the carpenter from Nazareth, inviting the most exalted religious leaders in Israel to give up everything they counted dear in order to follow Him and become like Him. No wonder they were aghast. No wonder they wanted to kill Him. People who do not know who Jesus is cannot take His invitation to follow seriously. Imagine a person knowing that it is God who invites him to follow and choosing not to follow!

Jesus promised that those who followed Him would have the light of life. That means that He promised to give what everyone wanted. There is something in nearly everyone's soul that cries out for relief from the effects of sin. The contrast between light and darkness points up the problem. The world is steeped in the darkness of sin. The entire creation is under the ban and subject to the pains and deficiencies of sin. By nature every person is given over to sinning. It is not that we are simply born as sinners, but that as sinners, we sin—all the time! Do sinners truly enjoy that condition? That is darkness. It is a foreboding darkness that seasoned sinners consider to be normal.

Not only is the world wrapped in the darkness of sinning, but the world continues to stumble in the darkness of ignorance. They are ignorant of their need. They are ignorant of the hope Christ gives. Yet at the same time, the world knows it is in trouble and seeks many various means to escape the trouble. Satan tries to keep people from thinking about reality by distracting them with fun, lights, sounds, and the entertainment of Vanity Fair. But when trouble comes, when the sinner is all alone with his thoughts, he knows that something is missing. When people grapple with the reality of death, they know something needs to change. When people are all alone with their thoughts, when the party is over, the music has died, and the lights are turned off, sinners feel the darkness.

Where do people turn when they realize how dark their world is? False religion is another ploy of Satan to keep people from following Christ and escaping the darkness. The true words of Jesus still offer escape. Antonio Moyano, a missionary in Spain, was reared in a Catholic home in Spain. When he was a teenager, the family became part of the Jehovah's Witnesses for three years. One night he was sitting in a service in a different setting where a preacher preached the gospel. As Antonio heard the Word of God, he realized, "I need that." He embraced it immediately. His life changed forever. He lives to serve the Christ He found in the Bible. That is following Jesus. That is escaping the darkness to walk in light.

Jesus invited the religious people to find in Him what only God can do. The Rabbis had taught for generations that Messiah would be God's Light. Now here was Messiah offering exactly what He ought to offer. How would the sinners respond? Maybe in the depths of their hearts they knew that only God can offer the light of life. The light of life is light which flows from the source of life, that is, from God Himself. The light of life is the light which is the source of life. Only God offers the source of life. Jesus invites sinners who walk in darkness to come to Him and find light that is life. Jesus invites sinners to embrace Him as God, the author of life. Why do sinners prefer eternal death to life? Why don't they embrace Christ's invitation?

### Religious People Chose to Argue Rather Than Follow (vv.13-20)

When the religious leaders heard Jesus' offer, they chose to argue about witnesses according to the law (vv.13-18). Instead of accepting Jesus' invitation and thanking Him for being so kind to offer it, they asked Him to produce His witnesses. They required Jesus to back up His claim with witnesses (v.13). This was a requirement of the law. God's law for the nation of Israel required, "A single witness shall not suffice against a person for any crime or for any wrong in connection with any offense that he has committed. Only on the evidence of two witnesses or of three witnesses shall a charge be established" (Deuteronomy 19:15). That is not an unusual law. Any civil society will have similar laws in order to ensure orderliness and to avoid anarchy. Even the Church operates with this law. Looking forward to the modus operandi of the coming Church, Jesus taught the disciples, "If your brother sins against you, go and tell him his fault, between you and him alone. If he listens to you, you have gained your brother. But if he does not listen, take one or two others along with you, that every charge may be established by the evidence of two or three witnesses" (Matthew 18:15-16). Paul wrote to Pastor Timothy telling him, "Do not admit a charge against an elder except on the evidence of two or three witnesses" (1 Timothy 5:19). Such laws are necessary for societies, organizations, and even churches in order to counteract natural tendencies of sin.

Sinners appeal to "law" when it is to their advantage. The Pharisees loved to appeal to laws that made them look good. But at the very same time, they shattered the two most important commands in the Bible—love God with all your heart and love your neighbor (Matthew 22:38-39). Hypocrites like the Pharisees still appeal to traditions and rituals in an attempt to lay claim to righteousness. In this case, the Pharisees attempted to move the discussion out of the supernatural realm (God giving the light of life) to the human realm (living by the law). In similar fashion, the sinner who is not really born again appeals to the date written in the front of his Bible. Or she asks her mother who was "there when the decision was made" to verify, to witness her salvation. Religious, but unrighteous people, depend heavily on human witness. Jesus pointed out this fact when He told the religious people, "You judge according to the flesh " (v.15).

The leaders chided Jesus for not producing witnesses who would validate His claim to being the Light of the World. In reality, Jesus didn't need anymore witnesses because His claim was clearly substantiated (vv.14-18). The first witness is found in the fact that Jesus Himself bears witness to His claim (v.14). Is the person making the claim allowed to verify the validity of that claim? Yes, when He is God. Because God is true, His witness must be true. He doesn't need another witness.

Second, Jesus told the religious people that God the Father bears witness to His claim (v.18). This is the same thing He pointed out in an earlier argument with the Pharisees when He said, "The Father who sent me has himself borne witness about me. His voice you have never heard, his form you have never seen" (John 5:37).

Beyond Himself and God the Father, Jesus had other witnesses. There was the witness of John the Baptist (John 5:33) and other prophets who foretold His coming. He had the witness of Scriptures (John 5:39). He had the witness of His works (John 5:36). What more did these fellows want? They had all the evidence they needed to confirm that Jesus is the Light of the World. They preferred not to believe it.

The religious leaders argued because they were ignorant (v.19-20). When Jesus called God the Father as witness, the leaders asked Him who His father was. They were really not seeking information. They had already made up their minds. They had already decided to kill Jesus. They looked very much like sinners who have already decided not to follow God's way to salvation. Proud sinners are really not interested in truth.

Rather than seeking information, the Pharisees were being sarcastic. Their retort was a reminder that they were convinced that Jesus' father was Joseph the carpenter in Nazareth. Joseph was probably dead at this point in history. When truth backs error into a corner, error retaliates with sarcasm, an attack against the person. Though the Pharisees demanded a witness, that was really not sufficient. They responded according to the flesh. They were like other people who say, "We disagree with what you say." Then they say, "Prove your point." If you give them proof, they say, "We don't think your proof is valid." People like that seem to personify a cute, but truthful saying, "Never wrestle with a pig. You both get dirty and the pig likes it."

The religious leaders would not accept Jesus' invitation because they did not know Jesus or His Father. They were ignorant about Jesus of Nazareth. Like many sinners, they knew much about Jesus. Certainly these leaders did what liberals do today when they vehemently disagree with someone who tells the truth. Surely, they went to Nazareth and dug up all the "dirt" they could find on Jesus. Yes, they knew a lot of things about Jesus, but they didn't know Him. Like sinners today, they did not know the most important things about Jesus. They did not know that He is God. They did not know that He came to die to provide a covering for their sins. They did not know the truths that will save their souls from hell.

They were also ignorant about God. They had a god who followed them, a god they kept in their neat little theological box. They had a little god they kept in their phylacteries. A true view of the true God is a frightening thing. Their god didn't frighten them. To see God, outside of Christ, is to know the certainty of hell for eternity. God's perfect holiness demands eternal punishment of sin. These religious folks were ignorant about that kind of God, and they were ignorant about God's plan. God's plan demands eternal punishment of sinners. Often sinners disagree with that. Or sinners don't see themselves as sinners and, therefore, deserving of hell. They are ignorant of God's plan.

God's plan provides the covering for the offense of sin, the sacrifice of Christ. Sinners are proud enough to try their own way. Sinners attempt to adjust the requirement to follow Christ to make it a more convenient association with God. God's plan requires His timing which the Pharisees did not understand, nor do sinners today. The Pharisees were not ready for Messiah, even though He stood before them. He offered them the light of life, and they wanted to kill Him. But they could not kill Him because it was not time for that according to God's plan.

How foolish sinners are to refuse Christ's invitation. Life and light is in His hand. He holds it out to the very people who cannot save themselves. Why would a reasonable man or woman reject the offer?

# 32

# THEY WERE STABBED
# THOROUGHLY

## ACTS 2:37-41

Arminians call me a Calvinist. Calvinists call me an Arminian. Am I confused, or are they, or does it matter at all? I have also been called worse things, but not in the context of theology. Why does this happen? I am a firm believer that the Word of God is true and that the preacher should preach the Word of God as it is written. Obviously, when a preacher is true to the text, there is no conflict. Maybe, maybe not. There is certainly never any conflict regarding God's plan, His work, His will, or with anything He has recorded in His Word. However, because God's ways are not our ways, and His thoughts are not our thoughts (Isaiah 55:8), there are times when the human mind is taxed beyond capability to comprehend.

For example, the preacher must preach that marvelous promise that Jesus gave to Nicodemus when He said that whoever believes in Him should not perish but have eternal life (John 3:16). And when the preacher finds himself in John chapter six some time later and reads that Jesus told the crowd that only those who the Father draws will come to Him, he must preach that too. Can the human mind marry such contradictions? Not easily. God is God, and we are His creation.

Human responsibility and sovereign control in salvation is not a conflict in truth but is an example of antinomy. Antinomy is 1) the opposition of one law, regulation, etc. to another 2) a contradiction or inconsistency between two apparently reasonable principles or laws. (Webster's New World Dictionary) Human responsibility in salvation compared to God's sovereign control in salvation creates several examples of antinomy.

J.I. Packer in his book, Evangelism and the Sovereignty of God, illustrates the idea like this:

> Modern physics faces an antinomy, in this sense, in its study
> of light. There is cogent evidence to show that light consists of
> waves, and equally cogent evidence to show that it consists of
> particles. It is not apparent how light can be both waves and par-
> ticle, but the evidence is there, and so neither view can be ruled
> out in favor of the other. Neither, however, can be reduced to
> the other or explained in terms of the other; the two seemingly
> incompatible positions must be held together, and both must
> be treated as true. Such a necessity scandalizes our tidy minds,
> no doubt, but there is no help for it if we are loyal to the facts.
> (J.I. Packer, Evangelism and the Sovereignty of God, Downers
> Grove, Ill.: Inter-Varsity Press, 1961, p. 19.)

Scientists who analyze light might need to deal with antinomy. Christians, on the other hand, are interested in telling people the good news
about Jesus Christ with the desire that they will embrace the truth and be
born again. Is antinomy an issue for us? Is there an apparent contradiction in this work? That does seem to be the case in this text taken from
Peter's sermon at Pentecost. At one point Peter told the crowd that "everyone who calls on the name of the Lord shall be saved" (v.21). But later,
according verse thirty-nine, Peter told the people that "the promise is
for . . . everyone whom the Lord our God calls to Himself." Which is it?
Who is doing the calling? Is a sinner saved because he calls on the Lord,
or is a sinner saved because the Lord called him to Himself? Yes, most
definitely. No one calls on the Lord unless the Lord calls him or her, and
everyone who the Lord calls to Himself calls on the Lord.

## HUMAN RESPONSIBILITY IN SALVATION

Peter preached a great sermon that brought conviction to the hearts of
all who heard (v.37). It had to be a good sermon because Peter preached
Christ crucified. That would not be a popular topic for a sermon in Jerusalem during the Feast of Pentecost. Popularity not withstanding, Christ
crucified is always a good and necessary topic. Peter told the crowd that
Jesus of Nazareth was affirmed by God to the people through mighty
works, wonders, and signs (v.22). It was the Jewish people who had deliv-

ered up Jesus to the Roman authorities just fifty days earlier to have Him crucified. Peter reminded the listeners that they were responsible for that very crime (v.23). However, God raised Jesus up from the dead (v.24) even as He had promised to do according to David's Psalm in the Old Testament (vv.25-28). Because God promised it through His prophet, it had to happen.

Peter continued the sermon preaching that God not only exalted Jesus of Nazareth by raising Him from the dead, but He is now seated at the right hand of the Father (v.33). From that exalted position, Jesus sent the Holy Spirit to be the encourager even as He had promised the disciples He would do (v.33). The people were observing the evidence of that Holy Spirit even while Peter spoke. Therefore, the only right conclusion for Peter to draw was that Jesus of Nazareth is Lord and Christ (v.36). He is the very one "you" crucified (v.36).

That was a rather unkind thing to say. Why did Peter do that? Why was he even preaching to those people who had crucified the Savior? Why didn't he mind his own business? Peter and the apostles were simply doing what Jesus told them to do. Before He ascended to the exalted position at the right hand of God, Jesus told His followers, "But you will receive power when the Holy Spirit has come upon you, and you will be my witnesses in Jerusalem and in all Judea and Samaria, and to the end of the earth" (Acts 1:8). Jesus plainly instructed His servants to "go therefore and make disciples of all nations, baptizing them in the name of the Father and of the Son and of the Holy Spirit" (Matthew 28:19).

Peter put forth much human effort to do exactly what Jesus told him to do. He and the other apostles were doing the same thing Paul would do after he was converted. They did what all other true servants of Christ do. Paul explained the work like this: "But we preach Christ crucified, a stumbling block to Jews and folly to Gentiles" (1 Corinthians 1:23). Declaring the gospel is hard work. It is necessary work. It is good work. It is God-ordained work.

As a result of Peter's sermon, the listeners were cut to the heart. What does that mean? It means they believed that Jesus of Nazareth was indeed the Christ. They believed that God raised Jesus from the dead. They believed that Jesus of Nazareth is Lord. That is what Peter preached. The words smote them. They were in the process of doing what Paul taught: "If you confess with your mouth that Jesus is Lord and believe in your heart that God raised him from the dead, you will be saved" (Romans

10:9). Peter preached the gospel and the truth penetrated the listeners' hearts. They did not simply draw right conclusions in their heads alone. Many people go that far with the gospel and, as a result, become religious but are never born again. No, in this case, the truth penetrated all the way to the depths of their being. These people believed with their hearts.

A very literal translation of the words in this verse might read, "They were stabbed thoroughly." These people were agitated vehemently in their hearts. They were thoroughly convinced that Jesus of Nazareth was God in the flesh, and they killed Him. They were thoroughly convinced of the gravity of their actions. They were thoroughly convinced of their sins. They were thoroughly convinced of their guilt!

Right away the convinced sinners wanted to do something (vv.37-41). They concluded that they needed to make a change (v.37). Their sin was obvious to them. God's righteous plan was obvious to them. They had no choice but to wonder what they must do in order to get right with God. A true servant of God, a person who is truly saved, longs to see this kind of response from sinners. It is not something the preacher or evangelist or friend can force, but something the sinner must conclude. The sinner who has been thoroughly stabbed in his or her heart (conscience) will reach this conclusion. But what can such a person do?

Peter told the convicted sinners that they needed to repent (v.38). Notice that, according to the text, no one asked Peter what he meant by that. Apparently, they were familiar with repentance and knew exactly what Peter instructed them to do. Some religious people today claim that the preachers of the gospel must remove all such theological language from their messages because the people of the world do not understand the terms and will be offended by them. Actually, most relatively intelligent people know what repentance is and what it requires. Peter's audience was familiar with the term because a few years earlier John the Baptist, a very popular preacher, had taught the need for sinners to repent. The essence of his message was, "Repent, for the kingdom of heaven is at hand" (Matthew 3:2). How interesting that Jesus picked up where John left off and preached the same message when He began His ministry. Matthew recorded that Jesus began His ministry in Galilee and "from that time Jesus began to preach, saying, 'Repent, for the kingdom of heaven is at hand'" (Matthew 4:17). The people knew about repentance. They had heard that message before.

The smitten sinners wanted to know what they had to do to change, and Peter agreed that they needed to change. When he told them to repent, he required that they change their minds for the better. To repent is to feel remorse because of sin and desire to change one's relationship with God. That definitely implies a change in the way one lives. Sinners need to do something. They need to repent.

Furthermore, Peter told them that they needed to be baptized (v.38). This was another work with which the audience was very familiar. Jews understood baptism well. No doubt they had observed Gentiles who were baptized in order to make a public declaration that they wanted to be identified with Judaism. Those Gentiles could never change their lineage and be reborn as Jews. But they declared that they wanted to be reckoned along with the Jews from then on.

Peter told these sinners that they needed to make such a public declaration regarding the name of Jesus Christ. They needed to publicly side with Jesus of Nazareth and His followers. They needed to publicly state that they understood their guilt of sin and that they repented of it. They needed to make this public statement on the basis of the forgiveness of sins. Peter did not tell the convicted sinners to be baptized in order to gain the forgiveness of sins. He didn't even hint that they would receive forgiveness of sins in exchange for the ritual of baptism. Rather, Peter taught them to be baptized because of or on the basis of having received forgiveness of their sins from God. This little preposition in the Greek language is translated nearly twenty different ways in the English New Testament. Apparently, it was the word people used in order to say almost anything. Maybe it was like the English word, "Whatever." Among the acceptable translations of the word is "because of," "on the occasion of," or "for the purpose of."

Furthermore, Peter could not have told the sinners to be baptized in order to receive forgiveness of sins because all of Scripture argues against any idea that a ritual or human work of any kind gains salvation. Paul reminded Christians, "For by grace you have been saved through faith. And this is not your own doing; it is the gift of God, not a result of works, so that no one may boast" (Ephesians 2:8-9). He told Titus that God "saved us, not because of works done by us in righteousness, but according to his own mercy, by the washing of regeneration and renewal of the Holy Spirit" (Titus 3:5). Yes, the people needed to be baptized. But only because they had already been converted.

Peter told the people that they also needed to accept God's promise (v.39). This was the promise of sins forgiven. Notice that Peter said the promise was for those sinful Jews gathered at the Feast of Pentecost and for their children. It is an everlasting message. Since it is an everlasting message, the promise is also for those who are far away. That might be a reference to Jews who were scattered all over the civilized world at that time. It is almost certainly a reminder to Bible readers in every age that God also gave the promise of salvation to the Gentiles who were separated from the Jews by their traditions. This is still a promise intended for sinners in this age. Who will tell them?

Peter also told those thoroughly stabbed people that they needed to save themselves from the crooked generation (v.40). The first necessary thing in order to carry out this command is for sinners to acknowledge that their world/culture is "crooked" or "bent." It would be nice if even professing Christians would acknowledge this reality. But how is a sinner supposed to deliver himself from the bent world? The passive voice verb is better translated be saved from this crooked culture. It is a command to have someone or something rescue you. Sinners must do this!

They also needed to receive the word (v.41). Sinners hear the Word of God, the gospel, communicated by God's servants. The messenger is responsible to tell the good news, but the sinner is responsible to "welcome it thoroughly" for himself (middle voice participle).

Finally, Peter told the convicted sinners that they needed to call on the name of the Lord (v.21). The name of the Lord refers to everything that characterizes God. Sinners must cry out to God because they trust everything that God says. These are the things people must do in order to have salvation.

## GOD'S WORK IN SALVATION

God's work begins in Christ (vv.22-36). He approved Jesus of Nazareth to offer the sacrifice for sins (vv.22-28). By the time Peter preached this sermon, God had already affirmed Jesus' work through signs and wonders (v.22). Humans did not do that. Humans could not do that. In fact, humans, as a whole, rejected Jesus. God used their rejection to continue His plan. He allowed Jesus to suffer at their hands according to His plan (v.23). After humans had killed the Son of God, God the Father raised Him from the dead (v.24). Only God could do that.

Then, having exalted Jesus of Nazareth through resurrection from the dead, the Father exalted Him more by seating Him at His own right hand (vv.29-36). From the position of authority, Jesus Christ has sent the Holy Spirit who indwells, teaches, and encourages the people God saves. Only God can do that.

Furthermore, according to God's plan, Christ intercedes for sinners by pleading the sacrifice of His blood to the Father. Paul asked, "Who is to condemn? Christ Jesus is the one who died—more than that, who was raised—who is at the right hand of God, who indeed is interceding for us" (Romans 8:34). Everything about the plan of salvation depends on God's work. If He did not create that plan, provide the Savior, approve His sacrifice through resurrection, there is no hope for the sinner. If God did not establish the plan, the sinner has no reason to call on God, nothing to believe, no promise to accept, no reason to repent, no means for forgiveness, and no purpose in being baptized.

More than that, God works in the individual sinner's behalf (vv.37-41). Why did these particular people believe Peter's sermon? Because God gives the gift of faith (v.37a). Not everyone came to the same conclusion. Why did 3,000 of the people believe what Peter preached while the rest did not? Paul would say a few years later that it was because "by grace you have been saved through faith. And this is not your own doing; it is the gift of God" (Ephesians 2:8). Notice that grace is not the individual's own doing—it is God's gift. Likewise, faith is not the individual's own doing—it is God's gift. For a sinner to believe the Word of God unto salvation is God's gift. In that vein, Paul reminded the Christians in Philippi, "It has been granted to you that for the sake of Christ you should not only believe in him but also suffer for his sake" (Philippians 1:29).

Second, these convicted sinners demonstrated that God also gives the gift of repentance (v.38). He gives the gift of "turning away from sin" to Jews. A few days after this grand revival, Peter reminded the religious authorities that "God exalted [Jesus] at his right hand as Leader and Savior, to give repentance to Israel and forgiveness of sins" (Acts 5:31). Apparently, apart from God's work through Christ, there is no repentance to be had. And we rejoice that God gives the same gift to Gentiles. Peter explained to the Church leaders how God saved Cornelius and his household. And "when they heard these things they fell silent. And they glorified God, saying, 'Then to the Gentiles also God has granted repentance that leads to life'" (Acts 11:18). God continues to give this gift through His kind convicting processes. Paul asked, "Or do you presume on the riches of his kindness and forbearance and patience, not knowing that

God's kindness is meant to lead you to repentance?" (Romans 2:4). He told Pastor Timothy that he should be "correcting his opponents with gentleness. God may perhaps grant them repentance leading to a knowledge of the truth" (2 Timothy 2:25).

Third, God gives the gift of forgiveness (v.38). Forgiveness is not deserved, but punishment is. Forgiveness cannot be earned. God gives it. That is the wonderful story in Paul's letter to the Christians in Ephesus. He reminded them, "And you were dead in the trespasses and sins in which you once walked, following the course of this world, following the prince of the power of the air, the spirit that is now at work in the sons of disobedience— among whom we all once lived in the passions of our flesh, carrying out the desires of the body and the mind, and were by nature children of wrath, like the rest of mankind. But God, being rich in mercy, because of the great love with which he loved us, even when we were dead in our trespasses, made us alive together with Christ—by grace you have been saved—" (Ephesians 2:1-5). Thank God for His gift of forgiveness. The only way any sinner is able to get it is because God gives it.

Fourth, God gives the gift of the Holy Spirit (v.38). Jesus promised the disciples that God would do this through Him. He told them a few hours before He was crucified, "But when the Helper comes, whom I will send to you from the Father, the Spirit of truth, who proceeds from the Father, he will bear witness about me" (John 15:26). Notice that Peter promised these repenting sinners, "You will receive." They would not gain the Holy Spirit by chanting a mantra, or by praying a special prayer, or by reciting the right kind of formula. No, the person of the Holy Spirit is God's gift. At regeneration believers receive Him.

Fifth, God gives the promise of salvation (v.39). It is God's promise. Only He who promises is capable of providing.

Sixth, God calls sinners to Himself (v.39). Peter made a very tight argument at this point. He told the people that the promise of salvation is for everyone who God calls. In fact, every person who God calls receives the promise, the Holy Spirit, and forgiveness. God calls to Himself sinners. These are the same ones God draws to the Savior as Jesus taught the multitudes in John 6:44, 65.

Finally, Peter explained that it is God who adds to the Church (v.41). He did not tell the people that they could assuage their guilt if they would only add themselves to the church. That is a modern perversion of truth. People join religious organizations, but only God is able to join converted sinners to His Body.

God added three thousand souls that day. But how many heard the same sermon and did not believe, were not thoroughly stabbed, sensed no conviction, or felt conviction and walked away? Jerusalem typically had a population of 55,000. During the feasts, the population swelled to a minimum of 185,000. Some estimate that during Passover there would be a million people in Jerusalem. Here, fifty days after Passover, there must have been several thousand people swarming the city. How many heard the Apostles preach the gospel? God's people rejoice that God poured out His grace on 3,000 sinners in one swift movement. But when one considers that multiplied thousands more heard the same sermons and did not respond, he is forced to acknowledge the limitations of the human factor in salvation. We, the servants of God, preach, teach, reason, argue, and present the gospel clearly and repeatedly, longing for sinners to get the message and repent. God uses His Word, thoroughly stabs certain sinners, and adds them to the Church. That is what the Bible teaches about salvation.

# 33

# AND THE SPIRIT SAID . . . .

## ACTS 8:26-40

The night before Jesus was crucified, He promised the disciples that when He went back to the Father in heaven, He would send the Helper, the Comforter, the Holy Spirit to take His place. He promised that the Holy Spirit would dwell with the disciples (John 14:17). He promised that the Holy Spirit will make His home with believers who do Christ's word (John 14:23). He promised that God the Holy Spirit is one with God the Father and God the Son (John 14:23). He promised that the Holy Spirit would teach the disciples all things and help them remember what He had taught them (John 14:26). Jesus also promised that the Holy Spirit would bear witness of Him even as the disciples would do the same (John 15:26-27). He promised that the Holy Spirit will convict the world of sin, righteousness, and judgment (John 16:8-11). Jesus promised that the Holy Spirit would guide disciples into all truth as He speaks with the authority of the Triune God (John 16:13-14). Can a sinner come to Christ in this age apart from the work of this Holy Spirit?

The history of the Church, the Book of Acts, opens with the last scene of Jesus with the disciples on earth. They were standing together somewhere on Mt. Olivet, and Jesus offered the last words of instruction before He rose into heaven to sit down at the Father's right hand. He told the disciples, "But you will receive power when the Holy Spirit has come upon you, and you will be my witnesses in Jerusalem and in all Judea and Samaria, and to the end of the earth" (Acts 1:8). This command is very similar to Christ's previous command to His followers, "Go therefore and make disciples of all nations, baptizing them in the name of the Father and of the Son and of the Holy Spirit, teaching them to observe all that

I have commanded you. And behold, I am with you always, to the end of the age" (Matthew 28:19-20). Based on these commands one must conclude that Christ is with His followers and servants in the person of the Holy Spirit even now.

Therefore, since the Holy Spirit must be present with the preacher of the Good News, it must also be true that a sinner is regenerated only through the work of the Holy Spirit. That is the story of Acts. It is the story of the early Church and lays the foundation for all Church history. The Acts of the Apostles records some remarkable stories about the beginning of the Church. There were the miracles of the disciples preaching in foreign tongues at Pentecost (2:1-47), the healing of the lame beggar (3:1-10), the death of Ananias and Sapphira (5:1-11), many signs and wonders (5:12), and Peter's miraculous release from prison (12:6-18). All of these miracles have the fingerprint of the Holy Spirit on them.

But the greatest miracles in Acts are the stories of sinners being converted. God the Holy Spirit regenerated 3,000 souls the day of Pentecost. He removed the spiritual blindness from Saul of Tarsus and gave him a new heart in a moment. He stepped outside Jewish traditions and saved the Gentile Cornelius and his household. Throughout the Book of Acts, the reader discovers multiplied evidence of the work of God accomplished through the person of the Holy Spirit. That is His ministry. Paul reminded the Corinthians that some of them were once vial sinners, "But you were washed, you were sanctified, you were justified in the name of the Lord Jesus Christ and by the Spirit of our God" (1 Corinthians 6:11) . He told Pastor Titus that regeneration is the work of the Holy Spirit (Titus 3:5).

Since salvation is the work of the Holy Spirit, His work ought to be obvious in the case of the Ethiopian nobleman's rebirth. It is. This short story is replete with the work of the Holy Spirit. Almost everything that Philip and the Ethiopian did was prompted by God the Holy Spirit. It is a wonderful demonstration of how God prepares the table before He gives the invitation for hungry sinners to come and dine.

## THE HOLY SPIRIT PREPARED THE CIRCUMSTANCES (VV.26-29)

God told Philip to go to the desert (vv.26-27a). How did God communicate this plan? The text says that the angel of the Lord sent the evangelist to the desert road (v.26). However, that should not cause the reader to picture a heavenly being with wings flying around Philip's head telling him what to do. That is modern mythology. The word translated "angel" means messenger. God's messenger might have been an angel who appeared in a vision, he might have been the Holy Spirit Himself telling Philip where to go.

It is not surprising that God chose Philip for this task. This evangelist had recently been involved in a great work of the Holy Spirit north of Jerusalem (8:4-25). According to the fifth verse of the chapter, when Saul's persecution broke upon the church in Jerusalem, Philip went up to Samaria and proclaimed Christ. God used the event, and crowds were transfixed because of the message and mighty works (vv.6-7). Many believed and were baptized (vv.12). News about God's work got back to Jerusalem, and immediately Peter and John joined the team (vv.14-24). Then when it appears that God ceased working so vigorously in Samaria, Philip and the team returned to Jerusalem, preaching in villages along the way (v.25).

No one knows how long Philip had been back in Jerusalem before the Lord's messenger brought him instruction about his next mission. In this case, God instructed Philip to go to a far different kind of situation than he had experienced in Samaria (v.26). Samaria was a city and great crowds gathered to hear the gospel message. Now God told the evangelist to go to the road that ran from Jerusalem to Gaza.

Actually there were two such roads. One of the roads ran through Hebron in the desert. That is the one God told Philip to take. It went into the old city of Gaza. The old city, the one that had been part of the five leading Philistine cities, had been destroyed in 93 B.C. The new city of Gaza was built on the coast. The remains of the old city were about three miles inland, and the old road ran right through the ruins. In ancient times, "the Way to the Land of the Philistines" was a major road to Egypt. But that was in ancient times. Now this road was generally deserted. Why did God send Philip to the desert road, the infrequently used road?

Furthermore, God's messenger told Philip to go "toward the south." Granted the old road to Gaza was south of Jerusalem. But this phrase can also be translated to say, "go at noon." It would be nonsensical to human wisdom for a proven, effective servant of God to go to the seldom-used, desert road at high noon in order to do the work of an evangelist.

Regardless of the conclusions of human wisdom, the evangelist went (v.27a). His response was immediate and purposeful. The test says that he rose and went. The verb form indicates that "having stood up he traveled." Unlike many modern servants of God, Philip did not debate the sensibility of the task. Of course it didn't make sense. But it was obvious to Philip that this was God's will. It is obvious to the modern reader that God moved him. But how did Philip know it was God's messenger who brought him this message? Granted, that was the age of miracles and maybe the messenger of God was as real as a person who sits next to us in a church service. However, in any age, close fellowship with God allows for accurate communication from God. David Williams observed, "God's guidance is always most evident where there is a willingness to follow" (David J. Williams. New International Biblical Commentary, "Acts." Peabody, Mass.: Hendrickson Publishers, 1990, p.160.). God uses willing servants, obedient servants, holy servants to do His will. Probably in this case it was an actual angel who God might have sent to Philip in a vision.

God sent the messenger with the plan and Evangelist Philip rose up and went immediately. While he was walking along the deserted, dusty road, probably somewhere between Hebron and Gaza, an entourage with a chariot, or covered cart, came lumbering along. If you were the evangelist sent by God with His message to a particular place, what would you assume at this point? Would you be looking for the opportunity to tell someone in this group the good news of salvation?

Again God the Holy Spirit spoke to Philip and told him to approach the Ethiopian (vv.27b-29). The Ethiopian was an important man (vv.27b-28). Therefore, there was certainly an entourage that accompanied this court official from Ethiopia. He would not have been out in the desert alone in his chariot reading the Bible. He was a very important court official who came from a kingdom that was roughly located about where modern Ethiopia is. Homer referred to this ancient kingdom in his poem, The Odyssey (c.a. 800-600 B.C.), as "the ends of the earth." Certainly that statement is not to be taken literally, but the reference does make an interesting comparison. It could mean that Philip's influence with the gospel on this official from Ethiopia had affected Jerusalem, Judea, Samaria, and now "the ends of the earth." Is that not what Jesus told him to do when He ascended into heaven (Acts 1:8)?

The kingdom of Ethiopia was ruled by queens called "Candace." It was not that all the queens shared the same first names, rather "Candace" is a title similar to "Pharaoh" or "Caesar." This particular man was in charge of the kingdom's treasure. In other words, he was the Minister of Finance.

He was the equivalent of the United States Secretary of the Treasury, Henry M. Paulson. In other words, this was one very important guy. Under most circumstances, he would have been unapproachable.

He was an important figure in the kingdom, but more important than his importance was the fact that the man was a "God-fearer." Because he had deep respect for God, he had been to Jerusalem to worship. This is a good example of a person who is seeking for a right relationship with God. He knew that something was missing. He was obviously looking for that thing that would establish peace in his heart. He was doing what the prophet Jeremiah foresaw when God promised Israel, "You will seek me and find me. When you seek me with all your heart" (Jeremiah 29:13).

The man acted on what little light of revelation he had. Maybe all he had was the certainty that there is a Creator. Maybe he responded to the law in his conscience. He demonstrated the truth that when sinners act on the light God gives, God gives more light. That is what Jesus meant when He told the doubters in His day, "If anyone's will is to do God's will, he will know whether the teaching is from God or whether I am speaking on my own authority" (John 7:17).

But in Judaism, this man could only be a God-fearer. He had a deep respect for God and sought to worship Him. He was much like another Gentile man named Cornelius (Acts 10). Cornelius could have become a proselyte to Judaism, but this Ethiopian official could not even do that. He was not only a Gentile and outside the natural pale of Judaism, but he was a eunuch which precluded him from ever fully identifying with God's people. He could not become a proselyte. He could not even enter the temple (Deuteronomy 23:1). Nevertheless, the man went to Jerusalem to worship as much as he could. Was he disillusioned by the hypocrisy he saw in Jerusalem?

On the way home, the official was reading the Scripture or possibly having it read by an attendant. He was reading Isaiah's prophecy because he continued to search after God. Reading Scripture is the best place to find God. But where did this man get this scroll? Did he just recently buy it while he was in Jerusalem? Not everyone was privileged to have their own copy of the Scripture. In fact, such ownership was rare. How much did a Gentile eunuch have to pay for it? Money was probably no object because this man was important.

The important man was almost certainly surrounded by his attendants, but that did not deter Philip. The evangelist had an important message to deliver (v.29). The second impression Philip received from God the Holy Spirit was as plain as the first: "Go over and join this chariot." Was Phillip awed by the nobleman's entourage? Awed or not, Philip obeyed again and ran up to the cart. How could this stranger get an immediate audience with such an important official? The Holy Spirit was in control. He had been preparing this man's heart. He sent the man to Jerusalem on purpose. He prompted the man to buy the Scripture. He sent Philip with the Good News. He caused the man and Philip to meet at precisely the right place and right time.

### The Holy Spirit Had Prepared the Invitation (vv.30-35)

The Ethiopian was reading what the Holy Spirit had written long before this event (vv.32-33). Isaiah would certainly be a book of comfort to such a man. If he continued reading from the point where he was when Philip found him, the eunuch would read, "Let not the foreigner who has joined himself to the LORD say, 'The LORD will surely separate me from his people'; and let not the eunuch say, 'Behold, I am a dry tree.' For thus says the LORD: 'To the eunuchs who keep my Sabbaths, who choose the things that please me and hold fast my covenant, I will give in my house and within my walls a monument and a name better than sons and daughters; I will give them an everlasting name that shall not be cut off'" (Isaiah 56:3-5). There he would have seen a reminder of God's kindness and grace.

But he had not read that far. At this point, the man was reading about Christ. This is an exact quote of the Greek translation of Isaiah (Septuagint). It is the great story of Christ's suffering to make atonement for the sinner's sins. What a coincidence? No, the Holy Spirit had prepared the heart of the messenger and the recipient of the invitation (vv.30-31; 34-35). This was not a coincidence at all. The official no doubt noticed Philip and called the evangelist alongside himself (vv.30-31). That was an amazing thing. But then again the man was hungry for truth. What made him think that Philip would know the truth? One can be quite sure that Philip was not wearing a clerical collar and holding a Bible in his hands. The Holy Spirit directed the man to invite Philip to teach him.

The man was curious about what he was reading. At least Philip obeyed the Holy Spirit, approached the cart, and asked the man if he understood what he was reading. What if he just waited by the roadside without taking the initiative? He did not and, therefore, Philip had the privilege of leading the man to Christ (vv.34-35).

The official asked Philip, "About whom does the prophet say this, about himself or about someone else?" That was a common question of the day regarding this passage of Scripture (v.34). It falls within the context of the Servant of Yahweh songs. The Jews debated much about who or what the "servant" motif referred to. Some taught that the suffering servant was Isaiah himself. Other Rabbis concluded that it was the nation of Israel. Some even applied it to Messiah. Jesus appealed to this prophecy stating that it referred to Him (Luke 22:37). The natural sinner cares nothing for such truth. But the person whose heart the Holy Spirit prepares wonders, like Pilate, "What shall I do with Christ?"

Philip used the question as a springboard (v.35). Jesus had showed the disciples how to start at "the" question and use Scripture to reveal Christ. The day of His resurrection Jesus met with the two disciples on the road to Emmaus, "And beginning with Moses and all the Prophets, he interpreted to them in all the Scriptures the things concerning himself" (Luke 24:27). "Then he said to them, 'These are my words that I spoke to you while I was still with you, that everything written about me in the Law of Moses and the Prophets and the Psalms must be fulfilled.' Then he opened their minds to understand the Scriptures" (Luke 24:44-45).

Philip learned well from such examples and used the same method with the Ethiopian (v.35). He had a working knowledge of the Scripture which allowed him to take the official from where he was to where he needed to be. Christians should be this familiar with Scripture. That was Peter's thrust when he taught, "But in your hearts regard Christ the Lord as holy, always being prepared to make a defense to anyone who asks you for a reason for the hope that is in you" (1 Peter 3:15). Starting at the sinner's question and unfolding Scripture will present Christ. The gospel message preaches Jesus. The real gospel, unlike the chatter of modern religionists, shows Christ from the Scripture. Modern chatter talks about doing good works and is content to challenge needy sinners to "do your best." It talks about commitment to a religious organization and encourages the seeker to "join our church." However, true servants of God must be like Paul and "preach Christ crucified, a stumbling block to Jews and folly to Gentiles, but to those who are called, both Jews and Greeks, Christ the power of God and the wisdom of God" (1 Corinthians 1:23-24).

### THE HOLY SPIRIT OVERSAW THE RESPONSE (vv. 36-40)

The entourage just happened to arrive at a place with water at exactly the right time what a coincidence (vv.36-38). No, what work of the Holy Spirit. The new believer desired to be baptized. The born again man said to Philip, "See here is water! What prevents me from being baptized?" According to the Jews, two things prevented it. First, he was a eunuch; and second, he was a Gentile. But God's mercy and grace in salvation is broader than Jewish laws.

This is a common response to the gospel in Acts. When Peter presented the gospel to the Gentile Cornelius and his household, they believed and were saved. Therefore Peter wondered, "Can anyone withhold water for baptizing these people, who have received the Holy Spirit just as we have?" (Acts 10:47). The Seminary students ask, "Where was the water in the desert place?" What difference does it make? What really matters is what happened in the water and why. That is the important issue. The sinner confessed Christ and desired to be identified with Him.

How do we know the man confessed Christ? Verse thirty-seven, which reads: "And Philip said, 'If you believe with all your heart, you may.' And he replied, 'I believe that Jesus Christ is the Son of God'" is missing from some English translations. That is because this verse is missing from the oldest manuscripts. The earliest manuscript to include it is dated around the 10th century. That is one thousand years after the story was originally written down. Obviously this is a scribal insertion with good intentions. However, it is not necessary because the conclusion is obvious and assumed. Do we think Philip would agree to baptism if the man did not believe and confess Christ as Son of God? Also in the Pentecost sermon account (Acts 2:38-41), "Believe in the Lord Jesus Christ" does not follow "What must we do?" But in Acts 16:31, "Believe in the Lord Jesus" follows "What must I do?" and precedes baptism.

Because the Ethiopian believed in Jesus Christ, God the Son, Savior from sin, Philip baptized him. That they "went down into the water" implies immersion. So does the word baptizo.

The Holy Spirit sent Philip to do more work (vv.39-40). He miraculously swept Philip away (vv.39-40). It appears that Philip preached in the cities that are destined for destruction (Zephaniah 2:4,12). He was found first at Azotus (ancient Ashdod) which is twenty miles north of Gaza. Finally he made his way along the coast northward to Caesarea which is about fifty miles north of Azotus. It appears that he spent the next twenty years living in that city. As he preached in the once Philistine cities that were marked out for destruction, he demonstrated that God's mercy is extended to those who need it.

What did the Ethiopian think when Philip suddenly disappeared? The new saint rejoiced even though the evangelist was absent (v.39). That is because a signal sign of the new birth is joy.

Telling the Good News is not about slick sales pitches and irrefutable arguments. It is about the servant of God being in such fellowship with God that the Spirit of God arranges his or her life's circumstances and words to the effective work of bringing others to Christ.

# 34

# GREAT SHAKES

## Acts 16:25-34

How many people were born again as a direct result of the 9-11 tragedy? Surely, no one but God knows the answer to that question. Maybe no one actually turned to God in saving faith, but it is quite likely that some folks did. Did anyone receive Christ as Savior from the power and penalty of sin because of the Christmas Tsunami that devastated Sri Lanka and Indonesia a few years ago? Why even expect such a response to the catastrophe?

Human tragedy tends to force people to face the fragile nature of life. Common, everyday, boring life often lulls the human mind to sleep. It is easy to begin to believe that as it was yesterday, so it shall be tomorrow. Life becomes very predictable. When life is predictable, when life has settled down into a rut, it can be managed pretty well without any outside help from God. But when all of the props have been knocked out and life as we know it suddenly comes crashing down, people tend to look for help from someone or something outside themselves. Yea, if the tragedy is bad enough, people might even look for supernatural help. In desperate times like that, folks have been known to turn to God.

No doubt it is fairly common for people make a profession of faith as a direct result of a personal tragedy. There are people who have humbled themselves before God when they learned from the doctor that they have a terminal disease. Others turn to Christ in faith believing when a loved one is taken from them in death. Others "get religion" when they lose their jobs, endure a divorce, or are forced to declare bankruptcy.

But are decisions for Christ made under duress the same as salvation? Actually, "decisions for Christ" are always suspect. A new heart is always genuine. Religious decisions are the things Jesus described in the parable of the Sower and the seed. He taught that the seed that fell on the roadside, on the rocks, and in the weeds represented folks who either ignored the gospel as it was shared, with the result that it was unproductive, or quickly embraced the gospel message, only to realize that it never took root.

That kind of thing happens frequently in "E.R." salvation. In the heat of the moment when life is falling apart, it is easy to decide to follow Christ. Something in the person's conscience quickly reminds him of the gospel story he heard in the past. Maybe for many months or years this person had been bothered by the certainty of sin's guilt. When the tragedy occurs, the person quickly makes a decision regarding the gospel message he had heard.

However, as the story about the Sower and the seed reveals, when the problems of life or the distractions of Vanity Fair arise, such decisions seem unimportant and the person lays it aside. Living life is more fun or more important to those people than living for Christ. The good news in the story is that the seed of the gospel does take root in some people who here it, and they produce various amounts of spiritual fruit.

That kind of thing can happen with people who are jerked out of the rut of life by a catastrophe. It is the kind of thing that happened to the Philippian jailer. He had a pretty good job. Probably life was tolerable, and he was able to keep things under control. Then suddenly everything changed. In a moment, he found himself in a life-or-death situation. In response to the cataclysm of life, the man was born again. It is quite obvious that he was truly changed because he immediately began to live out the love of Christ that God poured into his heart. The circumstances leading to salvation might be important, but they are not nearly as important as the subsequent evidence that proves the reality of salvation.

## GOD GAINED A SINNER'S ATTENTION (vv.25-29)

God's servants praised God in spite of their circumstances (v.25). Paul and Silas had been faithful in God's service ever since the church in An-tioch sent them out (Acts 13:1-3). But now in Philippi, their service to

God was rewarded with imprisonment. How could things have gone so wrong for these faithful men? Maybe "wrong" is not the right word to describe their apparent dilemma.

Actually, God used Paul and Silas for His glory in the city of Philippi. Soon after they arrived in town, they met Lydia, a God-fearing woman, and led her to salvation in Christ (v.14). Then it appears that on a regular basis they met with other God-fearers to pray (v.16). However, it is not uncommon for Satan to step up and oppose God's servants wherever God is granting success. So in this case, Satan sent an evil spirit to indwell a girl who then harassed God's servants (vv.16-18). In a marvelous miracle of kindness, Paul released the girl from the demon's control (v.18). What was kindness for the girl was the source of anger for the fortune-teller merchants because it caused them to lose money (v.19) They forced the authorities to arrest God's servants on trumped-up charges (vv.19-22). The authorities beat the servants and put them in the inner prison where they were chained to the wall and had their feet locked in stocks (vv.22-25).

What would you do if you were Paul or Silas? Many modern Christians would quit serving God on the spot because it is a common misunderstanding that it is not God's will for His people to suffer. Others would quit the God-serving business because they would conclude that suffering indicated they were out of God's will. Still others would contact their Christian law association and sue the Philippian authorities because they have rights too. Some Christians might even go so far as to organize a boycott against all Philippian fortune-tellers. Maybe the really devout servants of God would sit quietly in prison and pray imprecatory prayers against the magistrates.

Paul and Silas must have been rather odd. At midnight, with backs bruised and bleeding; with their wrists chained to the wall and their feet in stocks, these guys prayed and sang to God. There is no indication at all in the text that they prayed for their release. As the text reads, it is altogether right for us to think that maybe they thanked God in prayer, concluding that it was a blessing that God counted them worthy to suffer for Christ. Their friends, Peter and John, reacted like that when the authorities punished them. Luke tells us, "They left the presence of the council, rejoicing that they were counted worthy to suffer dishonor for the name" (Acts 5:41). Maybe they were praying for opportunities for the gospel.

The servants were also singing hymns of praise. The word translated "hymns" speaks of songs of praise. That word would describe words from the collection of Psalms such as, "Let the righteous one rejoice in the Lord and take refuge in him! Let all the upright in heart exult!" (Psalm 64:10). Servants who really believe God can really praise Him even in suffering because servants who really believe God believe that He oversees all things for His own glory. People like that agree with Paul who was confident that "we know that for those who love God all things work together for good, for those who are called according to his purpose" (Romans 8:28).

While Paul and Silas were singing praises to God and praying for God to receive glory in all that transpired, the other prisoners kept on listening to them. It was midnight. The servants could have been yelling or complaining about their unfair treatment. But the other prisoners heard only praise to God.

In that setting, God changed the circumstances (vv.26-29). He sent a great shaking that set the prisoners free (v.26). Earthquakes were common in Macedonia in those days. But this earthquake was not just another earthquake, nor was it a mere coincidence. This was a miracle. God is free to use any part of His creation that He chooses to bring about His plans. It was a miracle because God shook the earth at just the right time. He shook the earth at just the right place. He shook the earth just the right amount. And yet, according to the story, no one was killed or injured. The jail did not fall down on the prisoners. God moved the doorjambs just enough to let the cross bar fall out and the doors to swing open. God cracked the walls enough to let the chains fall free. God did everything just right to get the jailer's attention.

The jailer, who was responsible for keeping God's servants secure under arrest, suddenly submitted to the prisoners (vv.27-29). Probably he lived in a house next to the prison. No doubt he was jarred awake by the quake, ran outside, and immediately checked the prison to make sure that no one had escaped. The potential for injury to the prisoners would not be his first concern. Escape would be. Through the dust and moonlight the jailer saw that the prison door was open (v.27). Knowing that it was likely that he would be killed for allowing the prisoners to escape, he was going to kill himself.

Apparently, the Roman law generally applied at that time was that the keeper of prisoners would receive the punishment intended for a prisoner if the jailer allowed him to escape. For example, Herod ordered the execution of the sentries who were responsible to guard Peter, whom God released from prison (Acts 12:19). Likewise, when the ship full of criminals wrecked during a storm, the soldiers planned to kill the prisoners rather than let them escape (Acts 27:42).

Life was suddenly a wreck for the Philippian jailer. Surely the question, "Why me?" ran through his mind. Surely he wondered, "How could this have happened on my watch?" The fact that he was ready to kill himself indicates how discouraged he was. That was a good thing. The man's spirit was so crushed that he bowed before the servants of God (vv.28-29). Paul also looked through the dust and could see what the jailer was going to do. He cried out to stop him telling him that none of the prisoners had escaped. It was a miracle that all of the prisoners stayed put. Were they so impressed with these singing preachers that they deemed it better to stay in the prison?

The jailer got some lanterns and rushed in to bow down before Paul and Silas. Why did he do that? Obviously, he was aware of their relationship with the true God. Obviously, their testimony had paved the way for this response. Apparently, he knew that he and the magistrate were wrong for treating these men this way.

It is true that the story of Acts is all about miracles. God did many unusual things as He established the Church. In this case, God put Paul and Silas in the right city at the right time. He allowed Satan to stir up trouble at exactly the right time. He allowed His servants to suffer for Him. He gave them grace to pray and sing praises to Him, He shook the jail open, He made sure that Paul saw what the jailer was going to do, He restrained the prisoners from running away. Everything worked to the humbling of this one man at this moment. Why?

## THE SINNER WAS BORN AGAIN (vv.30-34)

The humbled jailer wondered what he needed to do in order to be saved. God's servants told him how to be saved (vv.30-32). Where did he even get the remotest understanding of the need for salvation? At some point, he heard about salvation. Maybe he had heard the servant girl as "she followed Paul . . . crying out, 'These men are servants of the Most High God, who proclaim to you the way of salvation'" (Acts 16:17). If so, he would not have been too much unlike the folks with whom we live. Most Americans know something about salvation; and when the crisis comes, they are prone to ask questions like this.

The jailer's question provided a wide-open door for Paul and Silas. They instructed the sinner from God's Word (vv.31-32). First, they told the man that if he wanted to be saved, he needed to trust Christ (v.31). The said, "Believe in the Lord Jesus." That seems simple enough. What is true belief in Jesus? The sinner must believe that Jesus of Nazareth is God in the flesh. He or she must believe that Jesus died in order to provide the covering, the atonement for sin. He must believe that Jesus rose from the dead to validate that covering. He must believe that Jesus is in heaven interceding. But maybe the first thing the sinner must believe is that he needs the covering that Jesus alone provides for sin.

Furthermore, Paul and Silas told the humble sinner that his entire household could trust Christ (v.31). This was not a promise that the entire household would be saved if the head of the household expressed faith in Christ. Each person in the household could be saved on the basis of individual faith. At the same time, this is an interesting promise because it teaches that one person's faith can effect the entire household. That same principle came to light when not only Cornelius, but his entire household, that is his wife, sons, daughters, and even servants, were born again at the same time (Acts 11:14). A few days before this event in Philippi, the entire household of Lydia was saved (Acts 16:15). Later the record in Acts 18:8 reveals that the entire household of Crispus was saved. The same must have been true regarding the entire household of Stephanas according to Paul's testimony (1 Corinthians 1:16 ).

They taught the Word of the Lord to him and his household. This is the most critical part of Paul's and Silas's communication with the jailer. It is critical because "faith comes from hearing, and hearing through the word of Christ" (Romans 10:17). Paul could not give the humbled man the assurance he needed through a program. He could not offer him assurance that he was okay as is. Paul and Silas made no attempt to soft-pedal the gospel. The guy was in greater eternal trouble than he was temporal trouble. He didn't need temporal help. He needed eternal help. He needed help, and help is in God's Word. Obviously the man did what Paul said. The text doesn't say that he confessed with his mouth and believed in his heart, but the fact that Paul baptized him proves that he did. That was the same conclusion Philip drew regarding the Ethiopian's faith (cf. Acts 8:37).

The jailer was born again, and immediately he began to live like he was saved (vv.33-34). First, he was baptized (v.33). The text makes it clear that he and his family were identified with Christ immediately after they were saved. Of course, one wonders where the baptism took place. It could have been in a cistern in the courtyard, if there was a courtyard and a cistern. Where it took place is not nearly as important as what took place.

Second, the new Christian showed pity for the suffering (v.33). It appears he took the servants up out of the prison into his own house. There he did what he could to relieve suffering.

Third, the jailer helped meet the servant's needs from his own resources (v.34). He gave them a simple meal. But Jesus taught that a simple meal offered to Christ's servants brings a great reward. "For truly, I say to you, whoever gives you a cup of water to drink because you belong to Christ will by no means lose his reward" (Mark 9:41). Hospitality is a good sign of salvation. Notice that Lydia responded the same way when she was converted (v.15). It requires the sacrifice of time, energy, and money. But Christian hospitality spends these resources because it believes that the other person is more important than self. Yet most people who call themselves Christians will not even speak to the person who sits beside him or her in church.

The fourth evidence of new life is in the fact that the man rejoiced (v.34). Frequently, the New Testament describes the born-again person with this characteristic. When Paul wrote the letter to the Christians in this town, he used the word "joy or rejoice" sixteen times. Where there is no joy, can there be salvation?

In religiously-educated circles, we know that these four traits characterize Christians. Therefore, church-going people decide that if they are going to be Christians, they need to do things like this. With all their might they try, but generally fail. Why? Either they are not truly saved, or they are quenching the Spirit. What should such people do? Paul told the Corinthian Christians to "examine yourselves, to see whether you are in the faith. Test yourselves. Or do you not realize this about yourselves, that Jesus Christ is in you?—unless indeed you fail to meet the test!" (2 Corinthians 13:5). If the person is not saved, it is possible that he or she will also lack joy. Furthermore Paul warned Christians, "Do not quench the Spirit" (1 Thessalonians 5:19). Quenching the Holy Spirit's influence will rob a Christian of joy. The person who finds obedience to God (baptism), love for others (care and provision), and joy missing in their lives needs to take the exam.

Each person who is truly born again through the miracle of God's grace must testify to God's amazing work. God arranged for us to be born where we were, meet the people we met, hear the gospel when we did, and on and on the miracles go. Human wisdom can arrange for a person to make a decision about religion and engage a lifelong journey of doing religious stuff that has no power, no purpose, and no joy. But when God shakes a sinner's life to the point that He saves that soul, the results are self-evident and the regenerated saint has no need to argue that he or she is really born again. The evidence speaks loudly and clearly!

# 35

# WHO IS ON TRIAL?

ne of the best ways to share the gospel is to simply tell
others how God gave you a new heart. A simple testimony
is something that other people often understand easily. It
does not condemn the sinner nor is it meant to make the sinner feel
uncomfortable. And yet while a personal testimony offers the great
invitation for salvation in non-confrontational terms, it also puts the
listener on trial. When a redeemed sinner explains to an unredeemed
sinner how he or she was redeemed, it causes the listener to reflect on
his own unforgiven sin. A simple testimony of salvation puts the sinner
on trial because he must reflect on why the same kind of change has
never occurred in his life.

That is the scene in this story about Paul the Apostle. Verse nineteen
of this chapter breaks in on a setting where Paul is standing before some
very important dignitaries defending his actions against the accusations
of the Jewish leaders. Paul, who had been Saul of Tarsus, was once the
darling of the Pharisees. He was highly educated, devoutly defended the
Pharisaic traditions, and spearheaded persecutions against Christians,
whom he and his fellow Pharisees considered to be heretics.

One day God broke in on Saul's life, gave him a new heart, gave him
a new name, and gave him a new purpose in life. Saul, the one time persecutor of Christians became Paul, the great spokesman for the gospel.
He preached the Good News of forgiveness all over the Roman Empire.
This infuriated the Jews. They concluded that Paul was a turncoat and
a traitor to the great cause of Judaism. They finally had opportunity to
apprehend Paul one day while he was in Jerusalem presenting an offering in the temple. They incited the Roman authorities to arrest Paul on
trumped up charges that he desecrated the temple by taking Greeks along

with him when he entered the sacred shrine (21:27-36).

The Roman authorities put Paul in prison in Jerusalem. But soon they learned of a Jewish plot to kill Paul (23:12-22). Upon learning of this plot, the commander in charge of 1,000 Roman soldiers in Jerusalem sent Paul, under guard of 470 of his solders, to Governor Felix in Caesarea (23:23-35). The emperor himself had appointed Felix to rule over the imperial province that included Judea. This was the job Pilate held in Jesus' day.

The next week, the Jewish authorities came from Jerusalem to Caesarea in order to formally charge Paul of profaning the temple (24:1-21). Felix listened to the charge and then listened to Paul's defense and chose not to make a decision. For the next two years he and his wife Drusilla, who was a Jewess, called for a conference with Paul in order to hear him teach (24:22-26).

In the mean time, the emperor replaced Governor Felix with a new governor, Festus. Festus had been in office only three days when the Jewish authorities confronted him about the Paul issue (25:1-5). He went back to Caesarea, and the next week the Jewish authorities came to Caesarea and again formally charged Paul with profaning the temple. Paul defended himself again. But this time Governor Festus forced Paul into the ultimate appeal for justice. As a citizen of Rome, Paul appealed to Caesar. Caesar himself would pass judgment on Paul's case.

Several days had passed since Paul had appealed his case to the highest court in the land when King Agrippa and his wife Bernice showed up in Caesarea to visit Governor Festus. Agrippa was king over the Jewish people in Palestine. He ruled under the authority of Festus. Festus shared the Paul dilemma with this Jewish king and confessed that he did not think Paul had committed a crime serious enough to deserve punishment. As a result, he wondered what he was supposed to write as an accusation in the letter when he sent Paul to the emperor. King Agrippa agreed to hear Paul's defense (25:13-27).

That brings us to the point in the story where chapter twenty-six begins. The scene smacks with the flaunting of royalty. The most important people of the province were present at this meeting. It began with much pomp and circumstance (25:23). The most prominent men of the city were present, which must have included the Jewish leaders of Caesarea (25:23). King Agrippa and Bernice would have entered the room dressed in the royal purple robes, wearing gold crowns, and accompanied by their entourage of advisors, guards, and servants. Governor Festus would have entered wearing his royal red robe and crown of authority. He too would have been surrounded by his court officials. The room overflowed with dignitaries and significant people.

Then the governor gave orders to have the prisoner brought in. Scripture seems to indicate that Paul was a slight man. Tradition holds that he was bald and given to poor eyesight. According to his own admission, he was not a skilled or powerful orator (1 Corinthians 2:4). Imagine this insignificant man as the focus of the attention of all these dignitaries. The governor gave Paul permission to speak, and Paul launched into the story he must have told many times before. He simply unfolded to the most important people of the land how God had changed his heart and how he lived because of that change. Paul left a wonderful illustration of how to invite sinners to the Savior.

## Paul's Defense (vv.19-24)

Paul's defense was not a legal maneuver through which he hoped to be set free. His legal defense would come when he faced Caesar. He had already appealed to the right channels to have Caesar hear and decide his case. This appeal was Paul's right as a Roman citizen. However at this point in Paul's life, he was waiting for the governor to send him to the emperor in Rome with a letter explaining the charge and the reason for Paul's appeal. It would be possible, yea likely, that Paul would have legal counsel or representation in that defense.

This story describes Paul's personal defense (vv.19-23). He did what Peter wrote about when he challenged Christians to "in your hearts regard Christ the Lord as holy, always being prepared to make a defense to anyone who asks you for a reason for the hope that is in you" (1 Peter 3:15). That is exactly what Paul did in this case. He gave an apologia. The word means to make a defense. The king and governor probably saw this as Paul's personal defense. Most people would naturally see it as his personal defense.

But Paul saw this as an opportunity to present the gospel. Then again, an opportunity for a Christian to present the gospel is a personal defense. The person of Paul and the gospel of Christ were so intertwined, so much one, that the defense of one was the defense of the other. For the Christian, merely living should be a defense of the gospel. That is what Paul explained. He answered by describing life for Paul from Tarsus. Paul told King Agrippa how God had interrupted his life and changed his heart one day as he was traveling toward Damascus (vv.12-18). Did the king understand this miracle? It's doubtful. Paul went on to relate how God gave him specific instruction about how he should serve his new Lord and Master.

Coming to verse nineteen, Paul confessed that he was obedient to God's instruction (v.19). He was in trouble with the Jews because he did precisely what God told him to do (vv.20-21). In obedience to God's plan, Paul began to preach repentance in Damascus. His gospel message required that sinners turn away from sin and toward the Savior. He started by declaring the message at home. Then Paul went right to the heart of Judaism in Jerusalem. He told the good news to Jews and Gentiles alike. His influence with the gospel reached throughout Judea though there is no record that he preached there himself. Paul taught that a changed heart results in a changed lifestyle (v.20).

The witness also explained how God kept helping him by giving him strength for the task, abundant grace, and the ability to do miracles (v.22). This is the man who God used to heal the sick and raise the dead. Paul understood the power of God working through him as he preached and taught. He had learned how to draw on God's sufficient grace (2 Corinthians 12:12).

As Paul obeyed the Lord's command, he went everywhere teaching about Jesus of Nazareth, who is the Christ (vv.22-23). He testified to all people about Christ as an eyewitness who had first-hand knowledge of the facts he related. He explained how Jesus fulfilled all of the promises of Christ from Moses through the Prophets. That is to say that Paul used the entire Old Testament to unfold the truth about Jesus who is the Christ. He learned this method from Jesus Himself. Jesus used this method when He unfolded the truth about Himself to the two disciples He met on the road to Emmaus. "And beginning with Moses and all the Prophets, he interpreted to them in all the Scriptures the things concerning himself" (Luke 24:27).

Paul confessed to King Agrippa that he taught all people everywhere that Christ must suffer and die, that Christ must be the preeminent one to rise from the dead, and that Christ would proclaim the light of truth to Jews and Gentiles.

This is the Christian's apologetic. This message of Christ is our defense, our explanation for a changed life. If a Christian is not obedient to God's word, he or she has no reason to speak and nothing to say. Obedience to God's Word marks the obedient one as being quite different from the rest of the world. In fact, it is the Christian's obedience to God's Word that often causes unregenerate people to ask for an explanation. If a professing Christian fits well with his world, it is doubtful that anyone in that world will ever ask him to explain the difference. Who would ask the reason for the difference when there is obviously no difference. How often does someone ask you why you live the way you live? A compromised lifestyle almost never opens the door for us "to make a defense to anyone who asks [us] for a reason for the hope that is in [us]" (1 Peter 3:15).

Paul's explanation about why he was so odd in a world of conformity stirred the governor's ire (v.24). Festus interrupted with a loud voice. He shouted at Paul and accused him of becoming foolish through his much study of the Scripture. It is important to remember at this point that Paul had been addressing King Agrippa, the Jew (v.19). However, it is obvious that as Governor Festus listened to this eyewitness testimony, he grew intense and agitated. Common sense concurs with the governor. Why shouldn't he be agitated? Here were some of the most important people in the empire trying to decide what they should do about this Roman citizen's appeal to the Emperor. When asked to explain, Paul went off on what appeared to be a wild goose chase talking about a man from Nazareth, a carpenter and teacher who rose from the dead! No one believes that!

Paul's words sounded senseless to the governor. He quickly and confidently concluded that no reasonable person believed this kind of stuff. Ultimately, Festus must have been frustrated because Paul was not giving him any reasonable material to put in his letter of accusation to the Emperor. Here was his chance to help his case and Paul was talking crazy about Jesus rising from the dead! Therefore, the governor accused Paul of being insane. Often the world doesn't understand faith in Christ. It is a miracle that escapes human comprehension.

Notice that Paul was not fazed by the governor's interruption. Why not? Maybe it was because Festus' loud interruption was expected in an age when men were men. Probably Paul was not even taken by surprise. The text indicates that he took it in stride. Christians in this modern age must be prepared when the gospel has this effect on some hearers. We should not be shocked and offended when our gospel testimony causes others to be agitated. How Paul responded to this abrupt, emotional interruption is an important lesson for everyone who desires to tell the

Good News to sinners.

## PAUL'S RESPONSE (vv.24-29)

First, consider what Paul did not do. Paul did not respond to the governor's explosion in kind. He did not yell back at the emperor and get embroiled in a mindless argument where he and the governor would attack each other's mothers or lineage. That is not because Paul was a weakling or incapable of raising his voice. The Bible records the fact that Paul was known to raise his voice when the circumstances warranted such a response. For example, when the jailer in Philippi was going to kill himself because he thought the prisoners had escaped, Paul thought that was an important enough issue to get animated (Acts 16:28). He cried out and told the jailer that he and the prisoners where still there and that he must do himself no harm.  In the early days of this saga about which he now answered, when the members of the Sanhedrin falsely accused Paul of profaning the temple, he deemed the situation fitting for him to cry out, "I am a Pharisee, the son of a Pharisee. . ." (Acts 23:6).

Other good men in the Bible did not hesitate to get animated when the cause required it. When the Jews were stoning Stephen because of his faith, just before he died he got vocal. "And falling to his knees he cried out with a loud voice, 'Lord, do not hold this sin against them.' And when he had said this, he fell asleep" (Acts 7:60). John the Baptist was so convinced that Jesus was superior to him that he cried out the testimony of Jesus Christ to religious hypocrites who thought they were the most important people in life (John 1:15). Indeed, Jesus Himself "cried out and said, 'Whoever believes in me, believes not in me but in him who sent me'" (John 12:44).

In this case Paul did not cry out to match the governor's response. Neither did Paul walk away and sulk. He did not get offended and pout. When another person boldly, even loudly, confronts with a cause or without cause, many Christians tuck tail and run. They act like they are afraid to give an answer for the hope that is within them. Paul did not shout back, and he did not cut and run. Paul understood that this man was his authority, and he dared not show disrespect by arguing. But he also knew that Jesus was his Lord, and he needed to represent Him well.

Consider what Paul did (vv.25-29). He responded with settled confi-

dence and deep respect. Paul showed respect to the governor who interrupted him and yelled at him (v.25). He affirmed that his words were
true and reasonable (v.25). And then he continued to address the king
(vv.26-29). Paul didn't let the governor's outburst get him off track.

He complimented the Jewish king reminding him he is observant
and fully aware of what was going on. The Church was growing—by
now it was worldwide. Surely Agrippa saw the evidence of this growth.
What had started in Jerusalem in A.D. 35 had spread like wild fire. Paul
reminded the king that the message of the gospel had spread through
Judea, Samaria, and Galilee. By this time in history, the gospel had gone
to Phoenicia, Cyprus, and Antioch. It had spread through Asia Minor,
Macedonia, Achaia, even to the emperor's door step in Rome. Paul reminded King Agrippa that he knew this.

Most sinners are aware of the gospel's effect on the world. They cannot
deny the effect the gospel has on individual's homes and entire nations.
Christians do well to call their attention to unavoidable facts. Show sinners that the light of the gospel is dispelling error wherever it goes. Tell
them how the gospel changed your life and that it continues to change
lives all over the world.

Paul appealed to the king's faith (vv.27-29). He laid out the great invitation in the form of a question: "Do you believe the Prophets?" This was
a well timed, well stated question. It was like an arrow from a bow directed at an exact target. As a king ruling over Jews Agrippa had to say, "Yes, I
believe the Prophets." To deny that faith would be political suicide. However, if Agrippa said, "Yes, I believe the Prophets" then he must accept
the Christ of the gospel Paul just presented. He was definitely stuck on
the horns of a dilemma. Paul helped the king by answering the difficult
question for him. He said, "I know in my heart that you believe."

Agrippa was stunned by conviction. What could he say? How would
he respond? He chose to interrupt Paul with a question (v.28). Would
Paul convince him to become a Christian? His response proves that he
understood what Paul had said. The prisoner invited the dignitaries to
become like him. He invited the most important people in the province
to receive Christ as Savior. Only a person confident of his relationship
with Christ will invite others to become like him. "Become like me"
flows from "I was not disobedient."

The Christian who does not live obediently regarding Christ's Word,
has no defense and no invitation. The Christian who lives a life of obedi-

ence to the gospel because he is saved by the gospel will put sinners on trial with his life. In fact, that kind of life is the best witness against sin and for the gospel. The conclusion is obvious. God desires for His people to so order their lives that those lives will produce evidence against the sinner's sin. God desires for His people to live in such a way that the details of their lives strike conviction in the sinners' hearts.

# 36

# EVERYWHERE IT IS
# SPOKEN AGAINST

## ACTS 28:17-27

L ife must be discouraging for modern evangelists. Knowledge of
the inner workings of evangelistic meetings and the evangelistic organizations that traverse the country, proves that modern
evangelists are under constant pressure to get results. Local church pastors are the lifeline for these servants of God. If the pastors don't invite
the evangelists to come to their churches for meetings, the evangelists
will virtually go out of business and be forced to look for some other line
of work. Many pastors invite well-known evangelists to their church in
order to "get results." Imagine how many invitations an evangelist is going to get if he must tell the interested pastor that he hasn't seen anyone
walk the aisle in the past three months. That fellow better start looking
for a new job.

Because of this pressure, evangelists often force themselves and the
other members of there teams to do everything in their power to generate
decisions. Some evangelists have resorted to pep talks before the meetings
begin in order to stir up the team members to get some results. These
meetings are much like a pep rally before a football game or a pep talk at
a sales convention. Apparently, some evangelists feel a need to get themselves psyched up in order to produce some decisions because failure to
produce decisions is going to make folks very discouraged.

Since that is true, one would expect that Paul the Evangelist must have
been discouraged a lot in life. This was the man who had been a member of

the Pharisees' "Who's Who." He was pegged as the most likely to succeed in Judaism. He was the front man for those who defended "the truth" of the Old Testament. He was the chief investigator, inquisitor, and persecutor of false teachings like the Christian sect. He would, no doubt, be in great demand as a teacher in Israel in the years to come. He was almost certainly wealthy. He was well liked. He was respected in his circles of influence.

Then one day when he was just going about his business, God interrupted his life. God changed Saul's heart, gave him a new direction in life, gave him a new purpose, and changed his name to Paul. From that moment everything in Paul's life changed. His friends not only rejected him but became his enemies. The very people who he once saw as his enemies became his dearest friends. He now promoted the "sect" he used to persecute. The success Paul enjoyed in the past was long gone.

For the next thirty-plus years, Paul wandered all over the Middle East telling people the good news that Jesus, the man from Nazareth, was really the Messiah. He taught everyone who would listen, everywhere he went, that Jesus the Messiah died for their sins and that they, by expressing faith in Christ's finished work, could be reconciled to God and receive the promise of eternal life. Would this not be good news in the sinner's ear?

That good news sounded as farfetched to many people in the first century as it does to people today. The ancient people were also slow to embrace this teaching. The majority of people who heard the good news refused to believe it. Some did. But for the most part the gospel was, as the Jewish leaders described it in this text, "spoken against everywhere." People just weren't standing in line to accept this teaching. Was Paul discouraged, having given up a promising career to preach a gospel that most people didn't want? Not at all.

This text finds Paul sitting in a rented house under house arrest by the Romans. Is that a fitting end for such a fine ambassador of Christ? The world would say, "No." Most people would conclude that Paul's circumstances were tragic. A man who had sacrificed as much as Paul did should be honored, not sent to prison! But Paul wasn't discouraged. The reason he was not discouraged is because he understood the nature of God's good news and the plan God ordained regarding that good news. The fact that Jewish people concluded that the Christian sect was spoken against everywhere, and the fact that the truth of the gospel always seemed to cause a division, didn't surprise Paul at all. He understood God's promises in the Old Testament.

Therefore, when Paul met the Jewish leaders in Rome, he went out of his way to assure them that he was not their enemy. He did all that he could to help the larger body of Jews understand that Jesus of Nazareth was actually the Messiah God promised in the Old Testament. Some of the Jewish people were convinced. Others refused to believe. Paul addressed the unbelievers with words from the Old Testament that should have cut them deeply. He simply revealed to those stubborn people that God had already promised that they would respond just like that. They were hopeless—utterly hopeless. Paul was not surprised because he realized that this "sect" was "spoken against everywhere." Be that as it may, it is still the good news of eternal life. It is still worth dying for. Popular acceptance was never a consideration when God laid the plans for salvation.

## Paul Had a Cordial Visit With the Jewish Leaders (vv.17-22)

The evangelist invited the leaders of the Jewish community in Rome to the house where he was staying in order to explain his current circumstances to them (vv.17-20). This is a clear attempt on Paul's part to win their confidence. It is critical for people who share the great invitation to win the confidence of the listener. Most people do not quickly embrace a radical message they hear from a stranger. People need to know what effect that radical message has had on the soul-winner's life before they will embrace it for themselves.

Paul tried to win the leaders' confidence (vv.17-19). He had been in Rome only three days. In that short time, he had recovered from a very difficult trip that included being shipwreck (27:39-44) and being bit by a viper while trying to dry out on the Island of Malta. He had stayed through the winter (three months) on Malta (28:11). Then he was transported the rest of the way to Rome where he would carry out his appeal to Caesar. When he arrived in Rome, Paul secured a rented house where he could stay under house arrest (28:16). The fact that Paul had endured so much and yet so quickly called a meeting with the Jewish leaders indicates that he was quite convinced that what he had to say to them was very important. Paul always felt a keen responsibility for the Jews. They were his kinsmen. He longed to see them saved from sin. For whom do Christians feel a keen responsibility to tell the good news?

Right away after arriving in Rome, Paul called a meeting of the local leaders of the Jews. Ancient historians indicate that as many as 40,000 Jews lived in Rome at this time. It was also a known fact that there were at least ten synagogues in this city. Paul wanted to talk to the leaders of his relatives. Notice that he began the meeting with the leaders by appealing to his Jewish lineage (vv.17b-19). He called them brothers which was literally true. Paul could not have done anything to become more Jewish than he already was. He explained to the leaders that he was innocent regarding the customs of "our fathers." That was also true. Paul's use of the term "our fathers" is very significant. He equated himself with those leaders and indicated that they had all come from the same lineage.

Paul related how the Jews had delivered him into the hands of Roman authority. And yet it is obvious that Paul did not accuse these Jews directly in his statements. He told them that the Roman authorities had examined him and desired to let him go since he had not done anything worthy of the death penalty (v.18). A quick review of Paul's history reminds the reader how important these conclusions were. First, there was Claudia Lysias, a Roman commander of 1,000 soldiers, who considered Paul innocent and sent him further up the chain of command to the governor. Governor Felix found him innocent, but he wanted to play up to the Jews and left Paul in prison. The governor who replaced Felix, Governor Festus, also found Paul innocent. King Agrippa found him innocent.

Paul should have been set free on several occasions. But, as God's will would have it, Paul was forced to appeal to Caesar. He explained that it was not his first choice to appeal to Caesar, but that he had no other options when the Jews from Jerusalem pressed their case (v.19). Paul made it very clear to these leaders that he had no grievance or accusation against "my" people. He wanted the Jewish leaders to know that he still loved his people and held nothing against them.

Paul attempted to win the confidence of the Jewish leaders through this conversation. However, as soon as possible, he directed the conversation toward the greater goal—to tell the gospel (v.20). Paul was open and frank about this as he explained the purpose of the conversation. He did not wish to be accused of playing tricks. There was no subterfuge or bait-and-switch tactics on Paul's part. He taught the soul-winner some important lessons about presenting the gospel. He taught us to be kind, be cordial, and be open.

How Paul turned the conversation to the gospel is also instructive. He simply explained that he was in prison because of the hope of Israel. Any

Jew who had been educated from the Scripture knew that this phrase referred to the Messiah who was promised in the Old Testament. Paul was up front about wanting to talk to the Jewish people in Rome about Messiah, His kingdom, His work, His suffering and His resurrection.

This is another example of Paul's desire to give the gospel to the Jew first. He knew that God had called him to evangelize Gentiles. When God saved Saul of Tarsus, He instructed one of His servants, Ananias, to go and encourage the new saint and tell him what God's plan was for the rest of his life. Ananias hesitated to go and tell God's message to Saul the persecutor. "But the Lord said to him, 'Go, for he is a chosen instrument of mine to carry my name before the Gentiles and kings and the children of Israel'" (Acts 9:15) . Paul heard what God said through His messenger and accepted it. He was so convinced of God's calling that some years later he confessed to Christians that God "was pleased to reveal his Son to me, in order that I might preach him among the Gentiles, I did not immediately consult with anyone" (Galatians 1:16).

However, while Paul understood that God's plan sent him primarily to the Gentiles, he also knew that God planned for the Jew to hear the gospel first. That confidence is evident when Paul told Roman Christians, "I am not ashamed of the gospel, for it is the power of God for salvation to everyone who believes, to the Jew first and also to the Greek" (Romans 1:16). Therefore, one sees much evidence that Paul presented the gospel to the Jews first and then turned to the Gentiles when the Jews rejected the message. That was his practice in Cyprus (13:5), in Pisidian Antioch (13:14), in Corinth (18:6), and in Ephesus (20:21). No doubt that was Paul's practice nearly everywhere he went.

Modern Gentile believers should be very thankful that God sent the gospel to Gentiles. We should be thankful enough that we would continue to give out the same gospel message that saved our souls.

In response to Paul's appeal, the leaders explained their ignorance (vv.21-22). They confessed that they were virtually ignorant about Paul (v.21). They had received no information from the Jews in Jerusalem about this so-called rabble rouser. Actually, the history reveals that it was not the Jews who lived in Jerusalem, but the Jews from Asia Minor who were responsible for Paul's arrest in the first place (21:27). They were painfully aware of Paul's ministry in Asia Minor where they argued with him, dogged his trail, and stirred up trouble wherever Paul went. They happened to be in Jerusalem for Pentecost and found a convenient opportunity to falsely accuse Paul. Then the Jewish leaders in Jerusalem took up the cause in an effort to get rid of Paul once and for all. However, since that time, over two years previous to this meeting, the Jewish leaders in Jerusalem had not contacted the Jews in Rome about the problem.

This lack of information might be explained by the fact that not enough time had elapsed since Paul had left Caesarea. He was one of the first travelers to get on the seas after the winter sabbatical. However, it seems more likely that the reason the Jews in Rome were ignorant concerning Paul is because the Jews in Jerusalem lost interest in the guy. It is possible that they thought, "out of sight, out of mind" regarding Paul. Since he was now out of Jerusalem and Asia he was of no concern to them. Furthermore, those Jews would not have been willing to take a weak case to Caesar. They did have a weak case, and maybe they realized it. By this time Nero was on the throne, and the Jerusalem Jews didn't want to take a chance on upsetting the volatile emperor unnecessarily.

In similar fashion, it appears that these Jewish leaders in Rome were being coy about establishing any kind of connection to or association with this Paul fellow. At this point in history, the Jewish leaders in Rome would just as soon not be involved in anything that had to do with Caesar. It had been just ten years earlier that Caesar Claudius had temporarily thrown all of the Jews out of Rome because of their constant arguing. These guys no doubt wanted to keep their noses clean. So their attitude toward Paul was, "We don't even know who you are." Maybe they also thought, "And we would prefer to keep it that way."

Instead, the leaders made it clear that they desired to have Paul dispel their ignorance about Christianity (v.22). They admitted that they knew that this "sect" was spoken against everywhere. It is obvious that they were convinced that Paul had an opinion about this sect, and they wanted to hear his opinion. Their request opened the door for Paul to share the gospel.

## Paul Rebuked the Unbelieving Jewish People (vv.23-27)

Paul bought up the opportunity to reveal Jesus the Messiah from the Jew's Scripture (vv.23-24a). According to the first part of verse twenty-three, great numbers of Jews arrived to hear Paul's explanation of the "sect" (v.23a). The leaders agreed on a particular day that they would hear

Paul's view of the gospel (though they would not have said those exact words). On that appointed day, many of the estimated 40,000 Jews in Rome showed up. It is amazing that the Romans allowed this. Obviously they assumed that Paul was innocent.

Paul taught the gospel and some were convinced by his teaching from the Old Testament (vv23b-24a). In fact, Paul continued to expound (unfold) the gospel throughout the entire day (v.23b). He gave testimony and challenge regarding the kingdom of God. This is the spiritual kingdom where Christ rules in the hearts of His people not the physical kingdom. This was nothing new for Paul. It was the same thing he taught in Ephesus. Luke recorded that in Ephesus Paul "entered the synagogue and for three months spoke boldly, reasoning and persuading them about the kingdom of God" (Acts 19:8). Two verses later Luke explained in greater detail what Paul taught. He wrote, "This continued for two years, so that all the residents of Asia heard the word of the Lord, both Jews and Greeks" (Acts 19:10). Paul taught the kingdom of God by explaining the Word of God. Likewise, in this setting Paul was trying to convince the Jewish leaders about Jesus from their Scripture (Old Testament). As a result, some were convinced. God changed the hearts of these people (v.24a).

But the gospel always makes a division. Some of the Jews who heard the gospel that day did not believe. Paul revealed God's judgment against those unbelievers (vv.24b-27). They were the unbelievers who argued and left (vv.24b-25a). These were the people in the group who chose not to believe. The Bible puts the responsibility on the heads of the ones who rejected the gospel (v.24b). The verb is in the active voice which means that it was their choice, their action. They were choosing not to believe. In fact, it was not enough for them to choose not to believe, but they also argued with the people who were caused to believe. In that case, the verb is passive, meaning that God caused the other folks to believe.

The division the gospel caused was obvious. It still happens. Many people try to bridge this natural gap by claiming to believe the gospel but living like they don't. The fact is, a division exists in spite of the pretenders efforts to deny it. When the issue is pressed, often through persecution, the lines of division become very clear.

Before the unbelievers left, Paul applied the judgment God had leveled against THEIR fathers (vv.24b-27). He reminded them of what God said to their fathers. It is significant how, at this point Paul, contrasted their fathers with his father. Remember that at the beginning of the meeting with the leaders Paul spoke of "our" fathers (v.17). Now Paul put the unbelievers in the lineage of rebellious Israelites like those of Isaiah's day. When it became clear that some of the Jews rejected the truth, Paul described them as the recipients of God's judgment (v.26-27). He pointed out from Isaiah's prophecy that these people hear the words but never grasp their meaning (v.26). They see the truth but never perceive how it applies to them (v.26). The reason they don't get it is because their heart has been made dull (v.27). Again this is a passive verb indicating an outward source. As a result of their hardness of heart, they do not hear (v.27). As a result of not hearing, they have chosen to close their eyes (v.27). As a result of closing their eyes to the truth, they cannot be saved (v.27).

The New Testament reveals that God issued this warning and judgment against Jews repeatedly through His messengers. Jesus leveled this judgment against Jews when He taught the parable of the sower and the seed (Matthew 13:14-15). John the apostle explained that the people rejected Jesus because of this promise from God (John 12:37-40). Paul explained this connection in Romans 11:7-8.

People like this speak against the gospel. They do not understand it. They choose not to accept it. God makes their hearts dull. They are in serious trouble. No amount of human argument can help these people. People who have experienced the change the gospel brings should praise God. We should praise God for His grace that allowed us to hear the gospel, understand how the gospel applies, and be changed by the gospel. Praise God because He makes His people different through the very message that unbelievers speak against.

# 37

# THE LAST GREAT
# INVITATION

## Revelation 22:17,20

John wrote, "The Spirit and the Bride say, 'Come.' And let the one who hears say, 'Come.' And let the one who is thirsty come; let the one who desires take the water of life without price" (Revelation 22:17). "He who testifies to these things says, 'Surely I am coming soon.' Amen. Come, Lord Jesus!'" (Revelation 22:20) These are words full of hope and warning. They encourage obedient readers to look forward to the imminent return of Jesus Christ. They warn everyone to handle this Word of God with the most extreme respect in light of the fact that Christ is coming again. These words are fitting words to bring to a close the most astonishing writing mankind has ever known. The message of the entire book describes Christ's return. To that revelation Christ's people say, "Come quickly."

It is also fitting that this amazing testimony should end with a great invitation. After laying out the remarkable events that will characterize the last days, Jesus Christ invites thirsty sinners to come to Him and find relief. The invitation stands until the day that Christ returns to set up His kingdom. At that time, the invitation will cease and there will be no hope.

Surely the people who have responded to the Lord's great invitation look forward to His return. We should say with the Holy Spirit of God, "Come." We, the Bride of Christ, should long for the coming of the Bridegroom Jesus Christ. Each Christian should determine if his life indicates that he really is part of the Bride of Christ who longs for His return. Or does his life indicate that he is a thirsty sinner looking in every place imaginable for satisfaction? People who have responded to the great invitation are quick to invite Christ to come again.

## THE GREAT INVITATION (V.17)

Verse seventeen is a threefold invitation for Jesus to come to earth, which will ultimately result in the new heaven and new earth—the eternal kingdom of Christ. The Spirit invites Jesus. Probably these are a continuation of Jesus' words that began in verses twelve and thirteen. The personal pronouns in those verses could not possibly be John's references to himself. It is possible that verses fourteen and fifteen are the words of John or the angel, but in verse sixteen the speaker is most obviously Jesus. He identified Himself as such. Therefore, it seems likely that Jesus continued to speak in verse seventeen. But now Christ focused on the words and thoughts of the Holy Spirit, His people, and those who hear the words of this book.

But why would the Holy Spirit invite Jesus to come? It is true that the Holy Spirit is also part of the triune Godhead. That would be like my soul asking my body to go some place. However, the trinity involves three unique persons. The Holy Spirit is one of those persons. He ministers on earth at the present time, primarily in the hearts of Christians whom He indwells. However, His ministry on earth is also to convince sinners about their sin and to testify of Jesus. Jesus specifically promised, "When he [the Holy Spirit] comes, he will convict the world concerning sin and righteousness and judgment: concerning sin, because they do not believe in me; concerning righteousness, because I go to the Father, and you will see me no longer; concerning judgment, because the ruler of this world is judged. I still have many things to say to you, but you cannot bear them now. When the Spirit of truth comes, he will guide you into all the truth, for he will not speak on his own authority, but whatever he hears he will speak, and he will declare to you the things that are to come. He will glorify me, for he will take what is mine and declare it to you" (John 16:8-14).

God's people can be sure that God the Holy Spirit is resident on earth even now, convicting the citizens of this world of sin, proving righteousness, and guiding Christ's followers into all truth. Obviously then, since God the Holy Spirit is working among people in this world of sin, He longs for and invites God the Son to come and fulfill the divine plan. Christians long for the divine plan to come to completion. How much more is that true for a member of the Godhead?

The Bride also invites Jesus to come to earth. At this point, the Bride of Christ is the Church. Most people who have attended church services and Sunday school for many years have learned that the Bride of Christ is the Church. That is true, in part. Paul taught that Jesus Christ loves the Church so much that He gave Himself to purchase His Bride (Ephesians 5:23-24). Paul also pictured the Church as the Bride which he betrothed to Christ. He reminded the Christians in Corinth, "I feel a divine jealousy for you, for I betrothed you to one husband, to present you as a pure virgin to Christ" (2 Corinthians 11:2). Therefore, the Bride of Christ, the Church, will certainly be at the wedding feast Jesus described earlier in this testimony. In John's vision, the great multitude acknowledged this truth when they shouted, "Let us rejoice and exult and give him the glory, for the marriage of the Lamb has come, and his Bride has made herself ready" (Revelation 19:7). A couple of verses later the angel said to John, "Write this: 'Blessed are those who are invited to the marriage supper of the Lamb.' And he said to me, 'These are the true words of God'" (Revelation 19:9).

Based on this evidence, one must admit that the Bride of Christ is the Church. The Bride of Christ is the body of redeemed people who have been living since the inception of the Church and will be on earth until the rapture. However, the bride motif or picture will eventually include all redeemed people. This will be true after heaven and earth pass away and the final estate of the saints comes. John testified to this event when he wrote, "And I saw the holy city, new Jerusalem, coming down out of heaven from God, prepared as a bride adorned for her husband" (Revelation 21:2). Obviously, the essence of the New Jerusalem, the final abode of all saints, will be "bride-like." One of the seven angels, who had the seven bowls full of the seven last plagues, spoke to John saying, "Come, I will show you the Bride, the wife of the Lamb" (Revelation 21:9). What the angel showed John was the New Jerusalem. According to this part of the vision, the Old Testament saints will be part of the Lamb's Bride because in the New Jerusalem the twelve gates will be named for the twelve Old Testament patriarchs (21:9-13). Likewise all of the New Testament saints, whether from the Church Age or the Tribulation, will be part of the Lamb's bride. This truth is indicated by the fact that the New

Jerusalem's twelve foundations will be named for apostles (21:14).

Therefore, one must conclude that all of the people who are like Old Testament saints and New Testament saints, yea, all redeemed people say, "Come, Lord Jesus." That means that all of Christ's followers today truly long for Him to come and fulfill all of the promises of the Bible. Ideally, every person who is born again should be consumed with thoughts of Christ's return. But maybe being consumed with thoughts of Christ's return is asking too much. Then at the very least we should think about Christ's return daily. True Christians ought to be motivated every day to live purely in light of Christ's return. The Bride of Christ ought to hate sin so much that we long to live in a world where it is absent.

How many professing Christians can honestly invite Christ to return right now, or would they need to clean up a few things? Could you invite Him into your home right now? Dare you invite Him into the inner most secret room of your mind and imagination? Would you show him the pictures hanging on the wall of your memory? Many folks get edgy about someone stopping in unexpectedly. Most of people would find themselves apologizing profusely to an unexpected visitor for what they think is a messy house. The uninvited guest's remarks that it is nice to see that the house is "really lived in" do not lessen the embarrassment. No one expects a homeowner to keep the house spotlessly clean all the time. But the Lord expects His people to order their lives in such a way that they can honestly invite His literal return at any moment.

Everyone who hears the great invitation should respond like the Bride and the Holy Spirit. Everyone should hope for Christ's return. But who hears the great news? Jesus invites the needy to come to Him. One cannot help but draw the immediate connection between the people who were part of the literal seven churches addressed at the beginning of this testimony and Christ's invitation. The first and most logical application would be to people who were in those seven churches (2:1-3:22). Not everyone who attended the meetings of those churches was born again. That idea is bolstered by the significant verb change in the middle part of verse seventeen. John wrote that the Spirit and the Bride are saying (present, active, indicative) to Christ, "Come." However, the next time he used the verb John wrote that the one hearing ought to say (aorist, active, imperative) to Christ, "Come." This imperative verb explains how those who hear should respond. Obviously, not everyone who hears the great invitation is ready to respond properly.

The evidence is clear that some of the people in the seven different churches did not look forward to Christ's return. They were not interested in Christ's return because th they had left their first love and were distracted by their world (Smyrna, 2:4). There were other professing Christians who actually embraced false teaching (Pergamos, 2:14). Some of the religious people were so far from fellowship with God that they tolerated sexual immorality (Thyatira, 2:20). Were people like that part of the visible church in Thyatira? Yes. Did they invite Christ to come to earth? Not likely! Jesus upbraided other people in those churches telling some of them that they needed to remember what they had heard and repent of their sins (Sardis 3:3). He encouraged still others to hold fast because Christ is coming quickly (Philadelphia, 3:11). Some of the folks just needed to admit their wretched condition (Laodicea, 3:18).

People like those in the seven churches in first century Asia illustrate the condition of a large portion of church-goers in this age. They claim to be born again, or at least they claim to be religious. Yet they are completely distracted by their fleshly desires and their world. If these people are truly born again, they need to live like it. If they are really Christians, they need to re-order their lives so that it is obvious that they want Christ to come. That is what John meant when he wrote in his first epistle, "And everyone who thus hopes in him purifies himself as he is pure" (1 John 3:3). Professing Christians, who were very likely not Christians, in the first century church needed to be born again so that they would truly long for Christ's return.

The second application of this challenge is to everyone who hears the great invitation thereafter. Everyone who hears the words of this revelation should invite Jesus to come to earth. This would be especially true for Christians who ought to be so focused on His return that the invitation would be the normal response. But there are many people who are not able to invite Christ to come to earth. They might mouth the words. They might pray, "Thy will be done on earth as it is in heaven," at public events. But they are not ready for Christ to come to earth. They are not ready for His judgment. If Christ comes today, they will be eternally doomed. The intent of this "proposed" invitation is to get sinners to seriously consider their plight. They must see their condition, acknowledge that they are without hope, and turn to Christ.

Therefore, it is fitting for Jesus Christ to address the great invitation to the one who is thirsty. Jesus referred to spiritual thirst at this point. It is the kind of thing that everyone should understand because everyone experiences it. Everyone has a natural thirst for spiritual truth. That does not mean that everyone wants to be satisfied by God. The contrary is true. Each person is born unsatisfied because natural sin separates the person from God. At the same time, each person is constantly faced with abounding evidence of the true God in nature, in the conscience, and in the Bible. Therefore, thirsty people quite naturally question and search for something, anything that will bring satisfaction. In those circumstances, many people turn to manmade religion in an attempt to assuage that thirst. Others turn to sin, seeking some kind of satisfaction.

But the invitation that Christ gives is for the everlastingly satisfying water of life. This is the same living water that Jesus offered to sinners while He was on earth. For example, He promised the Samaritan woman that she would find everlasting satisfaction in Him. He told her, "Whoever drinks of the water that I will give him will never be thirsty forever. The water that I will give him will become in him a spring of water welling up to eternal life" (John 4:14). It was the same satisfying water Jesus offered to the devout religious people who attended the Feast of Tabernacles. Those people sought satisfaction in dead religious ritual, but Jesus offered the eternal satisfaction of the indwelling Holy Spirit. "On the last day of the feast, the great day, Jesus stood up and cried out, 'If anyone thirsts, let him come to me and drink'" (John 7:37).

This invitation is so incredible because it means that whoever desires can take of the water freely. However, by nature, sinful humanity is so sinful that everyone is dead and cannot even desire Christ. By nature, we are so dead that we cannot even decide where to look to assuage our thirst. We must have the invitation. But sinners typically desire everything except Christ. The good news is that God, through the Holy Spirit, draws sinners to Himself so that they do desire Him.

Therefore, Christ's invitation is for every sinner. Those who know the thirst of desiring Him must come to Him and embrace Him. A visit to many foreign countries helps American citizens understand the importance of drinkable water. We typically take for granted the simple convenience and pleasure of drinking water. Often while I am in a foreign country I fight a natural response to put a cup under the spigot and turn the tap to get some cool, clear water. People who live in those countries do that regularly. But people from this culture cannot do that in many foreign nations. Their water is not put through the same purifying processes that our water is put through. As a result, when Americans drink foreign water, it is common for them to get amoebas. If a visitor has ever had to suffer through one of these ailments, he or she takes great precautions not to get another one. Therefore, while it is an inconvenience, it is safer not to drink the water in many foreign countries. Imagine being very thirsty, longing for a cup of cool water, but knowing that if you drink what is offered you will actually be worse off than you are. Into that setting comes Jesus with the offer of everlasting water which gives everlasting satisfaction from spiritual thirst. Why wouldn't a sinner take it?

The great invitation from Christ is to come and take freely of the spiritual water only He offers to assuage the soul that is parched by sin.

## THE GREAT PROMISE (V.20)

The great promise, which follows the great invitation, is that the One who testifies is coming. Jesus is the One who has given the testimony of the Revelation. He is the speaker John saw in the beginning of the Revelation (1:12-20). He is the first and last; The One who was, is, and shall be (1:8). He is the One who is able to bring to pass everything that He promises in this amazing Testimony.

He has promised that He will come to earth in order to complete all of the unbelievable things He promised in this revelation. That is great news to the people who have responded positively to the great invitation. People who love His testimony say, "Come." That means that real Christians look forward to Christ's return. Paul said that people who are genuinely born again are "waiting for our blessed hope, the appearing of the glory of our great God and Savior Jesus Christ" (Titus 2:13). Certainly people who are waiting for the fulfillment of the blessed hope should live each day like it is the day the Lord will return.

How a person responds to the great invitation determines how he values Christ's return. People who have come to grips with their sinful condition, and have confessed their offenses against God, and by faith have embraced Jesus Christ as Savior, long to see Him face-to-face. People who have heard the great invitation, but have chosen to become religious at best or chosen to ignore the invitation at worst, really have no compelling desire for Christ's return. They are content to try to find satisfaction in the things of this passing life. Which description fits you best?

# OTHER BOOKS BY
# DAVID WHITCOMB

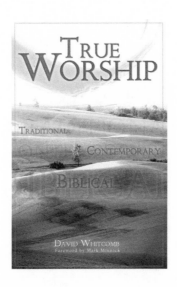

Discussions of worship often have a polarizing effect, doing little more than firming the impasse between the sides of "traditional" and "contemporary." Because meaningful discussion has become increasingly difficult, a book about worship that returns to the basics will prove useful to the body of Christ. This book avoids the rhetoric from either side, confining strictly to what is said in Scripture; the application of the scriptural principles in worship is left to the reader.

It is an effort to go beyond the categorizations of "traditional" and "contemporary" worship to explore what is "biblical." In doing so, important illustrations of worship in the Scriptures are discussed, from the foundational requirements of true worship to the distinctiveness of its expression. This book includes the basis, requirements, marks, and content of true worship. Each chapter contains questions, which makes this an ideal study for Sunday School, small group, or personal devotions.

Pages: 274
ISBN: 1932307303
Price: $14.99

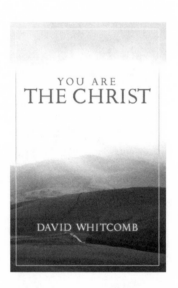

YOU ARE
## THE CHRIST

DAVID WHITCOMB

Was Jesus actually God or was He simply a man with an unusual teaching gift? Did He possess a divine nature that equipped Him to perform miracles, or were His miracles a slight of hand? Could He have actually been the incarnation of Jehovah? His conversations consistently pointed to the truth that He was indeed, God in the flesh. When Peter looked at this man who was very much like himself and concluded, "You are the Christ, the Son of the living God," he was exactly right. The plethora of modern theories denying Christ's divinity must be abandoned when we comprehend what He revealed about Himself through His conversations.

Pages: 236
ISBN: 1932307605
Price: $14.99